SEARCHING FOR BOKO HARAM

SEARCHING FOR BOKO HARAM

A History of Violence in Central Africa

Scott MacEachern

OXFORD

UNIVERSITY PRESS

Oxford University Press is a department of the University of Oxford. It furthers
the University's objective of excellence in research, scholarship, and education
by publishing worldwide. Oxford is a registered trade mark of Oxford University
Press in the UK and certain other countries.

Published in the United States of America by Oxford University Press
198 Madison Avenue, New York, NY 10016, United States of America.

© Oxford University Press 2018

Library of Congress Cataloging-in-Publication Data
Names: MacEachern, Scott, author.
Title: Searching for Boko Haram : a history of violence in Central Africa / Scott MacEachern.
Description: New York, NY : Oxford University Press, 2018. |
Includes bibliographical references and index.
Identifiers: LCCN 2017049317 (print) | LCCN 2017056111 (ebook) | ISBN 9780190492533 (updf) |
ISBN 9780190492540 (epub) | ISBN 9780190492526 (cloth : alk. paper)
Subjects: LCSH: Boko Haram. | Terrorist organizations—Nigeria. |
Terrorism—Nigeria—Religious aspects—Islam. | Insurgency—Nigeria.
Classification: LCC HV643.N62 (ebook) | LCC HV643.N62 .B657 2018 (print) |
DDC 363.32509669—dc23
LC record available at https://lccn.loc.gov/2017049317

1 3 5 7 9 8 6 4 2

Printed by Sheridan Books, Inc., United States of America

CONTENTS

Contents
vii

1

INTRODUCTION

WESTERNERS OFTEN ASSUME THAT THE lands of Boko Haram are remote and inaccessible, but getting to that part of Africa is actually fairly straightforward, in good times at least. Perhaps the easiest route starts with an Air France flight from Paris to Yaoundé, the capital of Cameroon, down in the forests in the south of the country. Those flights usually arrive late in the afternoon, so the next day a traveler would board the ninety-minute Cameroon Airlines flight for Maroua, the political and commercial center of Extreme North Province, about 135 miles (220 kilometers) south of Lake Chad and close to the Nigerian border. From there, they would need to hire a car and a driver from one of the local tour operators, taking the road out of town toward the Mandara Mountains, sprawling low on the horizon to the west. The road is paved, albeit badly, and the drive to the international border usually takes about four hours—or it did, at least, before terrorism and violence intervened.

In the plains that stretch between Maroua and the mountains, the highway winds through bustling villages surrounded by fields of sorghum and cotton, the roads crowded with farmers and travelers and made hazardous by potholes and some of the most stubborn donkeys on Earth. The twisting ascent up into the Mandara Mountains starts at the village of Mokong, close to a UN camp for refugees from the conflict with Boko Haram called Minawao that now holds about sixty thousand people. An hour or so into the mountains, the driver would trade the broken pavement for a dirt road in the plateau town of Mokolo. North from Mokolo, the going is slower, over tracks that are rutted and rocky but still quite passable, and with farmsteads crowded along the steeply terraced mountain slopes to either side of the road. Drop down out of the mountains again with the abrupt, switchback descent onto the plains in the village of Koza, little boys running beside the car as it slows for the turns, yelling pleas for gifts of coins or pens. Further on through the villages and fields, along the narrow valley that runs northwest through the mountains, and perhaps two days after leaving Paris, our traveler would arrive at the Nigerian border, in the dusty hill country just beyond Itéré.

Those unremarkable mountains three or four miles further to the west—Pulke, Zelideva, Dghwede—are in Nigeria (figure 1.1), and in mid-2017 they continue to be a refuge for Boko Haram. It would not be a good idea to attempt to cross the border: in fact, now would be probably a very good time for our traveler to leave. The Cameroonian military is wary of the sudden attacks that Boko Haram has been carrying out on their encampments and on local towns and villages, and people living along the frontier are understandably frightened of the attention that strangers can bring. Even just a few years ago, though,

Figure 1.1: The Nigerian Mandara Mountains, from just beyond Itéré in Cameroon

in 2011, I led field crews through this part of Cameroon searching for archaeological sites, and we were welcomed in the same villages that now endure attacks by Boko Haram raiders and suicide bombers.

This is a book about the lands of Boko Haram, the territory south of Lake Chad in Central Africa that has suffered under the terror inflicted by that organization. In it, I will focus on the parts of this region that I know best, the country between Lake Chad itself and the Mandara Mountains to the south where I have worked for more than thirty years. This is the area where Boko Haram's control over territory has gone on the longest, and it includes parts of northeastern Nigeria, northern Cameroon, and western Chad (figure 1.2). This book is not a comprehensive history of the Boko Haram insurgency itself or of the political processes that gave rise to it in Nigeria and around the Lake Chad Basin. Nor does it focus on the religious background or ideology of what is usually understood in the West as an Islamist insurgency. Religion is certainly a central element in any comprehensive understanding of Boko Haram, and other texts provide readers with crucial information on that aspect of this insurgency.[1] However, any large-scale social movement—and that includes terrorist movements—will probably engage many different motivations, some of which will be more or less salient in different circumstances. There are ways of thinking about Boko Haram that I do not often see covered by Western media and that I think help us to better understand this modern insurgency, the activities of its members, and perhaps even its future in the region.

In this book, we will examine Boko Haram by looking at the historical processes that brought this terrorist organization into being, and particularly by looking at the extraordinary human landscapes where it originated and where it still operates today. It is most importantly a book about the people who live in the lands of Boko Haram and the historical contexts of their lives—the centuries and millennia of human experience that have marked this area and molded its populations. The history of this region has been marked by horrific violence, ingenious adaptation, and fierce resistance to outside control, and memories of that history still affect how local people understand the scourge of terrorism that Boko Haram has brought to the lands around Lake Chad. I will argue that one productive way of understanding Boko Haram is as the latest expression of a set of social phenomena

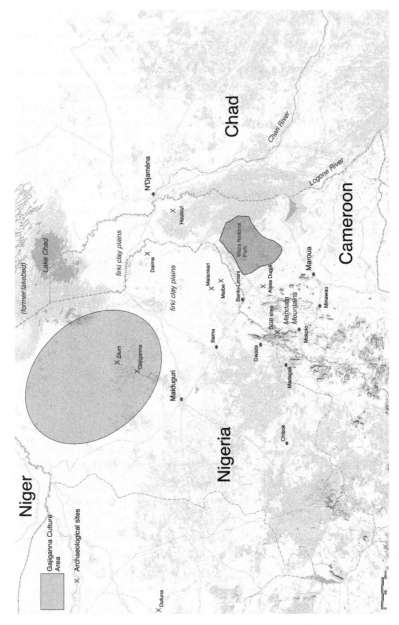

Figure 1.2: Map of the southern Lake Chad Basin

with very deep roots in the Lake Chad Basin, having to do with the opportunities and dangers of the frontier zones that have existed in the region for many centuries. These frontier zones are places of violence, but also of opportunity and the possibility of wealth and power that can be gained through violence. Boko Haram has shown an affinity for frontier zones through the history of the organization, and most of its activities today take place in such regions. This book will demonstrate ways in which we can understand those activities by looking at historical models of migration, state formation, slave-raiding, smuggling, and banditry in the regions where Boko Haram carries out its attacks in 2017.

I have worked in this part of Central Africa since 1984, doing archaeological and ethnographic research in and around the Mandara Mountains in northern Cameroon and Nigeria, and traveling more widely in those countries and in Chad. My work has involved the discovery and excavation of remarkable archaeological sites; conversations with old people about their memories of slave-raiding and colonial warfare; and a kaleidoscopic variety of encounters with farmers, soldiers, housewives, bureaucrats, smugglers, students, con men, missionaries, and entrepreneurs from all over this part of Africa. Those people are today all more or less embroiled in the terror of Boko Haram in different ways—but they all have their own stories to tell. In the course of my work, the people of the region have told me very modern stories of survival and striving and sometimes thriving, and occasionally of terror and politics, while making sense of the world they inhabit by recourse to their values and their history.

In doing so, they are no different than North Americans or Europeans or indeed people anywhere, working to reconcile the modern world of the twenty-first century with political systems and patterns of belief that have much deeper roots in history. Boko Haram insurgents themselves are equally a product of this region, and I expect that their stories would be broadly similar if we could listen to them, even though they play very different roles in those narratives. Through the last three decades, the lands now afflicted by Boko Haram have been a central part of my life, a region that I visit and where I do research, and they are inhabited by people whose courage and acuity strike me every time I visit. This land is not simply a blank slate, a savage and remote part of the world embroiled in terrorism, and I want to provide readers with a better sense of how Boko Haram fits within a long and complex cultural history in this part of Central Africa.

But what is Boko Haram in the first place? As we will see, this insurgency itself began about two decades ago in northeastern Nigeria, but its origins lie in a complex history of religious disputation and political competition that started centuries ago in the lands around Lake Chad.

Boko Haram: A primer

The organization that we now know as Boko Haram began at the end of the 1990s, in the city of Maiduguri, the capital of Nigeria's Borno State. Maiduguri is a hot, sprawling, and somewhat ramshackle city of just over a million people, draped along an ancient shoreline of Lake Chad called the Bama Ridge. The religious and political roots of Boko Haram extend much further back in time, however, to the coming of Islam to this part of Africa. People do not realize the long history of Islam on the African continent, especially between the Atlantic and Lake Chad in West Africa and along the East African coast. Muslims certainly lived in the ancient state of Kanem, northeast of Lake Chad, by the early eleventh century CE, and Hummay of Kanem was the first ruler in the region to convert to Islam later in that century, almost a thousand years ago (Lange 1977). Over succeeding centuries, most of the other rulers and members of their courts in the region around Lake Chad also became Muslims. There is no reason to doubt the sincerity of such conversion in many cases, but Islam also provided rulers with great advantages for international diplomacy and trade with the states of the Mediterranean, Nile Valley, and Middle East. Such advantages did not exist for ordinary citizens, however, and for centuries thereafter Islam seems to have remained an elite religion, not followed by the mass of common people in Kanem and other states— never mind the majority of populations in the Lake Chad Basin that lived beyond the control of centralized states at that time. Rulers of Islamic states made accommodations with the religions of their non-Muslim subjects, sometimes acting as participants in those rituals themselves when political advantage would follow. This was the case across West Africa, and in other parts of the Islamic world as well.

By the seventeenth century, controversies concerning Islam began to bubble up across this part of the continent. Reformist Muslim clerics criticized the reigning Muslim rulers, for being both wicked in their governance and lax in their duties as Muslims and in their responsibility for converting their citizens to Islam. They sought to replace the earlier elite tolerance of non-Muslim practice with a purer, more rigorous and more inclusive form of Islam, one that encompassed the entire state within the *dar al-Islam*, the global community of societies organized on Muslim principles. Muslim reformers put those critiques into action in a series of jihads, religious revolutions aimed at transforming societies throughout the lands of West and Central Africa. The first of these jihads took place in Mauritania and Senegambia in the early seventeenth century (Robinson 2000), and a series of jihadist states appeared across the savanna zones of West Africa during the succeeding two hundred years. As we will see, this current of religious and political critique reached the Lake Chad Basin by the late eighteenth century, when a reformist Fulani cleric named Usman dan Fodio overthrew the Hausa rulers of northern Nigeria and between 1804 and 1809 established the Sokoto Caliphate. That caliphate—the term was later used by Boko Haram to described the area briefly under its control on the Nigerian border—lasted until the coming of the European colonial powers a century later (Hiskett 1977).

It is important to remember the series of criticisms leveled by these jihadist reformers against the existing Muslim rulers: that they were lax and wicked and that their government was thus illegitimate. In some cases, this extended to debates about whether rulers and nobles were so contaminated by non-Muslim practice that they could not be considered as Muslims—in which case they would be excluded from a whole series of protections that free Muslims enjoyed in relation to other believers, most notably security against enslavement. These claims led to endless religious disputes, and neither the establishment of jihadist states like the Sokoto Caliphate nor the subsequent incorporation of those precolonial states into European colonies around Lake Chad ended those debates among prominent Muslim clerics from different schools of Islamic thought. This theological and political debate about the proper actions of Muslim governments and the proper role of believers faced with government misbehavior would continue through the twentieth century and form part of the intellectual environment within which Boko Haram originated.

Boko Haram itself first appeared in a period of extreme political and religious tension, associated with the expansion of sharia (Islamic secular and religious law) by the governments of different northern states within the Federal Republic of Nigeria, from 1999 onward. European colonial powers had incorporated very different African societies within the arbitrary borders of the new colonies that they carved out in the late 1800s. In Nigeria, as in many other colonies along the Atlantic coast of West Africa, this resulted in strong religious and cultural contrasts between the northern and southern parts of the colony. Islam predominated in the north, originally the Northern Nigeria Protectorate, which became a British colony in 1900, while the southern coastal regions that were progressively incorporated into the empire between 1861 and 1906 were increasingly Christian. There was sporadic violence between Christian and Muslim communities through the twentieth century, especially in the Middle Belt region of central Nigeria, where both religions are influential. That violence continues today. It has to be said, though, that in many cases this religious violence has taken place between groups that were hostile to one another long before their respective conversions to Christianity in the twentieth century or to Islam in earlier times. At the same time, some non-Muslim communities in the north, especially small populations at the margins of Islamic states, increasingly saw the advantages of becoming Christian themselves; that brought them closer culturally to their British overlords.

Independent Nigeria inherited these tensions between north and south, made stronger by increasing disparities in economic development between the different parts of the country. Some regions and some people in the south were becoming better off by the 1990s, especially because of oil wealth flowing from the Niger Delta, but northern Nigeria lagged further and further behind. This was especially evident in the federal educational system, so that Western education has never been really available or viable to the vast majority of people in northern Nigeria. The British colonizers had allowed existing sharia law to continue when they conquered northern Nigeria, because it was easier and cheaper to allow the pre-existing Islamic states to govern under British tutelage than to construct their own colonial institutions there—another contrast with the south. Family and civil law made use of aspects of sharia during the twentieth century, in the colonial and postcolonial periods, but secular northern state courts handled criminal law until a decentralization of federal power was introduced across Nigeria in 1999. When that happened, the increasing influence of foreign missionaries, some of them preaching a conservative brand of Wahhabi Islam from Saudi Arabia, led to popular pressure for the broadening of sharia, and the governors of northern states saw this as a way of gaining political support and demonstrating their adherence to Islam to the citizenry: between 80 and 98 percent of the population in the Nigerian sharia states are Muslim. In a rush, twelve northern Nigerian states adopted different aspects of both criminal and civil sharia law between 1999 and 2001 (Harnischfeger 2008).

These new laws re-energized those long-standing political and religious debates about the proper role of Islam in the nation. In preceding decades, northern Nigeria had seen a complex collision of different forms of Islam: *tariqa* brotherhoods with their background in Sufi beliefs, practitioners of inner, spiritual forms of Islam but politically and militarily powerful through much of West and Central Africa long before the colonial period; the Yan Izala, conservative Sunni clerics and legalists, critics of the *tariqa* but generally observant of the role of national law in Nigeria; and Wahhabi-inspired groups like the Ikhwan, which have often rejected cooperation with other groups and with the state (Danjibo 2009; Harnischfeger 2014). Sometimes, these debates could involve significant violence, particularly when reformist clerics preached radical criticisms of the existing relations between Muslims and the state and argued against the role of Western influences in society.

In the 1970s, a preacher named Muhammed Marwa had gained a large number of followers in northern Nigeria, especially in the metropolis of Kano. Marwa was nicknamed "Maitatsine" in Hausa, "the one who curses," for his habit of cursing people who disagreed with his teachings. In mid-December 1980, clashes broke out between Marwa's followers and the Nigerian security forces, and these escalated over the subsequent weeks. In all, between four thousand and five thousand people may have died in what is often called the "Maitatsine revolt," almost all of them the cleric's followers. There are striking parallels between the history of Maitatsine and of Boko Haram—including the fact that Muhammad Marwa is named for his hometown Maroua, the capital of Extreme North Province in Cameroon where our journey to the lands of Boko Haram commenced, and that he moved regularly back and forth across the frontier between the two countries during his lifetime. We will return to that frontier zone repeatedly in later chapters.

Followers of these different schools of Islam continued to fiercely debate theology in northern cities like Kano and Maiduguri after the crushing of the Maitatsine revolt. Some supported full integration into the Nigerian state apparatus, safeguarding the position of Islam through use of the instruments of the state. Other theologians rejected participation in the structures of the state to different degrees, from a quiescent withdrawal to active resistance. Some of the more extreme factions drew inspiration from Islamic fundamentalist and resistance movements in different parts of the world, and especially from the examples of anti-Soviet fighters in Afghanistan in the 1980s and the al-Qaeda movement in the 1990s and 2000s. There has been constant fracturing and amalgamation within and between these groups, with members following particularly eloquent and charismatic religious leaders, as was the case in earlier periods as well. Under these conditions of intense factionalism, it is hard to say exactly when Boko Haram came into being, but we can trace individuals and groups involved back into the mid-1990s at least.

In 2003, a small group of Muslims calling themselves the Nigerian Taleban, after the Afghani Taliban, moved from Maiduguri to Kanama, a rural area close to the border with Niger in Yobe State (figure 1.2) (Reinert and Garçon 2014). These were primarily young urban Kanuri, members of the predominant ethnic group in Borno State, and a number of them were from well-off and well-connected Kanuri families in Maiduguri. The Nigerian Taleban seem to have yearned for the establishment of a pure Islamic way of life on the remote Nigerian border, while at the same time carrying out attacks on police stations and other government institutions. The group was driven out of the Kanama area by Nigerian police and military forces in early 2004 and harried from place to place across the states of Borno and Yobe until they finally took refuge in the Mandara Mountains, on the Cameroon-Nigeria border, where the group was finally dispersed later that year. One of their sympathizers—although not a central participant in the Nigerian Taleban at that point—was a Kanuri preacher, Mohammed Yusuf, who had escaped arrest by the Nigerian authorities for his political activities by fleeing to Saudi Arabia. Mohammed

Yusuf would return to Nigeria in 2005, possibly in an agreement with the governor of Borno State (Mohammed 2014, 13), and would transform the remnants of the Nigerian Taleban into the Jama'atu Ahlis Sunna Lidda'awati w'al Jihad ("People dedicated to the propagation of the Prophet's teaching and jihad")—universally known in the West as Boko Haram.

Western media sources often translate the term "Boko Haram" as "Western education is forbidden," with the Arabic *ḥarām* meaning "forbidden" and the Hausa word *boko* derived from the English word "book." As the Hausa linguist Paul Newman has shown (Newman 2013), however, there is no particular evidence that *boko* is derived from "book." Scholars have been using books in the region for centuries, and there is a perfectly good old Hausa word, *littafi*, to describe them. Rather, the term *boko* has meanings of "deceitful" or "fraudulent," something that looks significant but is unimportant, a sham. Western education in northern Nigeria has been ridiculed as *karatun boko*—which Western commentators have sometimes translated as "education of the book" but which is probably better understood as "deceitful education" or "useless education," as opposed to traditional Koranic education. This is actually a fairly cutting description of the role that Western education has historically played in northern Nigeria, as the ornament of a few elite individuals but of little relevance to the lives of people in general, who must do without any except its most minor and superficial advantages. "Boko Haram" might thus more accurately be translated as "Deceitful education is forbidden," which does not fit quite as well with Western reductionist images of the group as fundamentally ignorant and backward.

Mohammed Yusuf reconstituted the Nigerian Taleban as Boko Haram in Maiduguri in the mid-2000s and immediately came into conflict with other Muslim clergy in the city—even very conservative ones. In religious terms, this conflict stemmed not only from Yusuf's demand that sharia law entirely replace secular law in Nigeria but also from his claims that any Muslim who opposed him was guilty of *taghut*, "idol-worship," if they supported any engagement with the Nigerian state. Such accusations of apostasy and unbelief are extremely serious in Islam, with a pedigree that goes back to the Kharijite movement of the seventh century CE, which held that dissent from their views was equivalent to apostasy. The Prophet Muhammad himself is supposed to have said that if a Muslim accuses another professing Muslim of being an unbeliever, the accuser is the closest to unbelief. These are, as we shall see, precisely the kinds of accusations that figured into historical debates about the orthodoxy and legitimacy of precolonial Islamic states in the region. After he returned from Arabia, opposing clerics sometimes accused Mohammed Yusuf and other Boko Haram leaders of being Kharijites, of conflating sin with unbelief—an accusation that so enraged Boko Haram leaders that they had some of their Muslim religious opponents assassinated in Maiduguri between 2006 and 2009. Those assassinations would, of course, seem to more or less substantiate the claims their opponents had made in the first place.[2]

Tensions were ratcheting up in Maiduguri in the brutally hot spring months of 2009. Clashes with other Muslim groups were increasing in frequency and seriousness, and Boko Haram was becoming more popular among disaffected youth, especially those drawn to the city from rural areas but unable to find employment there. The group became particularly popular among the *achaba*, the young men who drive motorcycle taxis in northern Nigeria. We will see these young moto-taxi drivers again in chapter 5, particularly in Cameroon, where their rides are called *clandos*. Moto-taxis, far more than automobiles, are a standard way for ordinary people to move around in this region, especially in urban areas. In mid-2009, the Nigerian security forces, with their long-practiced talent for making bad situations even worse, unleashed a crackdown on members of Boko Haram, harassing them as they went to preach, and on the *achaba*, beating or fining them for not wearing motorcycle helmets (Mohammed 2014, 24). Virtually no one wears a helmet while riding on a motorcycle in this part of Central Africa, especially not on moto-taxis, so this became a flashpoint in relations between the authorities and Boko Haram. Escalating, tit-for-tat violence culminated in a massive attack by Nigerian security forces on Boko Haram in Borno in July 2009, in which between seven hundred and nine hundred people, most of them adherents of Boko Haram, were killed. Mohammed Yusuf was captured and quickly "shot while trying to escape," and boys as young as twelve were accused of being members of Boko Haram and then executed by police in the main Maiduguri market. The Nigerian government declared victory over the menace of Boko Haram, and indeed for a few months everything seemed to be quiet.

Boko Haram returned with a vengeance in 2010, under the leadership of Mohammed Yusuf's deputy, Abubakar Shekau. The organization broke dozens of its members out of prison in Maiduguri and began a campaign of assassinations against government and security forces, as well as against civic and religious leaders who had been involved in its 2009 suppression. Again, the security forces responded with predictable heavy-handedness: in Maiduguri in 2010 and 2011 they were probably more feared than Boko Haram itself, because of their random killings of suspects and of anyone who happened to be in the vicinity of a Boko Haram attack. That perception changed, however, as Boko Haram began to diversify its earlier tactics of targeted assassinations and drive-by shootings with the increasing use of improvised explosive devices (IEDs) and suicide bombings. These escalating attacks through 2011 and 2012 resulted in the deaths of many hundreds of people across the country, from Borno State in the northeast to the Nigerian capital of Abuja in the center of the country (Pérouse de Montclos 2014).

The situation worsened in 2013 and 2014 when Boko Haram began to mount much larger-scale attacks, moving away from a concentration on urban terrorism to attacks on relatively isolated and unprotected rural settlements and security posts. These attacks demonstrated the group's increased membership and its ability to actually take and hold rural areas outside of government control, especially in and around the Sambisa Forest in Borno State, the highlands along the Mandara Mountains on the Nigeria-Cameroon frontier, and the grasslands and marshes around Lake Chad, where the borders of Nigeria, Niger, Chad, and Cameroon come together. These attacks on defenseless rural communities often involved great brutality, the instigation of terror through random killings, rape, and torture. Through such practices, but also through targeted alliances with some local communities, Boko Haram was able to create refuges in places like the heavily populated heights of the Mandara Mountains in Nigeria, where they still hold out today.

It was during this period that Boko Haram first really intruded on the consciousness of the Western general public, beyond those of us who work in the region and are personally and professionally involved with this part of Central Africa. Most notably, they kidnapped more than 250 young women from the Government Secondary School in the predominantly Christian town of Chibok, in Borno State. The kidnapping of those young women and their subsequent fate engaged the attention of the world's media and political leaders, in ways that the deaths of thousands of people in the conflict by 2014 had not. Many of those young women have not been released by mid-2017, despite the actions of the Nigerian military and American surveillance activities, or the Twitter campaigns of Western dignitaries. Their families and communities have spent the last three years hoping for their return and dreading what may have happened to them. Their fate has often been brutal, including rape and sexual slavery and possibly recruitment as suicide bombers (Bauer 2017).

During these years, the continuing ineffectiveness of Nigerian military and security forces raised suspicions, widely shared in northern Nigeria, of collusion between Boko Haram and high officials in the Nigerian government. Commentators also frequently raise the question of connections between Boko Haram and other Islamist terrorist organizations in different parts of the world: al-Qaeda, ISIS, al-Shabaab in Somalia, and so on. We have to treat such questions carefully, since both those terrorist organizations themselves and their opponents have a real interest in exaggerating their influence and their reach. The "alliance" between Boko Haram and ISIS that was announced in early 2015 and widely discussed in the West appears to be more or less rhetorical, with little evidence for cooperation between the two terrorist organizations, although the Nigerian government under Goodluck Jonathan made use of those claims to deflect criticisms of their security forces and to attempt to obtain advanced weaponry from the West. There is, on the other hand, good evidence that Boko Haram does interact with at least two other regional terrorist organizations in Africa: al-Shabaab in Somalia and al-Qaeda in the Islamic Maghreb (AQIM), which operates in the Sahara and the coastal zones of North Africa. The use of suicide bombers by Boko Haram, for example, was at one point unique in West and Central Africa, and may well have resulted from contacts with al-Shabaab.

That is the state of things in mid-2017. Offensives by the armies of other countries in the region over the last two years, especially that of Chad, and the use of "private military companies" by the Nigerian government (mercenaries, some of them from South Africa and associated with the apartheid regime of the 1980s) pushed Boko Haram out of some of their strongholds in the first six months of 2015, but the group still carries out dreadful terrorist attacks in Nigeria and in the other countries of the Lake Chad Basin. Boko Haram still appears to control some territory, especially in the northwestern Mandara Mountains near the border with Cameroon and along the margins of Lake Chad (Djanabou 2014; Seignobos 2014, 2016), but the extent of that control and the lives led by people living in Boko Haram–controlled communities remain unclear to outsiders. In part, this is because of the dueling propaganda claims generated by the group itself and by Nigerian authorities, but it also derives from the complex relations between Boko Haram and local populations, which as we will see in later chapters has involved both great savagery and intermittent accommodation. A market woman in Kolofata, a town in Cameroon just a few miles from the Nigerian border, told a French reporter in late 2016, "The prices asked by Boko Haram's wives are unbeatable. They need to sell their products very quickly, and they prefer to be paid in food."[3] How do we interpret this juxtaposition of everyday market haggling and terrorism (Tilouine 2016a)? What does it mean that Boko Haram, in all its savagery toward some women, including the young women of Chibok, also has wives who instead of running away at the first opportunity come across the international border to trade?

Between fifteen thousand and eighteen thousand people have been killed in the fighting since 2009, with perhaps two-thirds of that number killed by Boko Haram itself and the rest by Nigerian and other security forces (Amnesty International 2015). Millions of people have been displaced, both internally within Nigeria and across the border in Cameroon and Niger; when, in our traveler's imagined trip to the lands of Boko Haram, they came close to the Nigerian border at Itéré, they would have passed a series of formal and informal refugee settlements along the way, not just the huge camp at Minawao. Boko Haram has caused untold hardship across the region in the past decade, chiefly inflicted on people whose lives were already very hard. So how can we best understand the group and what they represent, and how do local communities in the regions where they operate understand them?

Historical and cultural frameworks

The lands of Boko Haram are not remote, nor are they in any way archaic, but history often does collide with the present there. Western witnesses in 2014, watching the sickening news reports of Abubakar Shekau as he threatened to sell kidnapped young women from Chibok as slaves in the marketplace, might be forgiven for thinking they were peering through a window into the deep past of African slave-raiding—but such slave-raiding ended in northeastern Nigeria and northern Cameroon only in the early 1930s. In chapter 4, we will meet a local warlord west of the Mandara Mountains, Hamman Yaji, who exploited his position on the colonial frontier to institute a reign of terror through his slave raids and attacks on neighboring communities. He kept a diary of his raids, a horrific and yet perversely boring account of houses burned, cattle stolen, men killed, young women taken as slaves. That diary was eventually translated into English and published by Western historians (Yaji 1995). Hamman Yaji's diary spans the period between 1912 and 1927, not so very long ago at all. Hamman Yaji was ultimately arrested by the British colonial government, not because of his slave-raiding but because they thought he had connections with Islamic extremists.

Very much of the present, too, is the statement of one of the young women captured at Chibok, who later escaped. She said that some of the Boko Haram attackers who took her and her schoolmates wore Nigerian military uniforms, and the young women first thought that the attackers were soldiers sent to protect them. One constant theme in conversations with common people in northeastern Nigeria and northern Cameroon is uncertainty about the relationships between the forces of the state—the police, military, and paramilitary units—and those who operate outside the law, the bandits and smugglers along the border, and now terrorists as well. There is always gossip in the markets and streets about bandits killed in the course of raids and found to be police officers, of highly placed state bureaucrats and well-off merchants who moonlight as smugglers of gasoline, stolen cars, and Kalashnikov assault rifles. In a brilliant ethnography of modern northern Cameroon, Janet Roitman writes about the *douaniers-combattants*, the "fighting customs officials," state officials in the region who engage in illicit trade and border banditry for their own economic and political ends (Roitman 2005). We will return to the *douaniers-combattants* and their equivalents in these different countries, and to these broader questions, in chapter 5.

The most recent leader of Boko Haram, Abubakar Shekau, is Kanuri, the ethnic group that originally formed the core of Boko Haram and that continues to play an important role in the organization. The Kanuri people ruled the empire of Kanem-Borno (figure 1.3) through the period before European colonialism, and as rulers they raided for slaves among the smaller societies at the frontiers of their empire, including in places like Chibok. The Kanuri are no longer rulers in northeast Nigeria, but when Shekau spoke like a Kanuri slave-raider about selling those young women from Chibok, people in the region listened and wondered if the days of the slave-raiders were coming back. In the past, most of the slave-raiders were Muslims, but by no means were all of them originally: members of other communities saw the opportunities, monetary and otherwise, of participating in the slave trade as well. Today, some of the people living in those hills across the Nigerian border from Itéré, where our traveler would have stopped their vehicle, seem to have converted to militant Islam and provided shelter for Boko Haram. That would have been unlikely a century ago—but this is 2017, and history does

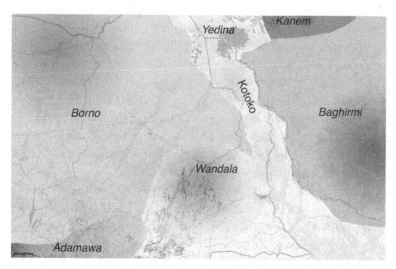

Figure 1.3: Precolonial states around Lake Chad

not entirely repeat itself. The positioning of such communities on the border may well have facilitated the smuggling of some of those kidnapped young Chibok women into Cameroon. We will look at these historical continuities involving Boko Haram in chapter 6.

As noted above, using a historical lens is certainly not the only way to try to understand Boko Haram. In fact, there are many different ways that we can try to understand this terrorist organization. We could—and undoubtedly should—examine Boko Haram from a religious point of view, as a particularly violent expression of an Islamist ideology that over the last few years has spread through the Middle East and beyond. Such an analysis would probably also lead us toward a better understanding of relationships between the different world religions in Africa and around the world more generally. We could take a military viewpoint and talk about insurgency and counterinsurgency and the strategy and tactics that might be used to defeat a terrorist organization in Central Africa. We could—and we certainly should—look to the history of chronic underdevelopment, political corruption on a baroque scale, and exploitation of common people that has marked the colonial and postcolonial Nigerian state and its neighbors in the region. Boko Haram is a movement made up of people, perhaps especially young men but also women, who see little hope in this world and the redemption of violence as their only means of making their way to the next. We might look at Boko Haram through the lens of gender roles, examining how men and women navigate their life histories and how particular crises in identity may predispose people to join such insurgencies. The events that I will describe in this book are often experienced very differently by men and by women, and those differences need to be kept in mind throughout.

All of those ways of understanding Boko Haram are valuable, and they all have their own strengths and weaknesses. For myself, I am an archaeologist, and I spend my professional life thinking about historical processes that play out over very long timescales. In this book, I want to provide readers with an understanding of Boko Haram by examining two closely related topics: the human landscapes within which Boko Haram operates and the cultural history of those landscapes. By "human landscapes," I mean not just the physical and environmental features that characterize a particular area of the Earth but the processes through which such landscapes have been dwelled in and understood by people through time. This might involve the exploitation of a physical landscape for food and raw materials, or it might involve the modification of the land itself, through clearing, agricultural, or building activities. For modern human beings, it always involves the incorporation of the natural landscape into our mental and ideological worlds, as we name places and designate them as familiar or foreign, friendly or threatening, and as we map our social relationships on to physical space and imbue particular places with supernatural power. As we will see, the human landscapes of the southern Lake Chad Basin, where Boko Haram operates, are partitioned in extremely complex and powerful ways: the variable boundaries of the great lake itself, plains areas that may be regarded as "bush" or cultivated lands, densely populated and domesticated mountains, and social and political frontier zones that are places of both great danger and great opportunity for the ruthless and the desperate. The development of these frontier zones, and the roles they play in individual and group calculations, will be a central issue through this book.

Landscape archaeology is an accepted subfield within the discipline of archaeology, and thinking about the history of human landscapes in order to understand the people who live in them is a method that I find both useful and congenial. However, there is more to it than just academic habit on my part, because this approach can help explain aspects of the Boko Haram terror campaign that may be otherwise difficult to explain. Why, for example, would a group of upper-class young urbanites in the Nigerian Taleban consistently move to remote rural areas to carry out their activities, and why does Boko Haram continue to operate so regularly in border areas? Why would modern African governments tolerate the activities of a group like Boko Haram on their frontiers, and under what circumstances? Why was Boko Haram originally so closely associated with the Kanuri ethnic group, and what other factors might lead other communities to support or resist this terrorist organization? To understand these and other questions, we have to broaden the horizons of our understanding, trying to understand the modern human landscapes in the region by reaching back from the twenty-first century into the precolonial and even prehistoric past of the lands around Lake Chad.

The lands and people of the southern Lake Chad Basin

For the most part, Boko Haram has operated where the terrorist group originated, in northeastern Nigeria and further along the southwestern margins of Lake Chad. Its attacks have frequently extended, however, into neighboring countries as well, into Cameroon, Niger, and most recently Chad. There is no real surprise in this: the countries of the southern Lake Chad Basin are closely connected to one another politically and historically. The events I describe here often take place over fairly short distances. When Boko Haram forayed into Chad for the first time in February 2015, the attackers probably traveled fewer than fifty miles from their Nigerian bases to the Chadian village of Ngouboua. A little further to the south, a twenty-five-mile trip will take you from northeastern Nigeria across the border into Cameroon and then across a second border into Chad, near the capital at N'Djaména—three countries in an hour or two, which is heaven for smugglers, bandits, and insurgents. The peoples who live across the region are also closely related to one another: before colonial and national borders were imposed on the lands to the south of Lake Chad, this region existed as a single cultural unit, so that modern populations share innumerable ties of culture, kinship, and sometimes enmity.

We can think of the southern Lake Chad Basin as divided into three broad zones, each with distinct environmental and cultural characteristics. The first of these zones encompasses Lake Chad itself, with its multitude of islands and ill-defined and variable shorelines. As we will see in the next chapter, Lake Chad is quite shallow and is fed by highly variable water sources (Brunk and Gronenborn 2004; Ghienne et al. 2002; Sikes 1972). This means that the size and extent of the lake changes dramatically; the Lake Chad that we see on maps almost never reflects the size of the lake at that particular moment. Between 1963 and 2007, for example, Lake Chad shrank to only a small percentage of its former size, with the former lakebed replaced by marshes and grassland. Historically, the islands and margins of the lake provided shelter for populations seeking refuge against stronger and aggressive neighbors, populations like the Yedina fishermen/

pastoralists, with their kuri cattle that are adept at swimming Lake Chad's waters from pasturage to pasturage while using their bulbous horns as flotation devices. Today, the new lands uncovered on the former lakebed provide refuge and staging points for Boko Haram.

The second of these three environmental zones is made up of the plains that stretch between Lake Chad itself and the Mandara Mountains to the south. Environmentally and culturally, this is a very diverse area, in part because of the fluctuations of the size of Lake Chad already mentioned. Seasonally flooded *yaéré* grasslands are found closest to the lake, although the extent of *yaéré* has shrunk significantly over the last decades with the decrease in the size of the lake. Further away from the lake, heavy clay *firki* soils mark areas of ancient lakebed, laid down when Lake Chad was much larger many thousands of years ago. These regions look dramatically different in the wet season, with pools of water and buzzing insects everywhere and vast stands of wild grasses towering over a traveler's head, and in the dry season, where all one sees is the expanse of baked, cracked clay and brush. The Bama Ridge runs northwest to southeast through the lands of Boko Haram and marks an ancient Lake Chad shoreline, dividing the clay soils of the former lakebed to the north from the sandy plains further to the south.

These plains have been the focus of human settlement south of Lake Chad for the last four millennia: during the last 2,500 years, they saw the appearance of proto-urban settlements, a political and military revolution when iron and horses were introduced, and the entrance into the region of expansionist, slave-raiding states (Connah 1981). Today, they are mostly occupied by Muslim populations belonging to a number of different ethnic groups, with very different histories in the areas: Kanuri, Hausa, Fulani, Shuwa Arab, Kotoko, and Kanembu. Interspersed around, between, and within these major ethnic blocs are a multitude of much smaller communities with different ethnic and linguistic identities, many of them peoples who historically have resisted the expansion of their far larger neighbors.

The final environmental zone is that of the Mandara Mountains and its environs. The mountains are the northernmost extension of the Cameroon Volcanic Line, an almost continuous line of mountains that stretches northeastward from the Atlantic coast of Cameroon along the spine of the Cameroon-Nigeria border, including Mount

Cameroon and its surrounding highlands, the Bamenda Grassfields, the Atlantika Mountains, and finally the Mandara massif. The mountains in this area are quite abrupt, with very little transition from the flat plains that surround them, although they are not very high. They rise steeply from about 1,400 feet (425 m) above sea level on the plains to just over 4,400 feet (1,340 m) at Mounts Oupay and Ziver. The result is a rugged network of mountains, ridges, plateaus, and internal valleys, often difficult to access except on foot, and a very easy place to lose oneself. Today, it is a landscape of homesteads, fields, and brush land, with the vegetation in many areas completely given over to human exploitation, but isolated stands of tree species now only found much further to the south in Cameroon indicates that the vegetation of the massif before human occupation was probably a more or less dense forest (Seignobos 1982).

The Mandara Mountains are one of the most complex human landscapes on Earth, in cultural and ethnic terms. They are occupied by a multitude of small populations, almost all speaking different Chadic languages (Boulet et al. 1984). For example, the homeland of the Plata people, where I did much of my dissertation fieldwork in the late 1980s, occupies an area of only about three by two miles (5 by 3 km)—but they are a population quite distinct from neighboring groups, many of which are not much larger. These mountain people (in the region, we often use the French term *montagnard* to encompass this very diverse set of communities) support themselves through intensive terrace farming of sorghum, millet, corn, and other crops on the rocky hillsides of the massif. Today, the northern Mandara Mountains are the most densely populated rural area in the southern Lake Chad Basin, with population densities of up to 650 people per square mile (250/km^2) (Boutrais et al. 1984). In many areas, this results in an almost entirely domesticated landscape, where every plant, every bush and tree, exists because it is meaningful and useful to local communities. The Mandara Mountains are the area where I have spent most of my time working in the southern Lake Chad Basin, and I find it an intensely interesting area.

On a larger scale, the southern Lake Chad Basin historically existed—and really still exists—as a crossroads for all of Africa north of the equator. To the north of Lake Chad lies the Sahara, a desert that has been dangerous and difficult to navigate for thousands of years. To the traders, missionaries, and explorers who crossed it, the Sahara could be thought of as a sea, a sea of rock and sand that could swallow unwary travelers, and the dry lands along its southern borders are still called the Sahel, from the Arab word *sāḥil*, "the coast." This desert sea could only be crossed by moving from one fertile island to the next, across the oases that dot the Sahara, and the location of oases strongly determined the presence of trade routes. One of the most important such trade routes ran from Tripoli on the Mediterranean in modern Libya, through the great oasis complexes of Murzuq and Kawar, to the northern edges of Lake Chad. Slaves and ivory were probably the most important commodities moved north along that route to the Mediterranean world, along with a whole variety of other goods moving in both directions: salt, hides, grain, ostrich feathers, manufactured goods, and much more. Even today, this remains one of the most important routes for moving illegal immigrants from sub-Saharan Africa to the Libyan coast, there to begin the dangerous voyage across the Mediterranean to Europe. Al-Qaeda in the Islamic Maghreb and related terrorist groups using these same routes have made the Central Sahara extremely hazardous for Westerners.

Contacts across Africa between the Atlantic and the Nile similarly focus on the lands just south of Lake Chad. In West and Central Africa, continental weather systems produce well-defined environmental bands that run east to west: moist tropical forests dominate the West African coast, with environments becoming steadily more arid as one moves north toward the Sahara Desert. In the intervening latitudes south of the Sahara, the savanna of the Sahel and Sudanic zones stretches eastward from the Atlantic coast of Senegal to the Nile and the Red Sea via Lake Chad, a great sweep of almost four thousand miles of grassland. These savannas provide a corridor for east-west migrations that people have used for millennia, and that were particularly important when cattle-using pastoralists moved into the region four thousand years ago. This east-west corridor passes to the south of Lake Chad, where movement is channeled between the lake to the north and the obstacle of the Mandara Mountains to the south. The hundred-mile-wide stretch of plains between lake and mountains is one of only two avenues for east-west movement between the Sahara and the Atlantic coast in this part of Africa, the other being the Benue River valley much further to the south. East-west passage across this region was focused on this narrow corridor around twelve degrees north latitude, between the Mandara Mountains and Lake Chad.

If only by virtue of its status as a crossroads, the southern Lake Chad Basin has for millennia been a focus of human migration, settlement, trade, and competition (Lange 1988). Fulani cattle pastoralists moved through the area in their enormous migration from Senegal to the Nile Valley and Ethiopia over the last millennium, while Kanuri and Hausa state-builders and Berber and Arab merchants extended trading and political networks across the Sahara. Muslim pilgrims on the hajj to Mecca have traveled back and forth between West Africa, Lake Chad, the Nile, and the Red Sea for just as long, and still do so today. After the Mahdist Islamist rebellion was crushed in Sudan at the end of the nineteenth century, British and French colonial officers in the Lake Chad Basin feared infiltration and subversion by Islamist agents traveling westward from Sudan through Chad and into West Africa. Today, regional governments and Western powers worry about the same thing, although the agents now would be members of al-Shabaab or al-Qaeda. History always yields to something new, but geography and landscapes impose themselves on the people who make that history, on their movements, their contacts, and their opportunities. In the next chapter, we shall see how transformations in the geography and environments of the region during the last ten thousand years set the stage for the historical moment in which Boko Haram appeared.

The weight of history in Africa

There are significant challenges in using a historical perspective to examine the actions of groups like Boko Haram, because European and North American commentators and the general public who read their work often make incorrect assumptions about Africa and its history. For the last two hundred years, Western commentators have most often described Africa as a continent more or less marooned in the past and in nature, full of "traditional" societies of noble savages hunting noble animals but not really a part of the modern world. In the early 1830s, the German philosopher G. W. F. Hegel famously dismissed Africa as "no historical part of the World," with "no movement or development to exhibit"—that is, he believed that human events in African societies did not involve any kind of historical development but rather a kind of cultural Brownian motion, Africans doing things randomly and meaninglessly, without any sense of progress or change. This claim that Africa has no history, no past and thus no future, has been endlessly repeated up to the present, to such an extent that it is part of the warp and woof of Western stereotypes about the continent. In 2008 in Dakar, Senegal, Nicholas Sarkozy, the president of the French Republic, apparently channeled Hegel directly: "The tragedy of Africa is that the African has never really entered into history. The African peasant, who for thousands of years has lived according to the seasons, whose life ideal was to be in harmony with nature, only knew the eternal renewal of time, marked by the unending repetition of the same epics and the same conversations. . . . The challenge of Africa is to enter to a greater degree into history" (Sarkozy 2007).

That is nonsense, and racist nonsense at that. When we study the African past with knowledge and without prejudice, we see a tremendous dynamism, and the ingenuity and persistence with which African communities and people have come up with their own solutions to the challenges of making their way in the world. Africa is not merely the birthplace of humanity, although that is significant enough. It has also seen some of the earliest experiments with what we would call modern human behavior: complex technologies, symbolism, sophisticated exploitation of natural and cultural landscapes. Africa has rock art that rivals European cave art in age. It was the home of diverse experiments in different forms of agriculture, far more varied than Europe ever managed. Africa saw the growth of cities and empires of great sophistication, indigenous developments that did not owe their beginnings to external influences from other parts of the world. It has seen wars and empires and savagery and heroism in just the same measures as Europe or Asia or the Americas have. That is real African history, not the timeless fantasy of Hegel and Sarkozy or the stereotypes of animals and savages that still too often color Western expectations of the continent. In this book, readers will encounter a complex history of the southern Lake Chad Basin that extends back for millennia. That history must be read just as we would read a Western history, as involving a past that may influence the present but does not determine it, just as it does not fix the future.

Westerners still often measure modern Africa in terms of violence, and I have subtitled this book "A History of Violence in Central Africa."

In fact, violence itself is not the central focus of the book, although it takes as a central question the ways in which people deal with the threats and opportunities that licit or illicit violence can provide. Rather, the book concentrates on the cultural logics within which violence takes place and asks why violence makes sense to certain people at certain times, and whether there are historical continuities in the way violence is used toward individual and communal goals in particular circumstances. I am not doing this to intellectualize violence, or to minimize the atrocities that Boko Haram terrorists or the security forces that oppose them have inflicted on civilian populations in the lands south of Lake Chad. But in lands that are so often dismissed by Westerners as simply savage places, prone to violence, I want to show readers how real, thinking humans—in Africa or anywhere else—can become enmeshed in such systems of violence, and for what ends.

Neither is this book a plea for salvation for Africans. Africa is a huge, diverse continent, and while in specific areas outside help may be needed and appreciated, the Africans I have met are not particularly interested in being "saved" by outsiders. They want to live their lives in security and prosperity, and they want the opportunities that would allow them to become actors in the wider world on their own terms. Today, in an age of African population growth and state retreat, they may seek those opportunities through dangerous and often tragic migrations across the Sahara and the Mediterranean into Europe—but such movements are born of calculation and often desperation, not by a desire for salvation. Nor would such salvation be forthcoming in any case: in the twenty-first century, Western powers are interested in the southern Lake Chad Basin chiefly as a safely distant battleground for fighting Islamist extremism, and to some degree for its potential for providing resources like petroleum. As we will see in later chapters, a century ago colonial powers in the region were preoccupied with more or less the same things.

In fact, this is not a book "about Africa" at all. Rather, it is a book about landscapes, societies, and circumstances that I have learned a little about through work over three decades in an area measuring about 150 by 180 miles (240 by 290 km) in area—in terms of the country that I live in today, somewhat smaller than the state of Michigan. Readers need to keep in mind these persistent stereotypes about the timelessness, violence, and scale of Africa while reading this book.

Like people everywhere else in the world, the inhabitants of the Lake Chad Basin often understand their present world using historical frameworks—but they are emphatically and entirely part of the modern world. There is a persistent Western tendency to falsely historicize and exoticize Africa, and that tendency needs to be resisted by both writers of books and their readers.

A note about terminology

The southern Lake Chad Basin encompasses four countries, three of which (Niger, Chad, and Cameroon) were formerly French colonies, while Nigeria was a colony of Great Britain. To make things even more complex, Cameroon (Kamerun) was a German colony for just over thirty years before World War I. Government administration and scientific publishing reflects this: French tends to be the language of government in the former French colonies, and English plays the same role in Nigeria. In addition, there are at least forty different significant languages spoken in the region covered by this book, from a number of language families, and the major ones sometimes have some official status as well.

This means that many locations, settlements, ethnic groups, and concepts have different names, depending on who is writing about them. I have tried in the text to keep naming as simple as is possible, using terminology that would be most familiar to an English-speaking audience. Thus, I refer to "Cameroon" and not "Cameroun," "Chad" and not "Tchad," "Lake Chad" and not "Lac Tchad." I call ethnic groups "Kanuri," not "Kanouri" or "Sirata," and "Fulani," not "Foufoulde" or "Peul." I use local spellings for place names. In one case, the town on the Cameroon-Nigeria border called Keroua in Cameroon and Kirawa in Nigeria, I have used the former spelling because I am more accustomed to it. For ethnic groups, I use the ways in which people most frequently identify themselves, although this is an extremely complicated issue that has generated a great deal of spilled ink in doctoral dissertations and scholarly articles. For the names of individuals, I use the forms most prevalent in Western media or academic literature. All measurements are given in both metric and imperial units, although the metric system is used across the region.

2

DEEP TIME, MODERN CONSEQUENCES

OUR INVESTIGATIONS INTO THE ORIGINS of Boko Haram begin in what may seem to be an unusual place—the bottom of an archaeological excavation in northern Cameroon, close to the *firki* clay plains that stretch away north to Lake Chad. Those clay plains were laid down between about ten thousand and seven thousand years ago, in far wetter times than today, when the lake was as large as the Caspian Sea and the Bama Ridge, extending northwest toward the modern city of Maiduguri, was its shoreline. At that time, even the Sahara to the north was green, covered with grasslands and river networks. As we dig up Neolithic or Iron Age archaeological sites in this area, however, we sometimes come down onto very different sediments deep in our excavation units, bright red sands that were blown into the region as desert dunes about sixteen thousand years ago. Africa was much drier during that period of prehistory, what archaeologists call the Last Glacial Maximum, than it is today, and the deserts of the Sahara correspondingly extended far to the south of their present limits. Lake Chad had more or less dried up, and there is no evidence that people lived in the region in those extreme desert conditions. The appearance of that old, weathered, bright red sand at the bottom of our excavations provides us with an unmistakable signal that it is almost time to stop digging: there will be no trace of humanity to be found within those sands. The great human complexity that we see in the region today has all developed after the Last Glacial Maximum, as the deserts shrank and people reoccupied the Lake Chad Basin.

This chapter examines the deep history of Boko Haram, and in particular the origins of the different cultural groups that have been swept up in the conflict. It does so through the lens of long-term environmental changes in the region, examining the ways in which humans dealt with the opportunities and challenges of those variable climates and resources. The timescales of these changes are much greater than those that we will deal with in later chapters, and even archaeologists find it difficult to conceptualize cultural adaptations that played out over millennia, not decades or centuries. On the other hand, we can think of these long-term cultural processes as the accumulation of events that take place on shorter timescales: as the saying goes, "Climate is what we expect; weather is what we get," and the same is true for the cycles of history. Historians and archaeologists look at long-term cultural changes from a multi-scalar perspective, as the accumulation and extension of shorter-term processes in the human world, from the events of everyday life, to economic and political processes that may play out over decades or lifetimes, to the far longer timescales of archaeology.[1] As we move through later chapters in this book, our timescales will shorten, moving from archaeology to history to current events, and these shorter timescales will probably be more familiar to the reader. But the challenges of understanding much longer-term processes do not mean that they can be ignored, because it is the long-term interaction of environments and people that set the stage for Boko Haram, ultimately producing the cultural milieu and the histories where their dreams and grievances began.

Many of these long-term environmental processes involve Lake Chad and its relations with the lands around it. Our knowledge of these processes comes from three different fields of research: archaeology, archaeogenetics, and historical linguistics. These three disciplines inform us about different aspects of the human experience. Archaeology provides us with material evidence of the technologies, economies, and cultural systems that ancient peoples used to cope with their environments. Archaeogenetics provides us with information on biological encounters in the past: the historical relations between modern human groups, the patterns through which their ancient ancestors migrated and intermarried, and their biological adaptations to their environments.[2] Historical linguistics studies language change over time and the histories of modern languages: their evolutionary relations, evidence for language splits, contacts and borrowings, and data on ancient cultural systems encoded in the ways in which ancestral peoples used particular words. Reconciling data from these different approaches to the past into a coherent historical narrative can be very difficult and is always subject to uncertainties, but it provides researchers with powerful ways of understanding how our ancestors lived, centuries and millennia ago.

Canoes and the Green Sahara

The Sahara Desert is one of the great geographical features of the globe, a vast and forbidding desert that stretches for thousands of miles between the Atlantic and the Red Sea. In the Western imagination, it is very frequently *the* iconic desert, so that our images of desert landscapes and desert peoples are derived from Saharan stereotypes—dune fields and endless skies, verdant oases, wandering nomads with their herds of camels, emptiness, and danger. In fact, the Sahara—like the "primeval," "timeless" tropics of the Amazon and the Congo—is a highly variable environment: it includes a great diversity of different landscapes and expands and contracts according to changing global climate regimes. As noted above, during the Last Glacial Maximum around sixteen thousand years ago, the Sahara expanded dramatically, and conditions throughout the desert became more extreme, hyperarid in fact. Mobile sand dune systems extended four hundred miles (650 km) south of their present limits, and Lake Chad and the river systems that feed it were either completely dry or reduced to only a tiny fraction of their modern extents (Armitage, Bristow, and Drake 2015). It would have been more or less impossible for humans of that time to live in what are now the lands around Lake Chad. Without camels, deep wells, and all the material accoutrements of desert life, and without the complex connections between oasis farmers and nomads that have developed in recent millennia, people could not have survived in those Last Glacial Maximum high desert conditions.

It is unclear exactly when people began to move back into the Lake Chad Basin after the Last Glacial Maximum, since colonizing groups, small in numbers and frequently very mobile, are always difficult for archaeologists to detect. However, we can measure the immense environmental change in the region by the fact that the earliest definite evidence of human presence after the deserts retreated is a beautifully made dugout canoe. The Dufuna canoe (Breunig, Neumann, and van Neer 1996) (figure 2.1) is the oldest watercraft known from Africa and one of the oldest in the world, constructed between seven thousand and eight thousand years ago. It is about 27 feet (8.4 m) long, carved out of a single mahogany tree trunk. It was found 16 feet (5 m) underground, by a Hausa farmer digging a well in the dry plains of Yobe State in northeastern Nigeria, west of Lake Chad and now well within the lands of Boko Haram.

The discovery of an ancient canoe, in a region that is now semi-desert and during the Last Glacial Maximum had been part of the Sahara, shows how dramatically environments of the Lake Chad Basin had transformed between about twelve thousand and ten thousand years ago. Lake Chad rebounded from its Last Glacial Maximum near extinction, so that by nine thousand years ago it covered an area vastly larger than today—140,000 square miles (360,000 km^2), a huge, shallow

Figure 2.1: The Dufuna canoe

lake that dominated the hydrology and weather patterns of Central Africa. Palaeoenvironmental researchers and archaeologists call this rejuvenated lake Mega-Chad. We can picture Lake Mega-Chad in our minds, and it makes an arresting image—the waters of a vast inland sea shining in the sun but striped with linear sand islands, the partly submerged Saharan dunes from only a few thousand years before. The location where the Dufuna canoe was found would have been close to one of the watercourses that would have fed Lake Mega-Chad, only about thirty miles (50 km) from the lake at that time. Today, the shores of Lake Chad are more than 190 miles (306 km) away from Dufuna.

While Mega-Chad was expanding, and probably in part because of the influence of the growing lake on weather patterns in neighboring regions, the Sahara began to shrink very rapidly, so that by nine thousand years ago its iconic desert landscape had been replaced by grasslands and semi-desert, laced with watercourses (deMenocal and Tierney 2012). An environment too extreme for human survival and a barrier to human movement had over a few thousand years been transformed into a vast corridor for human movement and encounter between the Mediterranean, Mega-Chad, the Atlantic, and the Nile. People came first as hunters, gatherers, and fisherman, and later as cattle pastoralists, and they flourished in the Green Sahara for thousands of years, their presence marked by innumerable archaeological sites and by joyous and accomplished rock art. The Green Sahara may have been a more attractive place to live than the lands around Lake Chad at this point, with the latter too unstable, too wet and marshy and prone to flooding, for large populations to thrive.

This may be why, beyond the fortuitous discovery of the Dufuna canoe, we know so little of the earliest human settlers in the Lake Chad Basin after the Last Glacial Maximum. One small archaeological site, Konduga, located on the Bama Ridge near Maiduguri dates to approximately seven to six thousand years ago and contains pottery that resembles ceramics of the same time period from further to the north in the Green Sahara. It would probably have been a lakeshore site when people lived there. The people responsible for Konduga and the Dufuna canoe were probably living in a number of fishing communities scattered at low densities along the lakeshore, in communication with their neighbors living in the grasslands to the north. At this point, we simply do not have enough information to link these early settlers to any of the modern populations living in the area, and it is possible that they were absorbed by later immigrant populations and left no distinct ancestors.

Like the hyper-arid deserts of the African Last Glacial Maximum, the Green Sahara was a dynamic ecosystem, and, like those earlier hyper-deserts, the Green Sahara also came to an end. Between seven thousand and five thousand years ago, rainfall across Africa north of the equator decreased significantly. As rainfall decreased, the river and lake systems that ran through the Green Sahara broke up, and grasslands shrank as arid conditions returned to northern Africa. The reappearance of the Sahara took less than two thousand years, although the desert that we see today is the result of gradually increasing aridity over the last six millennia. Lake Mega-Chad began to dry up as well, and, since it had been quite shallow, even minor decreases in water levels could result in dramatic contractions in the size of the lake. Starting around 6,500 years ago and as Mega-Chad retreated toward the size of historic Lake Chad, vast areas of former lakebed were exposed all around the peripheries of the lake, perhaps especially in the southern part of its basin. For human occupation of the region, the effects were synergistic: expansive grasslands, ideal for grazing cattle and hunting wild animals, were appearing on former lakebeds around the edges of the shrinking Lake Mega-Chad, at exactly the time that settlement in the Green Sahara was becoming more and more precarious because of drought. In response, people began to move into the Lake Chad Basin in much larger numbers, and it is at this point that the archaeological record in this part of Africa really begins.

Refugee encounters

Between about six thousand and four thousand years ago, researchers detect the initial cultural encounters and collisions in the Lake Chad Basin that lead us eventually to modern times, and to the social and political systems that give rise to Boko Haram. When we think of populations retreating in the face of a rapidly expanding Sahara in order to settle new lands around a shrinking Lake Mega-Chad, we should not abstract the situation too much. This is a process that would have played out over centuries, and it would have involved immense dislocation and suffering for peoples all over the region. Researchers estimate that perhaps one hundred thousand people died across West Africa as a direct result of the Sahelian droughts of the 1970s and 1980s, through famine and disease. Other, less direct effects of those droughts were also very damaging: communities that found it impossible to live in an area either permanently or seasonally, because of lack of food or water or grazing, were forced to migrate to areas with more resources—areas that were already occupied by indigenous communities. The violence caused by such encounters between settled peoples and involuntary immigrants and refugees contributed to widespread political instability throughout the Sahel in the 1980s and 1990s, and these stresses very probably contributed to the rise of groups like Boko Haram. There is some evidence from other parts of the world, like Syria and Iraq, that climate change is implicated in large-scale conflicts and civil wars today (Kelley et al. 2015). It is entirely possible that there were similar consequences of the Sahelian droughts of the twentieth century, and this situation may worsen in the future. We may well see a reprise of the human tragedies that I am describing in the coming decades of the twenty-first century.

To some degree, the people living in the drying Green Sahara between six thousand and four thousand years ago would have been better prepared to deal with dramatic deterioration in climates than would the sedentary farmers who endured the late-twentieth-century droughts. Many were already mobile or semi-mobile agro-pastoralists, moving with their herds of cattle for at least part of the year. In addition, they would have lived at lower population densities than modern farmers in Nigeria or the surrounding countries; there would have been more scope for them to move to more favored areas when environmental crises happened, and probably less conflict with other groups as they did so. On the other hand, the environmental transformations involved in the reappearance of the Sahara and disappearance of Mega-Chad and the water sources around it would have been far greater than anything we have seen in more recent times, and at some point those environmental transformations may well have overwhelmed the capacities of ancient populations to deal with them.

Archaeological, genetic, and linguistic data agree that when people began to move into the Lake Chad Basin between six thousand and four thousand years ago, they came from different parts of the

Sahara and Central Africa. This makes sense given what we know of more recent environmental dislocations, since the fertile new land appearing around the shrinking Lake Mega-Chad would have been a powerful attraction for people living in deteriorating Saharan environments. These kinds of crises are often catalysts for new kinds of social and cultural identities that emerge out of forced encounters between strangers. In this case, these encounters seem to have primarily involved groups of people belonging to two very different language families, not counting the scattered communities that were probably already living there, the descendants of the builders of the Dufuna canoe and the people of Konduga. These languages came from different areas of Africa, and their speakers had somewhat different cultures and economies (Ehret 2006, 2011).

This early immigration into the Lake Chad Basin involved populations speaking Afro-Asiatic and Nilo-Saharan languages, and these peoples play a central role in our story up to the present day. Today, the most widely spoken Nilo-Saharan language in the area is Kanuri. As we saw in the first chapter, Boko Haram originated in primarily Kanuri communities, and Kanuri people still make up an important element of its membership. Nilo-Saharan languages are today found in the areas of Africa that the name implies: along the Nile, from northern Sudan southeast into the plains of East Africa, in the desert north of Chad and neighboring countries, and scattered south of the desert between the Niger River and the Nile. In ancient times, Nilo-Saharan languages were probably spoken over even larger areas of the Sahara than they are today: speakers of Berber and Arab languages now dominate much of the desert, but those languages were only introduced to the area over the last 1,500–2,000 years. In fact, the overall distribution of the Nilo-Saharan languages leads researchers to believe that people speaking ancestral versions of these languages may have been some of the most important human groups in the southern Green Sahara (Drake et al. 2011), and thus likely some of the earliest environmental refugees flooding into the Lake Chad Basin as the desert dried out.

Afro-Asiatic is one of the great language groups of the Old World. The best known of its subgroupings is the Semitic language family, including Arabic and Hebrew, and ancient Egyptian was also an Afro-Asiatic language, but in the Lake Chad Basin the Chadic languages are most important. Chadic languages are spoken along the southern fringes of the Sahara from Niger and northern Nigeria to Central Chad; Hausa is the largest, with over thirty-five million first-language speakers and many millions more who speak it as a second or trade language. It is dominant in northern Nigeria and is in fact the lingua franca of that area and the western Lake Chad Basin: Boko Haram communiqués are sometimes delivered in Hausa spoken with a Kanuri accent, to reach as much of the region's population as possible. Kotoko communities living close to Lake Chad and the montagnard hill farmers of the Mandara Mountains, where our traveler drove at the beginning of chapter 1, also speak Chadic languages, many of them having only a few thousand speakers.

Difference and assimilation

Exactly where these different ancient populations came from is perhaps less important for our story than what happened to them when they encountered each other in the lands around Lake Chad. Here genetic and linguistic data are particularly informative, because they vary in ways that tell us about ancient social interactions between these different peoples. Many of the Chadic-speaking communities found around Lake Chad closely resemble their Nilo-Saharan-speaking neighbors genetically, particularly those populations that speak Saharan languages like Kanuri (Ehret 2006; Tishkoff et al. 2009). In fact, they seem to resemble those modern Nilo-Saharan populations in the Lake Chad Basin more closely than they do other Afro-Asiatic speakers along the Nile and in East Africa. Biologically, then, these groups around Lake Chad are closely related, even though the languages they speak are as different as English and Chinese. There are linguistic connections as well, because ancient word roots that originated in Nilo-Saharan are found in a number of Chadic languages. One way that linguists evaluate the intensity of prehistoric language contacts between different groups of people involves the examination of "core vocabulary," important concepts that are only rarely borrowed from another language. Core vocabulary is defined in a series of "Swadesh lists" of one hundred and two hundred words, named after Morris Swadesh, the linguist who developed the concept. These early Nilo-Saharan word roots that we find in modern

Chadic include a number of core vocabulary terms: "little, or small" "body," and "breast," along with non-core terms (Ehret 2006). To give a sense of how significant this is, the imposition of French-speaking rule on England after the Norman Conquest in 1066—with all of the dramatic consequences for English society that such conquest involved—resulted in the borrowing of precisely *one* word, "mountain," into English from Swadesh's one-hundred-word list (Ehret 2011). These groups evidently had a very great impact on one another's languages, but such transformations never involve only language. Like the Norman Conquest, they are also important cultural changes as well.

Taken together, the linguistic and genetic evidence implies a dramatic set of social processes in the ancient Lake Chad Basin at the end of the Green Sahara period. The first stage of this historical drama would have involved people speaking ancestral Nilo-Saharan languages moving into the region. Those people were cattle herders and probably also brought some knowledge of domesticated plant foods from their Saharan homes, even if they did not practice much farming. Sometime after they arrived in the new lands around Lake Chad, newcomers speaking very different languages, ancestral to modern Chadic, began to appear on the edges of these fertile lakeside grasslands as well. Their arrival had outsized effects, because a significant proportion of the earlier Nilo-Saharan-speaking population, probably people who for one reason or another had close contacts with the immigrants, stopped speaking their ancestral languages and instead adopted the language(s) of the Chadic-speaking newcomers. Their descendants carry the traces of their Nilo-Saharan origins in their genes, even though the languages that these people speak today are entirely different.

At this point, we do not know exactly why these Nilo-Saharan peoples would have ceased to speak their ancestral languages and begun to speak early forms of Chadic. There is an entire sub-discipline of sociolinguistics devoted to the question of the sociocultural circumstances in which people begin to speak new languages or maintain their old forms of speech. Invaders may conquer an area and impose their language through force, as was the case with the Anglo-Norman dialect that evolved after the Norman Conquest of England. Alternatively, this may be a situation in which some combination of the languages of the incoming Chadic-speaking groups were more prestigious for some reason, either immediately when they arrived or at some time thereafter. The newcomers might, for example, have been more proficient and more specialized cattle pastoralists than their neighbors, or they may have brought a new set of religious beliefs that seemed powerful and convincing to Nilo-Saharan peoples. Perhaps they brought initiation systems that led to young men cooperating more efficiently in raiding or warfare. Quite likely these different elements, violence and prestige, were all involved at different places and times—but there is no doubt that this process involved far-reaching cultural changes, not just a shift in what language people spoke from day to day.

The dynamics of difference

The parallels here with the present situation in the region, and with the development of Boko Haram, are striking. Five to six thousand years ago, populations around Lake Chad were marked not only by a diversity of origins and by very different cultures and languages but also by close biological relationships and intense interactions with one another. Any communal violence accompanying those interactions would probably have been wars between neighbors (and quite possibly relatives), and such wars of neighbors have often been characteristic of more recent times in this region as well. These are precisely the kinds of conflicts that can impel the vanquished, or even onlookers, to copy the habits and the languages of the closely observed victors. These kinds of cultural transformations are also characteristic of historical and recent conflicts in the region, up to and including Boko Haram. They also took place in a situation of dramatic environmental change and the economic and social dislocations that attended such change, and such dislocations have also resulted from environmental crises in modern times.

There are even parallels in the specific ethnic groups involved. The origins of Boko Haram are closely associated with Kanuri—and thus Nilo-Saharan-speaking—communities in northeastern Nigeria, and to a lesser extent in Cameroon and Niger. Many of the peoples who have been subject to Boko Haram attacks have been from Chadic-speaking communities, especially those montagnard populations from the Mandara Mountains and Hausa communities from across the region, although today there are other populations—Fulani people, for example, and Shuwa Arabs—that are also a part of this complex ethnic milieu. That being said, the conflict begun by Boko Haram over the last decade is not the latest installment in some kind of primordial confrontation between Chadic and Nilo-Saharan speakers in the region. For one thing, none of these oppositions today are set in stone. The vast majority of Kanuri people want no part of Boko Haram terrorism, and many have paid for their resistance with their lives, while elements of some Chadic-speaking communities have allied themselves with Boko Haram. In addition, the history of the Lake Chad Basin is one of complicated processes of competition and cooperation between all of these different groups, and some of the strongest sociopolitical oppositions existing today—those between mountain peoples and the plainsmen surrounding them, for example, or the rural-urban dichotomy that now dominates regional demography and modern politics—simply did not exist until much more recent times.

What we see here, instead, are *themes* that will recur in later times and in different ways. The first of these involves the close interactions between groups of people with different origins and economies that have existed throughout the history of the Lake Chad Basin. These interactions often developed because the economic and social practices of different groups were complementary, and so allowed more intensive use of landscapes and resources. Groups of socially and economically differentiated specialists—plains or mountain farmers, pastoralists, fishermen, and later people like blacksmiths and traders—can cooperate to exploit complex and varied landscapes far more efficiently than can homogenous groups of generalists, all trying to do different things at the same time. The other side of this coin, the second theme, is that the boundaries between these different groups are fluctuating and dynamic, and individuals and groups often find it very useful indeed to cross such boundaries and adopt (or invent) different identities. We will see this happening on numerous occasions, even with Boko Haram, in later chapters. That dynamism of identities is one of the most important characteristics of precolonial African social groupings more generally.

Third, these cultural identities can persist over the long term—but that does not mean that the populations that make use of these identities necessarily remain static. When, in the fifth century BCE, Herodotus described the Troglodytes of the Central Sahara, raided for slaves by Berbers from the north, he was possibly describing at third-hand people related to the modern Nilo-Saharan-speaking Teda people. The Kanuri are identified as a distinct population in the historical record by Islamic chroniclers and travelers at least 1,200 years ago, as are related Nilo-Saharan groups like the modern Zaghawa, even though they were sometimes located a long distance away from their modern territories and seem to have been behaving in quite different ways. However, there is no evidence that *membership* in these groups remained static, and there is a good deal of evidence from more recent times suggesting just the opposite. Identities in the Lake Chad Basin are always in a state of change, always in the process of becoming something else in response to changing circumstances. This is the paradox of ethnicity: such identities can persist over very long periods even in situations where the people who hold such ethnic identities, the "carriers" of identity, so to speak, may themselves be of quite different origins. We see this complexity play out in modern Western societies as well, as immigrant populations come to adopt the identities of "American," "French," or "Canadian"—rarely completely, often with strife and conflict, and always changing those values as they do so. People adopt cultural identities and are transformed by them, and they in turn transform those preexisting identities in the process.

Archaeological correlates

How does archaeological research correspond to the data from this recent work in genetics and linguistics? Reconciling archaeological with genetic and linguistic data is always challenging, and it can be difficult to link these latter patterns with the material traces of ancient people in the Lake Chad Basin. What the archaeological evidence indicates is that through much of the period between six thousand and four thousand years ago, as the Green Sahara was breaking up and Mega-Chad was shrinking, there were not many people living in the lands south of Lake Chad. This was probably because the focus of human settlement at that time was to the north of the lake; this would make sense, as we would expect the expanding desert to push populations progressively further south, while it would take some time for the wetter lands south of the lake to be suitable for use by cattle pastoralists. The difficulty for archaeologists is that virtually no research has ever been undertaken north of Lake Chad, because of the difficulty of accessing the region and because of banditry and political violence.

The earliest significant evidence for humans moving into the southern Lake Chad Basin comes from southwest of Lake Chad, on the sandy plains of northeastern Nigeria and indeed north of the Bama Ridge and Maiduguri, in exactly the territory where Boko Haram is found today. These early settlers belong to a prehistoric society that archaeologists call the Gajiganna Culture, after one of the earliest sites excavated, and Gajiganna sites date to about 4,000–2,500 years ago. The earliest Gajiganna people probably knew about cereal agriculture but they did not use it at first; instead, they combined cattle herding with the gathering and consumption of grain from the immense stands of wild grasses that are still abundant in the area around the lake even today. This was sufficient in the early phases of colonization, when population densities were low and communities were still mobile, but as Gajiganna settlements began to fill the area, people settled more permanently in one locality and planted fields of pearl millet as a staple crop. Gajiganna pottery looks like the pottery made by earlier groups through a wide area of the central and eastern Sahara, with the most similarities to material from modern Chad and western Sudan (Wendt 1997, 102). The archaeological data imply a lot of long-distance contact, interchange, and social maneuvering across this huge region six thousand to four thousand years ago, but they also make it difficult to positively identify Gajiganna peoples with either Nilo-Saharan or Chadic-speaking groups. That may well be just what we should expect: variations in material culture do not map onto modern ethnic or linguistic identities in any simple way, and there is no reason that they should do so in ancient societies either.

By about three thousand years ago, human settlements had also begun to spring up in other parts of the southern Lake Chad Basin, beyond the areas where Gajiganna settlements were found: on the heavy *firki* clay plains south and southeast of the lake, on the Diamaré Plain to the east of the Mandara Mountains, and increasingly around the mountains themselves. The pottery from these different regions is generally similar to that of the Gajiganna Culture and more distantly comparable to that of the central and eastern Sahara, but it shows a lot of variation, which again is what we might expect to see with complex ethnic relations developing in different parts of the Lake Chad Basin. These ethnic relations of the first millennium BCE represent the "filling in" by humans of many of the economic and environmental niches that were becoming available in the transforming landscapes south of Lake Chad. They are thus precursors to the kinds of relations that existed in the region during the historical period, which in turn provided the cultural setting for Boko Haram's appearance.

Gajiganna Culture sites persisted in northeastern Nigeria until sometime around 500 BCE. By that time, small Gajiganna sites had been replaced by large, complex settlements like Zilum, sometimes encircled by ditches and perhaps even walls and with some evidence for internal neighborhoods of craft specialists. At thirty to seventy-five acres (12–30 ha) in size, some of these sites were comparable to the large Iron Age *oppida* settlements being constructed in Western Europe at about the same time, and later encountered by Julius Caesar. For archaeologists, ditches and walls are particularly interesting, as people often build such structures for defensive purposes—which in turn implies the existence of a military threat, perhaps from other neighboring communities. These sites were substantial villages, surrounded in turn by smaller hamlets and farmsteads, and their existence bespeaks far more social and political complexity, and much larger populations, than anything that had existed in the area beforehand.

The spread of iron and politics

Gajiganna sites disappeared soon after 500 BCE, and there is some evidence for a very arid period, perhaps involving a long series of severe droughts, at about this same time. Those droughts would have led people to adjust to the changing climates and their economic potentials by living in new ways. One of the most transformative factors in those adjustments would have been the appearance of ironworking and iron tools. Iron begins to be found in southern Lake Chad Basin sites by about 500 BCE, at more or less the time that Gajiganna sites were disappearing, and this material can change societies in a whole number of ways. Iron tools make possible new kinds of agricultural techniques, especially through the use of hoes, which in this region allowed farmers to cultivate heavier soils on the *firki* clay plains than they could have with stone tools. Iron weapons increase the lethality of warfare, and within a few centuries of its appearance iron would be put to use making riding gear for horses.

Iron transforms society in less obvious ways as well, often becoming a central ideological and ritual focus for societies across the Old World. In historical times, south of Lake Chad, producing iron from ore was an economic activity but also a visual display and a highly charged ritual and technological performance. When a Mafa blacksmith re-created an iron smelt in the Mandara Mountains for a group of archaeologists in 1986, the spectacle of the process was in many ways as impressive as the outcome in cold iron. Through a long, hot day of grueling effort, the smith and his sons and male relatives continually pumped the bellows of the smelter, working in time to the music of pipes and zithers and singing battle songs as their colleagues fed the fire with ore and charcoal. The process continued into evening, and at its culmination, as a firehole in the front of the smelter burned away near the end of the smelt, a yard-long tongue of flame blasted rhythmically out into the gathering dusk, beating time to the bellows and the music. It seemed magical to me and to the other onlookers, Cameroonians and foreigners alike, a performance of fire, music, and human and supernatural power that could easily imbue iron—and the men who make it—with special, dangerous gifts.

The coming of iron accompanied a gradual change in ways of life for most of the ancient populations of the southern Lake Chad Basin, between about 500 BCE and 500 CE. Over this period, settlements became more permanent and far larger in scale, and we see the appearance of large tell mound sites, massive accumulations of the detritus of human habitation over centuries and millennia. As we shall see, these would later be associated with a semi-mythical race of people called the Sao, often described as giants. They are extraordinary places, crumbled mud-brick and discarded tools and ancient trash dumps piled dozens or hundreds of yards across and twenty to thirty feet (six to nine meters) high, their surfaces covered with innumerable pieces of broken pottery and iron slag. They are vivid testaments to just how dense and complex human life was south of Lake Chad a thousand and more years ago. There are scores of such sites on the plains between Lake Chad and the Mandara Mountains, and more running down the Chari and Logone Rivers that feed Lake Chad from the south. They again attest to far larger populations, and to more complex social and political relations, than outsiders might expect to have seen in the Lake Chad Basin through the first millennium of the Common Era.

That complexity manifests itself in other ways too. Elaborate clay figurines begin to appear on some of these larger, more permanent sites like Maibe and Malankari. Gajiganna people made small, simple four-legged figurines, probably representing cattle, which makes sense given the importance of cattle in their communities. The later figurines are more carefully made and sometimes larger, and they depict wild animals, including elephant, giraffe, and hippopotamus (figure 2.2), even though there is no evidence that these animals were being hunted or eaten more frequently two thousand years ago. These figurines imply that large wild animals, and perhaps the increased status associated with hunting them, were playing ideological roles in Lake Chad Basin communities. In more recent times, hunters have a special cultural and military role, in addition to their economic functions: they are the men who are courageous and knowledgeable enough to brave the natural and supernatural forces of the wilderness for the good of their community. They act as scouts during war, and in

Figure 2.2: Figurine of a hippopotamus from Malankari

many oral histories, wandering hunters played a role as explorers and community founders, often through relations that they established with indigenous groups that they encountered. Today, associations of hunters continue to play an important role in community responses to violence across the Lake Chad Basin, including the violence associated with Boko Haram.

There are also much rarer depictions of humans as well, and especially adult males. These may have been hunters; it is impossible to tell. But it does appear that individual prestige began entering into social calculations in these communities in complex ways about two thousand years ago: certain people were being deemed worthy of commemoration in ways that other people were not. This was also a period when beautiful depictions of individual people were being constructed in clay in the Nok Culture of central Nigeria as well, which may imply that societies were becoming more complex socially over a larger area (Breunig 2014). This implies the pulling apart of social identities, so that some few people will eventually be recognized as members of elites, while the vast majority of the population was seen as much more ordinary and less worthy of note. That differentiation, between elites and ordinary people, would be central to the structuring of violence and wealth creation that we will see in later chapters.

Archaeology in the Lake Chad Basin demonstrates these beginnings of social hierarchy in other ways, as well. About 700–800, there came a new development: ponies dating to that time are found on the Aissa Dugjé site in northern Cameroon (MacEachern, Bourges, and Reeves 2001). In later times, such ponies, and eventually full-sized horses, would become central to elite identities and state functioning through Central and West Africa more generally, because of their military functions and use in slave-raiding. For African aristocrats, fine horses played the same role as they did for their European counterparts, signaling status, wealth, and power. One of the Aissa Dugjé ponies was elderly and suffered from hip dysplasia; he could not have been ridden, but he was kept carefully and fed by his owner, which certainly implies a valued animal. It may also be significant that horses do not seem to have been kept on nearby contemporary sites in the region: either the prestige associated with them was not universally shared, or they were not available everywhere.

At about the same time, just after 800, there was another development: more and more foreign artifacts—bronze/brass and copper ornaments, and a great diversity and number of carnelian, stone, and glass beads—begin to appear in grave sites around the southern shores of Lake Chad. In the previous millennium, there was very little evidence of contact between the Lake Chad Basin, the Central Sahara, and North Africa: the situation had obviously changed since the days of the Green Sahara, thousands of years before. As we will see in the next two chapters, slaves would be the most important trans-Saharan export from the Lake Chad Basin in the historical period, and the appearance of exotic artifacts in the late first millennium CE may signal the very beginnings of that trade in humans. At this point, the region was being reknit into regional and even transcontinental exchange systems, as it had not been since the time of the Green Sahara.

But who were all of these people, these Iron Age farmers and pastoralists and blacksmiths, and eventually traders and chiefs, who inhabited the lands of Boko Haram in ancient times? All of the domains of research that we have looked at—archaeology, genetics, and linguistics—indicate that the communities that occupied Iron Age sites around the Mandara Mountains between perhaps two thousand and five hundred years ago were ancestral to the montagnard peoples who live in the mountains today. For reasons that we will go into in the next two chapters, many of those people seem to have moved into the mountains centuries ago, transforming that rugged and inhospitable terrain into a humanized cultural landscape and pulling apart plains and montagnard identities. Some of the Chadic-speaking peoples in the region, whose ancestors had spoken Nilo-Saharan languages at the end of the Green Sahara period, appear to have begun in turn to speak Kanuri—a Nilo-Saharan language itself, of course—during the last thousand years. This would almost certainly have been in response to the expansion of the Kanuri state in the area that we will examine in more detail in the next chapter, a succession of linguistic transformations that provide yet another illustration of the complexity and mutability of human identities through time. Arab and Kanuri chroniclers place the origins of the Kanuri people and the Kanuri state of Kanem on the southern margins of the Sahara, northeast of Lake Chad and perhaps two hundred miles (300 km) across the lake from the centers of Kanuri population today. The cultural and political center of gravity of Kanem shifted from north-east to southwest of Lake Chad—that is, into Borno and the modern lands of Boko Haram—in the centuries after 1200, likely because of increasing aridity and political instability north of the lake.

By the middle of the second millennium CE, then, many of the populations found around Lake Chad were broadly occupying the lands they held in more recent times. The Kanuri and their allies were expanding and raiding for slaves through Borno at that time, spreading fear and the knowledge of Islam among non-Muslim populations that had occupied the region for millennia. Iron Age peoples, almost certainly Chadic-speaking, were colonizing the heights of the Mandara Mountains, in a process we will examine in the next chapter. New peoples, mostly pastoral populations in search of grassland for their cattle, were immigrating into the region and would soon enter into complex relations of cooperation and competition with the people they found there. These new immigrants included the Fulani or Fulbe people, who spread eastward from Senegambia on the Atlantic coast, as well as Shuwa Arabs, who had migrated westward from the Nile valley into the Lake Chad Basin starting in the sixteenth century.

Through this period, Lake Chad itself continued to exist as a touchstone for people living on its shores. Those chroniclers of five centuries ago also wrote about the ancestors of modern Yedina fisher-pastoralists, Chadic speakers who had taken up an island way of life in resistance to the encroachments of their more powerful neighbors, and who in turn raided communities all around the lake's peripheries in fleets of war canoes. Between the sixteenth and nineteenth centuries, first Kanuri and later European writers described the Yedina as bandits and pirates, just as they did other border populations like the Melgwa, who we will meet at the beginning of chapter 5. Like the Melgwa, the Yedina are still seen as unreliable and somewhat dangerous people today.

The lake has remained through history one of the great frontier regions of this part of Central Africa, changing its extent and its shoreline, often over a period of mere decades. As it changes, it opens and closes navigable waterways, exposes hidden trails along partly submerged ridges and dunes and through reed-choked marshes, and provides both fishing grounds and fertile bottomland grazing for herds of cattle. It is a variable, fluid landscape in a modern world of fixed political borders, and that variability provides opportunities for people who exist at the margins of states even today. People move in droves to take advantage of those possibilities. In 1976, there were about seven hundred thousand people living around Lake Chad; by 2013, there were probably 2.2 million, mostly in the southern part of the basin. In modern times as well as in the past, the lake has served a refuge for political dissidents and fugitives. The islands of Lake Chad were one of the last bastions of resistance to the present president of Chad, Idriss Déby, in the early 1990s, after he had overthrown his rival Hissène Habré, and opponents to his regime have coexisted with the other inhabitants of the region ever since (Seignobos 2016). It is no wonder that the lake, its boundaries, and the people who live there preoccupy modern political elites even today.

Today, fishermen from the different countries around the lake venture further and further out past its contracting shorelines to catch fish, frequently coming into conflict with one another, sometimes violently. When fishing becomes impossible, they turn to other pursuits, including banditry and smuggling. In some areas, fishing has been replaced by cattle pastoralism, as water has been replaced by grazing land, and so pastoralists like the Udawa Fulani from Niger move onto the old lakebed and come into conflict with Shuwa Arabs from northern Cameroon and Chad. Over the last century, during the colonial period and into modern times, smuggling has flourished across the lake, both on boats and along the trails that skirt its changing shorelines. In most cases, this smuggling has been controlled by powerful businessmen and political leaders in the different countries around the lake; they make use of guides, boatmen, and drivers from Yedina and other local communities, who have an intimate knowledge of Lake Chad and its byways. Today, all of these different people are affected by the conflict between regional governments and Boko Haram. The militant group builds camps in the remote bottomlands of the former lake and makes use of smuggling routes to move people and weapons, while the security forces of Nigeria, Chad, Cameroon, and Niger pursue them with varying degrees of enthusiasm and effectiveness. The lake, like the Mandara Mountains that we turn to in the next chapter, stands to become one of the most important refuge areas for Boko Haram.

Deep histories in the Lake Chad Basin

An excursion into archaeology may seem like a curious place to begin an analysis of a modern Islamist terrorist movement like Boko Haram. However, there are deep historical resonances in the actions taken by Boko Haram insurgents and their leaders, in the way that they speak about their activities, and in the ways that regional populations understand those activities. It is impossible to gain a complete understanding of Boko Haram without understanding them, in part, as the most recent manifestation of social and political processes that have molded the peoples and the human landscapes of the Lake Chad Basin over different timescales, some of them spanning millennia. These have involved the reorganization of human societies in the face of changing environments, along the always shifting shorelines of Lake Chad itself and in the variable grasslands, woodlands, and mountains that border it. The movement of ancient populations with diverse origins into these different environments set off a series of social and cultural transformations, with people changing their languages and customs to conform to new realities. As time went on, their descendants differentiated economically and socially, becoming specialized farmers, herders, and fishermen to most efficiently exploit the diverse possibilities that these landscapes afforded. This process continues today. All of these identities at various times accommodated people moving across ethnic and cultural boundaries, when the dangers of a previous life or the attractions of a new one warranted such transgressions. We know that historically such transgressions caused conflicts as well. The adoption of early Chadic languages by former Nilo-Saharan speakers, six millennia ago, probably signaled the same kind of upheavals that we will see during the last two centuries, when people argued about who is a real Muslim and who is not.

These sociopolitical processes also involved new technologies, as iron and horses transformed social hierarchies and gender roles and made possible new political forms through the last 2,500 years. Today, Kalashnikov assault rifles, cell phones, and the internet furnish the possibility of similar transformations. Networks for economic and ideological exchange have expanded and contracted over long timescales, from far-flung cultural connections across northern Africa during the Green Sahara period; to the relative isolation of the Lake Chad Basin over the period 2000 BCE–700 CE; to the progressive globalization associated with long-distance contacts, Islam, and eventually European colonization through the last 1,200 years. This globalization affected different populations unequally and sporadically. Boko Haram itself is very much the product of globalizing processes of intellectual interchange, as it draws inspiration from Wahhabi preaching from Saudi Arabia, declares allegiance to ISIS, and fulminates against Christianity and the West—but it also places itself in violent opposition to more localized systems of belief that we will examine in later chapters, including the ideologies and religious beliefs of people who also define themselves as Muslim.

In timescales of decades and lifetimes, the development of Boko Haram will probably be most affected by political, ideological, and military decisions, some made locally and some in places far away from the Lake Chad Basin. But those are not the only timescales in play, and perhaps not even the most important ones. In a future world where climates become more unpredictable as a result of human activity and where technological changes and globalization continue to accelerate, people living in the lands of Boko Haram will of necessity continue to adapt to transformations of their natural and cultural worlds, just as their ancestors did after they entered the new lands laid bare around the lake many millennia ago.

3

FRONTIERS: MOUNTAINS AND PLAINS

WHEN TRAVELERS TO THE REGION look at the Mandara Mountains in the dry season, those heights often look more or less unoccupied—steep and barren slopes and ridgelines, inhospitable and desolate. This is an illusion: many parts of the northern Mandara massif are more densely populated than the plains around them, even after fifty years of colonial and national policies designed to force montagnard communities off the mountains. Occupation of the mountains is sustained by uncountable thousands of agricultural terraces running along the slopes, a continuous array of stone walls cunningly built to accommodate the granite outcrops and boulders. Mandara terrace agriculture is an extraordinary human achievement, supporting population densities that reach 450 people per square mile (150 people/km^2) in a hot and dry environment. Mountain people have over time converted this forbidding terrain into a domesticated landscape, one where every tree and bush exists because of its utility to humans and permeated with the values and beliefs of the people who live there. Cemeteries become orienting points for local communities, and rocks and trees are the abodes of powerful spirits of the land, who must be propitiated, entreated, and negotiated with according to the demands of the moment. When a person walks through the mountains, they walk through an entirely cultural landscape, full of meaning and the very opposite of wilderness.

In many ways, the terraces of the Mandara Mountains symbolize the impact that humans have had on this landscape—and also the impact that the landscape has had on the people who live there today (figure 3.1). Plata people, living in the northeastern part of the mountains where I did my doctoral research, called themselves and their montagnard neighbors *duw kunde*, "people of the rocks," and similar terms are used in other Chadic languages around the Mandara massif. Despite the lack of water and the ferociously hard work involved in farming and terrace maintenance in a mountain environment, Mandara people speak with pride and satisfaction about the comfort of their homes, the coolness of mountain breezes, the productivity of their fields, and the beauty of the landscape around them. Vistas across the mountains will also today take in the aluminum roofs of churches and homes of well-off families, glaring in the sun, and conversations (and archaeological excavations) may well be interrupted by the ringing of a cell phone. But centuries of life in the Mandara Mountains have led to a real attachment between mountain communities and the human environment that they have created under very challenging circumstances.

Today, Boko Haram finds refuge in parts of the northwestern Mandara Mountains, where it has gained support among some montagnard groups. It has attacked other montagnard communities savagely,

Figure 3.1: Mandara landscapes

while describing them in ways that hark back to the slave-raiders that afflicted the area until ninety years ago. The contrast between mountains and plains societies plays a central role in the violence that is going on in the region today, particularly since the Mandara Mountains also sprawl across the international frontier between Cameroon and Nigeria, adding jurisdictional issues and questions of state control over movement through the mountains to the complexity of dealing with Boko Haram.

In this chapter, this chapter describes the processes through which a dichotomy between different human landscapes of mountains and plains evolved through time, defining fundamentally important cultural frontiers in the region. To look at this, we will first examine a series of extraordinary archaeological sites, the DGB sites, that I and other researchers have investigated in the northwestern massif in Cameroon, only a few miles from the Nigerian border and the refuges of Boko Haram just beyond. (DGB is an acronym for *diy-ged-bay*, "ruins of chiefly residence," in the Chadic Mafa language now spoken in the area around the sites.) We will then consider in more detail the coming of Islamic states to the lands south of Lake Chad and the consequences of the appearance of these predatory states for the existing populations of the region.

The history of the DGB sites and of Islamic states provides us with important clues to how political power was conceived in this region at least five hundred years ago, and to the ways in which the identities of montagnards and plains-dwellers were pulled apart from their common Iron Age inheritance, described in the last chapter. That fracturing of earlier Iron Age identities would eventually result in a world when the Mandara Mountains and the shores and islands of Lake Chad would act as internal frontiers between states, places where slave-raiding state elites could seek their human prey but also where the losers in state disputes could find refuge. Today, they play the same role for Boko Haram.

Dichotomies of place

The distinction between mountains and plains is one of the most important geographical characteristics of the southern Lake Chad Basin, and it is also a cultural distinction, with human societies organized in very different ways in these different regions. This has been the case for the last five centuries at least. In the Mandara Mountain, people have historically lived at relatively high population densities in households dispersed across the mountain landscape, pursuing intensive terrace agriculture. There is a sense of social and ritual hierarchy that is understood across the mountains, although this can be expressed in different forms in different places. Mountain people may make a distinction between "chiefly" and "commoner" clans (Müller-Kosack 2003, 273), and particular prestige may be attached to individuals or families who can control the rains or other natural phenomena, like the "masters of the rains" found in many parts of the mountains. The first people to live in a particular territory may have different rights and obligations to the land and its spirits than do later immigrants, and blacksmiths and their families would often be treated very differently than non-smiths (David 2012b).

However, such ideas of hierarchy are usually only weakly expressed in the mountains. Mountain communities are often truculently egalitarian, and institutions based on the authority of chiefs, rainmakers, and other ritual experts have historically been quite unstable. Political hierarchy, where it does exist, is primarily based on privileged relations between people and local supernatural forces, spirits of particular places and circumstances. With such identity between power and place, such hierarchies do not tend to extend over large territories; the spirits of other places would not look kindly on such expansion. Although such power may be passed down from father to son, it may also be stolen or taken by trickery or violence, and so often does not last in one family for many generations: stories of families having such power and then losing it, falling precipitously from the top of the social heap to the bottom, are legion. The belief systems of mountain communities involve the maintenance of good relations with deceased ancestors and with local spirits and other supernatural powers, as well as ceremonies to ensure good health, good crops, and good luck for their communities. Over the last seventy-five years, many mountain people have become Muslims or Christians. Christianity in the mountains came originally with Catholic missionaries in Cameroon, and more recently via the different varieties of evangelical Protestantism that have flourished in both Cameroon and Nigeria in recent decades.

However, many of those earlier belief systems still exist in juxtaposition to the more recently introduced global religions, and it is not at all unusual to find people in the mountains whose religious practices encompass Christianity or Islam as well as traditional beliefs—and sometimes all three at once.

Unlike the mountains, the plains, which stretch from beyond Maiduguri in northeastern Nigeria far past Lake Chad in the east, have been controlled by centralized Islamic states for more than five hundred years. These states include Wandala at the northern edges of the Mandara Mountains, as well as the much larger Kanem-Borno and Baghirmi states that dominated politics around Lake Chad for much of the last millennium, and the various Hausa states—since the beginning of the nineteenth century amalgamated through jihad into the Sokoto Caliphate—that controlled much of northern Nigeria. The leaders of these states directed rule in their territory from towns of various sizes; urbanism is another characteristic of the plains that did not exist in the mountains before the colonial period. Rulers on the plains presided over courts staffed by a complex hierarchy of nobles and literate clerics and made use of the pomp and ceremony involved with being a Muslim sovereign in Central Africa. Their capitals were often walled in mud brick, and they sat at the apex of a complex settlement hierarchy, with administrative subdivisions at a variety of different levels. One important indicator of elite status continued to be the possession of horses, which as we saw in the last chapter are found at archaeological sites like Aissa Dugjé from between the sixth and eighth centuries CE onward, and which served both military and slave-raiding functions. Those horses, and the military gear that went with them, helped elites to lord over common people. As a royal praise song from Borno said, "The poor are grass: they are fodder for horses. Work, poor man, so that we may eat" (Reyna 1990, 134).

Beyond the state capitals and ornate courts, the commoners of those plains states lived at lower population densities than their mountain neighbors did, practicing similar kinds of cereal agriculture but much more extensively, over larger areas and without terraces. Plains villages today are surrounded by cultivated land, the fields extending out into the brush and the dust. The plains, through most of the last thousand years, have also been the home of specialized fishing communities, like those of the Yedina on the Lake Chad islands and Masa along the Logone River, and groups of cattle pastoralists, like the Fulani and Shuwa (Boulet, Beauvilain, and Gubry 1984). Farmers and fishermen lived in small villages distributed across the plains, again in marked contrast to the dispersed settlement patterns found in the mountains. Pastoralist groups were much more mobile, living in temporary camps and leaving fewer traces in the archaeological record.

The dichotomy between these two landscapes, mountains and plains, is thus a central geographical and cultural fact in this part of the southern Lake Chad Basin. It is not absolute—as we saw in the last chapter, boundaries between societies in this area are almost always permeable, because of the social possibilities that such permeability generates. In Wandala farming villages, on the plains close to the edge of the Mandara Mountains and well away from the state capital, common people share some elements of culture with their mountain neighbors. They still organize their kin networks according to lineage reckonings that do not fit well with Islamic belief, and their propitiation of spirits and ancestors is even more blatantly non-Muslim (Bourges 1996). Some plains populations, like the Melgwa and Marghi, resisted the spread of Islam and of states into the colonial period—and gained the reputation of being bandits and thieves, outlaws on the borders, at least in the eyes of Muslim rulers and chroniclers. That is a theme that we will encounter again later in this book.

Muslim states and mountain communities rubbed up against one another along the edges of the mountains, fighting at some times and trading and supporting one another at others (MacEachern 1993). Such paradoxes are to be expected when both societies need resources that only the other can supply, and when one such resource is the bodies of enslaved people from the mountains. Individuals and groups sometimes crossed the plains-mountain boundaries, frequently by becoming temporary or permanent refugees in mountain communities, and stories of such refugees can be found in settlements on both the plains and the mountains. Through all of this contact and interaction, however, mountain and plains landscapes have encompassed two different cultural worlds south of Lake Chad, for some centuries at least. How did this situation come to be? How did humans make the Mandara Mountains, and how did the mountains make them?

Processes of mountain settlement

It is hard for archaeologists to detect the very first human colonizers of a particular environment, as we have already seen around Lake Chad: such colonizers are few in number and liable to leave little in the way of material traces. This is a particular problem in the Mandara Mountains, paradoxically because of the intensity of occupation there today. The modern mountain landscape is full of people doing things—building homes, repairing terraces, planting and harvesting their fields—and it has been that way for a long time. All of that digging and moving of rock and earth damages archaeological sites; stone house foundations are dismantled and used in modern walls; pottery and other artifacts are broken and mixed in with the earth; and prehistoric garbage middens or house floors are chopped up or dug out entirely. It is almost as if the material traces of ancient occupation are gradually being run through a rather slow, but very thorough, farmer-powered blender. Unless researchers are very lucky, as they were with the accidental discovery of the Dufuna canoe, noted in the last chapter, then they will probably have to infer the processes of first colonization from later traces, working backward from the earliest archaeological sites that are known to us. Often those earliest known sites are simply those that were just too big, or that were seen by later people as too important, to destroy.

This is precisely the case in the Mandara Mountains. The earliest well-attested sites that we have discovered there are not the modest houses of pioneering farmers or ancient agricultural terraces, but rather an enigmatic and impressive class of stone ruins that I have already mentioned: the DGB sites, "ruins of chiefly residence" (figure 3.2 and figure 3.3). The phrase indicates the unusual nature of these sites, which are imposing complexes of dry-stone platforms, walls, and terraces situated in a densely settled area of the Mandara Mountains, only a few miles away from the Nigerian border and only about eight miles (12 km) away from the strongholds of Boko Haram in the mountains east of the Nigerian town of Gwoza. We have numbered these sixteen sites as DGB-1 to DGB-16 but also use their local Mafa names. DGB-1 and DGB-2 at Kuva are only 110 yards (100 m) apart, and they appear to have both been in use simultaneously, during the fifteenth century at least. They should probably thus be considered a single

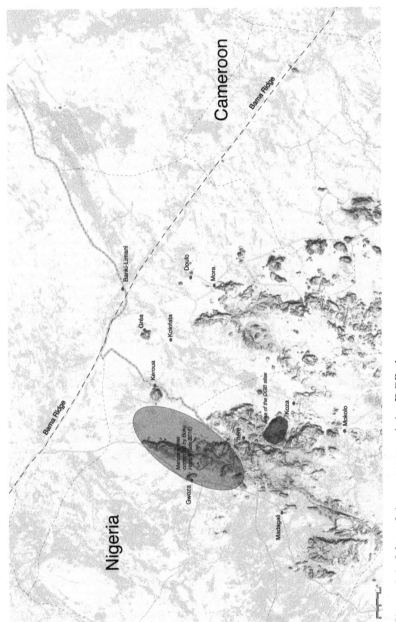

Figure 3.2: Map of the area around the DGB sites

Figure 3.3: The DGB-1 site at Kuva

monumental site complex extending over an area of about ten acres (4 ha), with just over half of that area covered by platforms and terraces. The other DGB sites are smaller and do not seem to be as complicated architecturally as DGB-1 and DGB-2, but that impression may be deceiving—most of their architectural complication becomes evident only once archaeologists started digging. Three of the DGB sites have been partially excavated to date, DGB-1, DGB-2, and DGB-8, and the approximately twenty-five radiocarbon dates taken from these sites indicate that they were probably occupied between the thirteenth and the seventeenth centuries, with a concentration of activity in the fifteenth century.

The DGB sites are almost unprecedented in Central Africa, in their size and in the sophistication of their dry-stone construction: the Kuva site complex of DGB-1 and DGB-2 taken together is perhaps the most impressive example of indigenous stone architecture in Africa between Ethiopia and Great Zimbabwe. Westerners knew about the largest of the DGB sites from at least the late 1960s, but they were identified as a coherent group of prehistoric sites and described in detail by archaeologists and ethnographers only in the late 1990s and 2000s (David 2004).

The DGB sites are striking, but they do not look at all like what we would expect of the earliest human occupation in the Mandara Mountains. For one thing, they are simply too large: it would be as if the first thing that Europeans did when they reached the New World was build the Empire State Building. There is, however, an even more convincing reason for thinking that people had already been living in the mountains for a long time before they started building the DGB sites. The Iron Age communities on the plains described in the last chapter exhibit the remains of an architecture made of earth, of coarse, sun-dried clay, and sometimes mud-brick. There is no significant tradition of stone architecture in the plains, in large part because there are no major sources of stone there. The DGB sites, on the other hand, are the product of skilled stonemasons, people who already knew how to choose and set stone together, fitting it so cunningly that they could build walls well over twenty-two feet (6.8 m) high without mortar. It seems highly unlikely that that skill could be acquired within only a generation or two, and far more likely that the ancestors of the people who built the DGB sites had already lived in the mountains, in a world of stone instead of a world of earth, for a substantial period of time.

The problem is that we have almost no information on what any earlier, pre-DGB settlement would have looked like. Decoration on pottery from the DGB sites suggests that the builders were the descendants of Iron Age plains people who moved up into the mountains for some reason. This would presumably have begun some centuries before the thirteenth century CE, when we find the earliest radiocarbon dates at DGB-1 in the mountains at Kuva. Modern montagnard pottery seems to be descended from the same set of traditions. There are hints of an earlier occupation at DGB-1, where I excavated between 2008 and 2011, small pieces of a different, finer pottery type that we found as we excavated underneath the DGB levels. However, we know almost nothing of what that earlier occupation might involve, and it is effectively undated. Stone grinding hollows that are found on rock surfaces in Sukur, southwest of the DGB sites in the Nigerian part of the Mandara Mountains, appear to be very old indeed (David 1998)—but, frustratingly, we cannot date the production of those grinding hollows with radiocarbon or other archaeological dating techniques.

Is there any other way to approach the question of when the Mandara Mountains were first occupied? We have other, indirect evidence that might help us solve this conundrum. As I noted in the last chapter, there is little evidence for external contacts in the archaeology of the southern Lake Chad Basin until about 800 CE. Before that time and since the Green Sahara period, communities in the region do not seem to have really participated in intercontinental systems of trade and exchange that were knitting together the Mediterranean world and the Sahara, and that had already begun to incorporate the Inland Niger Delta in Mali to the west by the beginning of the first millennium CE. After 800, however, exotic artifacts originating in North Africa or the Sahara—especially ornaments made of copper alloys and beads of carnelian, stone, and glass—begin to appear in increasing numbers in archaeological sites, particularly grave sites, from modern Nigeria, Cameroon, and Chad.

In the historical period, enslaved captives constituted the primary export from this area into the trans-Saharan exchange systems, and some of the earliest records associated with the rulers of Kanem, about a thousand years ago, mention their power over slaves (Lange 1988). By this time as well, some plains sites in the region have already acquired ditches and perhaps walls, which certainly appear to have been defensive features. It seems likely that these processes are related, and that the exotic imports found in the area after 800 were being paid for to at least some degree by selling slaves, as would be the case in succeeding centuries. In more recent times, living in the mountains served as a defense against slave-raiding; if such violence was beginning after 800, it might well have served as an incentive for people to retreat up on to the mountains.

Linguistic data also helps us approach this question. As with DGB ceramics and Iron Age plains pottery, the Chadic languages spoken in the mountains today are related to the languages that are spoken in the neighboring plains. Those mountain languages seem to have separated from one another between very roughly 900 and 1300. Estimates of the age of such linguistic processes are always approximate, but this fits with a scenario where people speaking ancestral Chadic languages had begun to colonize new mountain territories over that time period, spreading out and beginning to distinguish themselves from one another in their new communities by their changing accents and patterns of speech (Barreteau and Dieu 2000).

Finally, the end of the first millennium CE coincides with a very significant drought event across much of the Sahelian zone of Central/West Africa (Street-Perrott et al. 2000). As in more ancient and more recent times, this would have had political consequences across the Lake Chad Basin. It would also have had environmental effects, after a period about 1,500 years ago when climates in the area were wetter than they are now. The relict stands of woodland trees scattered across the Mandara Mountains suggest that the massif was probably forested during wetter periods in the past, but such forests would likely not have survived the droughts of the first millennium. In that case, humans moving into the mountains would not have needed to cut down the forests that seem to have existed there in earlier times. Colonizing the abrupt and rocky mountain landscape, a land of stone utterly unlike the plains below, was probably challenging enough as it was.

Taken all together, these different kinds of evidence converge on a date in the late first millennium, perhaps between 800 and 1000, for the first major occupation of the Mandara Mountains, by people coming from the Iron Age communities that had existed in the plains around the massif for centuries. This was a period when the political landscape of the region as a whole was growing more complex. New kinds of social differences were displayed in burials and figurines, at plains sites like Daima and Maibe in Nigeria; defensive features like walls and ditches were being dug around communities; horses were appearing at Aissa Dugjé and trade goods in numerous sites; and chroniclers wrote of kings, war, and slaves in the lands of Kanem. Even though powerful Islamic states were not installed at the foot of the mountains a thousand years ago, as they would be some centuries later, these different elements imply that hierarchy and probably intercommunity competition—if not violence—were becoming more important elements in the lands south of Lake Chad than they had been in previous centuries.

It is quite possible that the initial exploration of these empty mountain regions would have been undertaken by hunters, experienced in dealing with the potent natural and supernatural dangers of areas beyond human settlement; local legends of wandering hunters and their roles in founding communities may well contain a kernel of truth. The settlement of the mountains itself may well have been a gradual process initially, with people occupying foothills areas that provided both protection and easy access to additional farmland on the plains nearby. The occupation of the slopes of the mountains themselves, though, would probably have taken place relatively quickly. Sophisticated terrace systems cannot exist without a lot of people to support their construction and maintenance, and it would have been impossible to gradually construct terrace systems from the bottom of the mountain slopes up toward their crests: that would have destabilized those slopes from the bottom upward, causing catastrophic erosion and leaving crops vulnerable to animal pests like baboons and other monkeys (Hallaire 1976, 6). This points to a comparatively rapid increase in population and intensive exploitation of the environment in whichever areas of the mountains were first settled. At this point, archaeologists have no way of telling where exactly Mandara settlement began, but that settlement would culminate in a transformation of landscapes across the region.

Water, ritual, and theater

When Mafa people in the region today label the DGB sites *diy-gedbay*, "ruins of chiefly residence," they are making an inference about the functioning of these ancient structures. It is a somewhat surprising inference, since people in modern Mafa communities do not differentiate chiefs from commoners in architectural or material terms. In modern Mafa communities, members of chiefly lineages do not live in "chiefly residences," and indeed it seems likely that the unstable nature of political power among the Mafa would not allow them to direct the construction of such large houses. The biggest DGB sites, like DGB-1 and DGB-2 at Kuva, are much larger and more elaborate than any modern habitations on the region. The Mafa people living around the DGB sites deny that their own ancestors had anything to do with their construction or use; rather, they say that the sites were built by *ndoday*, more or less mythical people said to be white- or red-skinned and associated in various ways with horses, slavery, and cannibalism (Sterner 2008) and whose spirits still must be propitiated in those powerful places.

Mafa people call these sites places of chiefly *residence*. Leaving aside the question of chiefs (and white-skinned cannibals) for the moment, are these sites actually residences, places that people would live in or on? Mountain people today build homesteads as tightly integrated clusters of small, round structures with peaked thatched roofs. (Westerners might often call these individual structures "huts.") Each of these buildings serves a functional purpose, as sleeping and storage spaces, kitchens, granaries, cattle cowsheds, and so on. The external walls of this cluster of huts are usually themselves connected by walls in stone or earth, so that people can only enter a household through a well-demarcated single entrance, often located right beside the bedroom of the head of the household.

The DGB sites look nothing like this. They are clusters of platforms, terraces, and retaining walls, some very large indeed—the tallest walls of the largest DGB sites stand well over twenty feet (6.8 m) high, far larger than any domestic or terrace walls built by people in the region today. Most of the rocks used in these structures are local granites, some of them extremely massive. The impressive skill of the DGB builders lay in selecting particular faces of these large rocks and then fitting those faces together into smooth external facades, with rock wedges in between them and without mortar. The wall facades thus give a striking impression of smoothness and regularity, even though the individual stones that make up those walls are more or less unmodified. The bulk of DGB walls and the solidity of the platforms sometimes give these sites the air of being fortifications, especially when looking at them from below the hilltops that they usually sit on. In fact, the DGB sites would have made terrible fortifications, with no effective protection from attack from neighboring hills and no water sources or water storage facilities on the sites.

If the DGB sites are not residences or fortifications, what other roles might they have played that would justify the great effort made in their construction? There are two things that we can say fairly confidently: first, ritual and ceremony played some role in their construction and function, and, second, these sites were designed to impress. Obviously, those two characteristics are very often connected: places where rituals happen are often impressive visually or architecturally, for participants in such rituals and even for outsiders who may visit millennia later. Stonehenge comes to mind. Nicholas David, who has also studied the DGB sites, has spent years as an ethnographer, living and working in Mafa and other montagnard communities in both Cameroon and across the border in Nigeria. He thinks that at least some of the characteristics of the DGB sites seem to be related to modern Mafa rituals, especially those involving water and the rains—vital elements in this semi-arid mountain environment. Montagnard communities are constantly preoccupied with water and the coming of the rains, especially when they presage the beginning of the planting season in May and June. The first rains are often scattered and hard to predict: rain clouds may scud across the horizon, yielding nothing, or deposit their precious burden on the fields of neighbors or enemies. A farming season that starts with a set of good rains can ensure a plentiful harvest, but a first rain, even an abundant rain, that is followed by weeks without water can ruin crops and cause real hardship through the rest of the year. Food prices in that case may skyrocket; people will not have enough to eat; children, the infirm, and the elderly may die.

We found deposits of stones smoothed by the actions of streams or rivers, and streambed sand, as we dug on all three of the DGB sites excavated to date. However, there is no running water around the DGB sites, and these materials would have had to be carried in to the site from seasonal streams, some hundreds of yards away in the cases of the different sites that we have excavated (David 2008, 128). Water-smoothed stones and streambed sand are not essential to the construction of the sites, and in most cases they were either concealed by later layers of stone and earth or mixed in with other deposits in the course of construction. The builders of the DGB sites could not have directly perceived these materials while the sites were in use—but they would have known that they were there. Water is, at least metaphorically, incorporated into the foundations of the DGB sites.

As we saw in the last chapter, the fifteenth century, when the DGB sites were most intensively utilized, was a time of terrible drought in the Lake Chad Basin, when the land was so arid that Kanuri rulers may have ridden across the dry lakebed of Lake Chad when they moved from Kanem to Borno, to build their capital at Birni Ngazargamo. That timing might substantiate a relationship between the DGB sites and water or rainfall: if they were being used in some kind of ceremonies that at least referred to water, during a period of exceptionally intense drought, the connection seems obvious. At the same time, the situation must be more complex than this. DGB-1, at least, was in use for a much longer period of time, and there is no evidence that the thirteenth or fourteenth centuries—when building started on the site—were particularly dry in the region, nor was the sixteenth century.

If there is one adjective that comes to mind when archaeologists look at the DGB sites, and especially the complex of DGB-1 and DBG-2, it is always "theatrical." These sites seem designed to impress people, with their sheer, smooth, carefully fitted walls and their hulking platforms and terraces. They do not really resemble other architecture that we know of in the Lake Chad Basin at the time of their use, either in the Mandara Mountains or on the plains below. They have characteristics that seem more specifically theatrical as well: when the sites were in use, people standing on the DGB platforms would have been able to gaze down on onlookers, almost as if they were on a stage and confronting an audience. The passageways and sunken courtyards and stairways could well have had similar effects, allowing people to vanish from one place and move, unseen, to reappear in other part of the sites, and probably providing an impressive or even frightening experience for those people moving within the sites as well. I wonder what it would have felt like to enter one of the underground passages in the great central platform wall at DGB-1 at night, stooping or crawling up the passageway and through the dark heart of the site and then emerging into the sunken courtyard at its center, to face whatever would have awaited there.

At this point, we don't know exactly what such theatricality might have meant in the lives of the people who built the DGB sites. In Sukur, about twenty miles (30 km) to the southwest of the DGB sites and along the western edges of the Mandara Mountains in Nigeria, one of the most important rites of passage involves the initiation of boys into manhood, which is celebrated with elaborate communal rituals and the passage of the initiates through stone gateways that in some ways evoke the passageways of the DGB sites (Smith and David 1995). Perhaps similar sorts of ceremonies of initiation took place on the DGB sites; although Mafa people do not practice such rites today, Sukur is not far away. Among the Mafa and many neighboring ethnic groups, a set of ceremonies called *maray* cycles between different communities; it involves the killing of a bull and the consumption of its meat in a ritual that both honors ancestors and brings status to the man who provides the animal for sacrifice. *Maray* at least provides a conceptual framework for understanding ritual systems that might have knit together many communities in the region. None of these modern forms of ritual theater found in the northern Mandara Mountains precisely fit the archaeological evidence for what was happening on the DGB sites five centuries ago, but that is not particularly surprising: we should not expect any precise parallels, because Mandara communities have undoubtedly changed in their cultural practices over the last five centuries, just as they have changed in their architectural practices. Transformation and continuity coexist when we compare modern Mandara people to the people who occupied their territory in the fifteenth century, as is the case throughout the world.

The advent of states in the Lake Chad Basin

All of this evidence speaks to a variety of different indigenous cultural meanings associated with the DGB sites. However, we must also look at these sites as part of the wider sociopolitical world of the southern Lake Chad Basin during the centuries of their construction and use. In the early/mid-second millennium, the Lake Chad Basin was already part of the known world for Islamic and Christian European scholars, although the Mandara Mountains and the DGB sites sat just on the misty edges of that world. In about 1450, just when the DGB sites were being used most intensively, an Italian monk in northern Italy named Fra Mauro created an extraordinary world map, a *mappamondo*, in which he tried to summarize all of the geographical information known from across the globe (Falchetta 2006). The African part of this *mappamondo* incorporated some information from contemporary Portuguese explorations of the African coastline, as well as traveler's reports and classical and medieval authors, but Fra Mauro also claimed that some of the information that he gave for parts of Central Africa was derived from the accounts of native informants. On the portion of the African map that encompasses the lands to the south of the Sahara, approximately where Lake Chad would be located, he

Figure 3.4: Detail from the Fra Mauro *mappamondo*

placed a number of different toponyms; it is difficult to say whether he understood those toponyms as the names of nations, ethnic group territories, or geographical features. Among those names and in a roughly correct geographical relation to one another, we find "Bargemin" (modern Baghirmi); "Bolala" (Bulala—pastoralists living southeast of Lake Chad); "Mergi" (Marghi—non-Muslim populations still found living just to the west of the Mandara Mountains in Nigeria); and "Mandera," which given the other toponyms in the area must correspond to "Mandara" (figure 3.4).

This term "Mandera" also provides researchers with a clue to the networks through which Fra Mauro obtained his information about the lands south of Lake Chad. "Mandara" is the Kanuri name for one of the Chadic-speaking ethnic groups found directly north of the mountains. These people call themselves the Wandala. The Mandara Mountains are thus named, using a foreign, Kanuri word, for one of the important groups of people living on the borders of the mountains. Today, as we have seen, Wandala people live in the towns and villages at the edges of the Mandara Mountains and in the adjacent plains, in both Cameroon and Nigeria. Their territories are at the epicenter of conflicts between regional governments and Boko Haram, and some of their young men have joined the movement. The use of the term "Mandera" rather than "Wandala" as a toponym in Fra Mauro's *mappamondo* indicates that he obtained at least some of his information on Central Africa ultimately from Kanuri-speaking sources, although probably at third- or fourthhand. At this time, Kanuri traders were already part of commercial networks that linked the Lake Chad Basin across the Sahara to the Mediterranean world, so the transmission of the word "Mandera" (along with other toponyms in the region) to Fra Mauro makes a good deal of sense.

The language of the Wandala is very closely related to other Chadic languages spoken in the region, including those of plains groups like the Melgwa (see chapter 5), but also among montagnard populations just to the south like the Mafa and Podokwo. These different languages appear to have descended from a common Chadic ancestor about a millennium ago. Some ritual beliefs and practices also seem to be shared, including beliefs in the kinds of spirits associated with particular places that exist in the mountains. However, in recent centuries the roles and destinies of the Wandala and their neighbors were very different. By the eighteenth century, Wandala was a centralized Islamic state situated on the plains north of the Mandara Mountains and comparable to larger neighbors like Borno and Baghirmi. It had a complex administrative apparatus and a royal court centered on the *tlikse*, the ruler of Wandala. It engaged in warfare and diplomacy with other Islamic states on the plains of the Lake Chad Basin, and the Wandala also raided into the Mandara Mountains for slaves.

Historically and linguistically, then, Wandala poses a paradox—although the Wandala people speak a language closely related to that of their non-Muslim neighbors living in the mountains and have elements of non-elite culture in common, the culture of the Wandala nobility and the political systems of the Wandala state are very different, much more like those of other Islamic states on the plains south of Lake Chad. How did this happen? How were the Mandara Mountains and the people who live in them "pulled apart" from the surrounding plains and their Wandala inhabitants, so that the common Iron Age cultural inheritance that had developed in the region over millennia was sundered into those two contrasting cultural systems? Why did elites develop in the plains but not to the same degree in the mountains? How did it come to be that, in the course of that sundering, the plains became the lands of enslavement, while the Mandara Mountains and other marginal areas became slave-raiding frontiers?

We can trace these transformations of the Lake Chad Basin to the appearance of expansionistic states in the region in the first half of the second millennium. Walls, horses, and rich grave goods suggest that intercommunity conflict and social stratification were known in the region by the end of the first millennium, but there is little evidence that Iron Age communities south of Lake Chad were involved in sustained warfare or large-scale slave-raiding. Those innovations would require new elements in regional life, most importantly the development of complex military systems, economic networks that could make use of human beings treated as property (either by making use of their labor at home or selling them as property abroad), and ideologies that would justify the whole enterprise. These novel configurations of life in the Lake Chad Basin would emerge in the crucible of new cultural encounters, between the indigenous societies that had existed there through the Iron Age and encroaching political systems that obeyed quite different cultural imperatives.

This seems to have begun with the Kanuri, with later developments in Baghirmi, Wandala, the Sokoto Caliphate, and other states. As we have seen, the Kanuri state of Kanem, northeast of Lake Chad, was known to Arab chroniclers late in the first millennium, and the ruler Hummay became a convert to Islam toward the end of the eleventh century. Over the succeeding three hundred years, Kanem seems to have become progressively more involved in the lands south of Lake Chad, almost certainly for two reasons: first, because environments northeast of the lake in the homeland of Kanem were becoming steadily drier and less able to support agriculture and, second, because the lands south of the lake offered a rich supply of human captives, to be sold for slaves. Today, Kanem is a very dry Sahelian grassland environment, where agriculture is extremely precarious and mostly restricted to seasonal riverbeds. It is likely that this progressive aridification contributed to the decision by the Kanuri rulers of Kanem to move their capital to Birni Ngazargamo in Borno, southwest of Lake Chad, by about 1450. It would remain there until 1808 and the destruction of the dynasty. The economic and political fulcrum of Kanem-Borno was probably already in the process of shifting to the plains south of the lake two centuries before, by 1250 (Lange 1993, 1989).

Kanuri histories and Arab chroniclers often make reference to people called "Sao," the indigenous non-Muslim populations living in the lands south of Lake Chad when the Kanuri moved into the area. Those Sao would have been some of the late Iron Age populations of the region, descendants of the people who had lived there for thousands of years, who introduced iron, made the figurines found at Malankari, and kept horses at Aissa Dugjé. Four rulers of Kanem-Borno are supposed to have died in battle with Sao communities in

the 1330s and 1340s; in later centuries, such warfare would be intimately tied to state expansion, slave-raiding, and the extraction of
tribute from reluctant neighbors, and there is no reason to think that
such was not the case in the fourteenth century as well.

The Kanuri rulers of Kanem and Borno were Muslim, and rulers
of other states in this region were progressively converting to Islam
by the middle of the second millennium as well. (It took a little
longer for the Wandala, but even there the ruler and his court had
become Muslim by the early 1700s.) It is worth asking what role Islam
itself played in the expansion of Muslim states south of Lake Chad
through this period, beyond the claims of royal piety and orthodoxy
that were made by court writers and clerics (Lange 1987). As elite
groups in states throughout this region (and throughout the Sudanic
zone) converted to Islam, they had a ready-made justification for their
slave-raiding into non-Muslim communities: they were protecting or
even expanding the *dar al-Islam*, the global community of Muslim
societies, where Islam is practiced as the predominant religion. As we
will see in the next chapter, however, the incorporation of conquered
communities into the *dar al-Islam* would have rendered those conquered peoples immune to enslavement and thus undercut the economic and military structures that made state development and elite
display possible. It would also have complicated governance by rulers
who were for the most part careful to balance their commitment to
Islam with tolerance for—and sometimes active participation in—
preexisting, non-Muslim religious practices. Before the eighteenth
century, Islam was very much an elite religion, one associated with
the maintenance of the networks that allowed rulers to function in
regional and even intercontinental political and economic arenas. It
is unlikely that Islam was particularly significant to commoners even
within Islamic states like Borno and Baghirmi before the eighteenth
century. Under those circumstances, it seems quite likely that the
spread of Islam to "pagan" populations acted more as a rhetorical justification for state expansion, rather than an important impulse toward
such expansion.

Over the succeeding centuries, slave-raiding extended across the
lands of the Lake Chad Basin as an integral element of that state
expansion. It was most often directed by Muslim elites at marginal,
non-Muslim populations, and more and more of the enslaved captives

were sent across the Sahara to markets in the Mediterranean and the Middle East. Such raiding has regional consequences. The violence associated with enslavement is often something that takes place in frontier areas. Indeed, we might go further than that and say that in the Lake Chad Basin, frontiers were historically defined as the places where slaves—and the wealth to be gained from slaves—could be obtained. There are, however, logistical and military challenges to slave-raiding on frontiers, which are often distant from state capitals and difficult and dangerous to reach. West and Central African history abounds with accounts of communities that served as "sub-contractors" in both the trans-Saharan and transatlantic slave trades, enslaving people locally and then trading them onward for a profit with other groups that would feed them into the intercontinental trading systems. By the eighteenth century, the Wandala were well-known as middlemen, raiding for slaves in and around the Mandara Mountains and selling them to Kanuri and other slave-traders further to the north (MacEachern 1993).

Today, the Wandala court still exists, in a dramatically diminished form, in the town of Mora at the northeastern tip of the Mandara massif. Ask to see the *tlikse*, the Wandala ruler, at the door to his palace, and you will be asked to remove your shoes, then ushered through a series of dusty courtyards to his inner court. There you can approach to speak with him, surrounded by the half dozen elderly men who make up what remains of his courtiers. Through the nineteenth century, though, Wandala was still an independent state, ruled by the *tlikse* with real power and with Doulo and Mora as its successive capitals. The earliest known Wandala capital was located about twenty miles (32 km) further to the west at the modern town of Keroua, which is at the foot of another mountain on the modern frontier between Cameroon and Nigeria. Cameroonian "Keroua" is known as "Kirawa" in Nigeria, and by late 2017 it has been subjected to the terrorism associated with Boko Haram for four years.

Keroua was certainly an important Wandala center by the fifteenth century, at least. Wandala written traditions identify Keroua as the place where the Wandala state really began, and the closest linguistic relatives to Wandala are languages like Podokwo and Hidé that are today spoken to the east and the southwest of Keroua, respectively. While my crew and I lived in the Nigerian town of Gwoza in the early

1990s—twenty years later it would be the capital of Boko Haram's "caliphate"—we found sites around Keroua with pottery and architecture more or less identical to that found on Iron Age plains sites. This parallels the results of our work along the edges of the massif and inselbergs in other parts of the southern Lake Chad Basin: favored locations like Keroua, situated at the edges of mountains and inselbergs where soils were good and retreat to the heights was always an option, appear to have been an important focus of settlement over much of the last two thousand years. The Wandala elite liked to have mountains at their back for defensive purposes and to escape into, a behavior that they have engaged in periodically over the last five centuries.

And finally, Keroua is only about twenty miles (32 km) north of the DGB sites. A long valley within the Mandara Mountains just north of DGB-1 and DGB-2 crooks northwestward and then to the northeast, from close to the archaeological sites toward the plains on the modern Cameroon-Nigeria border. The journey toward the lands of Boko Haram that I described at the very beginning of this book followed that valley just below DGB-1, in the long trajectory from Paris to the Mandara Mountains and the Nigerian border. At the end of that valley, on the last stretch of hills in that dusty country just beyond Itéré and with the mountains of Pulke, Zelideva, and Dghwede close by to the west, a traveler might turn their head just a little and see the inselberg of Keroua looming away in the heat haze to the north, only fourteen miles (23 km) away. Thus for centuries there has been a convenient corridor for trade and exchange between Keroua and the DGB sites—indeed, such movement would almost have been funneled into this corridor between the plains and the neighboring mountains.

Today, this area is a borderland between the modern nations of Cameroon and Nigeria, as well as being a battleground between radically different visions of how societies should function, as national armies struggle against the Islamist visions of Boko Haram. It played the same role in the past as well: five centuries ago and more, this same region delineated the development of radically different social and ideological systems, born out of the collision between Iron Age traditions that had typified the lands south of Lake Chad for a thousand years beforehand and encroaching, centralized Islamic states. On the one hand, those centralized states would define the history of the plains of the Lake Chad Basin in succeeding centuries; on the other hand, mountain populations—as well as marginalized groups in other parts of the region—would stand against them.

The DGB sites were built and occupied in close proximity to the area around Keroua on the edge of the mountains, at just the same time that the Wandala state was developing there and generally in an ideal location for interaction between mountains and plains. The developing Wandala elites and the people who built and used the DGB sites would have been well aware of one another. It seems quite likely that the builders of the DGB sites spoke a Chadic language closely related to Wandala, which would be another signal of the close relations between these mountain and plains centers (Müller-Kosack 2008). In 2012, just before the border region became far too dangerous for archaeological research, my colleague Rébecca Janson discovered Iron Age sites along the flanks of the mountains leading north toward Keroua that may well be the remains of communities occupying that profitable and dangerous border position between two developing and increasingly antagonistic worlds. More work on those sites, and on the prehistory of this area more generally, must await the conclusion of the bloody saga of Boko Haram.

The relationship between Wandala and the DGB sites may well have involved slaves. As Islamic states like Kanem-Borno extended their reach—and their thirst for captives—across the lands south of Lake Chad, they would have required middlemen in more peripheral areas to fulfill their need for slaves. Wandala elites, positioned at the northwest of the Mandara Mountains and thus closer to the Kanuri center Birni Ngazargamo, were ideally positioned to supply those needs, in return for the exotic goods that proclaimed elite status throughout the region: horses, silk robes, exotic beads and jewelry, and perhaps eventually chain mail and firearms. What exactly the role of the DGB sites was in that interaction is at present unknown—although we need to remember the Mafa belief that the mythical *ndoday* people who built the sites, those white-skinned cannibals, were associated with horses, slavery, and the consumption of people, perhaps for profit.

There is no doubt that modern Mafa stories about the *ndoday* are palimpsests of different layers of montagnard experience, evoking the experiences of Mafa people with more recent exploiters, including nineteenth-century slave-raiders and even European colonial officers. At the same time, there is a sense of power and menace associated with the DGB sites that may have more ancient echoes as well. At one point during excavations on DGB-1 in 2008, excavators found a small human tibia—a shinbone, probably that of a child or adolescent—with a hole drilled neatly through it. The Mafa people working with us immediately associated this discovery with the menace of *ndoday*, and with a mutilation undertaken so that a cord could be run through the flesh of a captive to keep them in one place. Whether that was true or not, the discovery was certainly unnerving. Other researchers found iron chains while surveying close to DGB-10, one of the smaller DGB sites. Such chains are virtually unknown over the region as a whole, but they would have been useful in securing valuable captives, and people in the area around Keroua say that in the past they obtained such chains from the Wandala (David 2008, 107; Müller-Kosack 2010).

This provides us with a different understanding of the theatricality of the DGB sites. The sites certainly can evoke a variety of cultural references, and these may well include elements associated with water and abundant rains. However, we should not lose sight of the wider sociopolitical context within which the DGB sites were built. They were being constructed and used as one cultural order on the plains around the Mandara Mountains was ending and another was beginning. Substantial Iron Age farming communities had dominated the plains north toward Lake Chad through the whole first millennium CE. These people appear to have lived in permanent and sometimes walled villages and towns, with some degree of social and political hierarchy accompanied by fairly frequent but low-level warfare. Modern anthropologists would likely label such communities with the rather vague term "chiefdoms," not yet states but dominated by one preeminent individual or family. By the middle of the second millennium, that old Iron Age world order was crumbling under new pressures. Centralized and far more aggressive states like Kanem-Borno were expanding into the region from the north and east, bringing with them an expansion of trade and exchange systems, a vast increase in slave-raiding, and the temptations of wealth and status that the slave trade brought with it. They were forcibly absorbing indigenous communities into their expanding states as subjects or tributaries and selling many people as slaves. Those states and their actions would dominate the region until the coming of European colonial powers some five centuries later.

In the gradual separation and distinction of the Wandala from their Chadic-speaking relatives, we can see both the "making" of the Mandara Mountains and the plains around them by humans, as different identities coalesced in plains and on mountains, and the ways in which geographical positioning and proximity affected the destinies of both the Wandala and their close fifteenth-century neighbors—the mountain people who built and used the DGB sites. Under those circumstances, the DGB sites, with their massive walls and the theatricality of their platforms and passages, their caches of iron, and their exotic artifacts, would certainly have been part of the consciousness of the Wandala and their neighbors living in the plains below the massif. They are simply too unique, too remarkable in the region not to have played a role in the cultural and political understandings of both mountain and plains communities. As such, they would have served on the one hand as centers of ritual performance within a cultural world that was becoming distinctively "montagnard" and also as political statements directed at those strange and threatening new systems of power evolving at Keroua and elsewhere on the plains stretching toward Lake Chad.

Islamic states throughout the region created refuge zones and frontiers in a variety of environments, along the shores of Lake Chad and the banks of the Logone and Chari Rivers, for example. There is no reason to think that similar processes of cultural differentiation and accommodation to the appearance of predatory states did not take place in those areas as well, given that they all originally shared more or less the same Iron Age cultural heritage. However, for most of those other areas, we have relatively little archaeological data to analyze the precise processes through which such differentiation would have taken place. Perhaps the most important exception involves the territory of the Kotoko, a Chadic-speaking ethnic group that today occupies the *firki* clay plains just south of Lake Chad. Kotoko populations are primarily Muslim today, an outcome of their intense interactions with the Islamic states over many centuries, but they retain significant non-Muslim cultural practices and are best thought of as descendants of the "Sao" Iron Age populations of the region that have not been fully assimilated into Kanuri or Baghirmi identities.

Archaeological research on pre-Kotoko sites like Houlouf by Augustin Holl shows that processes analogous to those taking place in the Mandara Mountains were taking place closer to Lake Chad (Holl 2001). Work on these sites shows that population size and social/political complexity grew steadily through the first millennium. Intensity of settlement appears to have been greatest over the period 1000–1400, while the mountains were being settled and the DGB sites were being built and used. The discovery of a non-Muslim cemetery dated to the sixteenth century indicates that there was a significant degree of social stratification in the community at that time, with elite men buried with foreign, exotic grave goods and artifacts associated with horsemanship. There is even evidence that competing factions existed within Houlouf's elite. In very different contexts, the DGB sites and the contemporary Houlouf cemetery were complex developments of the Iron Age culture that had flourished south of Lake Chad for centuries. Both Kotoko and montagnards would be drawn, with or without their consent, into wider political and cultural worlds through their interactions with slave-raiding states, and both the Mandara Mountains and the shorelines of Lake Chad would become frontier zones in succeeding centuries.

Making frontiers: Montagnards and plainsmen

At the beginning of this chapter, we asked how the Mandara Mountains and the plains stretching north toward Lake Chad became separate human landscapes. In the mid-first millennium CE, the mountains were empty of human habitation, and a distinctive Iron Age agrarian culture had developed in the plains to the north and reaching to the shores of Lake Chad. A thousand years later, in 1500, descendants of those Iron Age peoples occupied both mountains and plains, but societies in those different environments were taking dramatically different forms: mountain communities were evolving toward the distinctive montagnard culture that existed in historical times (and creating the DGB sites), while the plains were coming under the control of centralized Islamic states. This trajectory of differentiation between mountains and plains progressively imposed on the region the frontier zones from which precolonial states would extract slaves, booty, and tribute, elements vital to the sustenance of state elites, through processes that we will consider in the next chapter.

That process of cultural change seems to have been a gradual one, beginning just over a thousand years ago as new dynamics of trade, exchange, and state violence started to encroach upon the Chadic-speaking farming communities that had domesticated the plains south of Lake Chad during the Iron Age. As the sociopolitical environment on the plains became more complex and probably more aggressive in the late first millennium, some people began to move into the hitherto-uninhabited mountains themselves, first along the foothills and eventually into favored landscapes like those around the DGB sites. We know far too little to call such people "losers" in conflicts on the plains, but this would have been a period when defensible and less accessible territories might well have looked quite attractive to certain groups, even given the challenges of mountain settlement. As this process continued, the distribution of land and the necessity of relatively higher population densities to sustain terrace farming produced different kinds of mountain communities than those on the plains below, with dispersed households scattered across the slopes and less scope for the aggrandizement of centralized power. Settlement in such new landscapes would have changed many aspects of daily life for mountain people, from the distribution of wood and fields, to the possibilities of architecture, to interactions with powerful new spirits of place. We can see those possibilities vividly expressed in the DGB sites themselves, and in the fully realized expertise in stone construction displayed by their builders, utterly unlike the construction techniques in use on the plains below—while at the same time, the pottery used by DGB people still bore significant similarities to that used by their plains neighbors.

When the DGB sites were being built and used, between the thirteenth and sixteenth centuries, significantly distinct mountain and plains cultures had already developed out of the common Iron Age cultural milieu that had existed on the plains in the preceding millennium—although of course those mountain and plains cultures would in turn change and develop further during the centuries leading up to the modern period. The descendants of the people who first settled the mountains were in the process of becoming montagnards, with cultures shaped by the possibilities and limitations of their physical environments at the same time that they in turn transformed those environments into landscapes amenable to human occupation and enjoyment. On the plains below, their cousins at places like Houlouf lived in a cultural landscape that was increasingly characterized by the expansionistic, slave-raiding states that were extending their control over the region through the same period.

Almost certainly, that differentiation between mountains and plains was mutually constituted: as in the historic Lake Chad Basin and everywhere else in the world, people defined themselves in opposition to those people who they saw as "outlandish," strangers, and possibly enemies. As noted above, mountain people today define themselves as *duw kunde*, "people of the rocks," and so fundamentally different from plainsmen, while plains groups insult mountain communities with the vile epithet of *kirdi*, "unbelievers," savage and uncivilized. Such would have been the case in the past as well—but we need to remember that both of these populations, montagnards and plainsmen, continued to interact and even to depend on one another in surprising ways through the succeeding centuries. As we shall see in the next chapter, one great paradox of human settlement in this region lies in the mutual interdependence displayed by these very different groups of people through the centuries, in circumstances where advantage and danger, cooperation and conflict, existed in the finest of balances, liable to be disturbed by even the most minor words or actions.

4

STATES, FRONTIERS, AND ENSLAVEMENT

August 16th, 1917: On Thursday the 27th of Juldandu
I sent Fadhl al Nar with his men to raid Sukur and they
captured 80 slaves, of whom I gave away 40. We killed 27
men and women and 17 children.

On the same day I sent a force to raid Dufur and they
killed eight pagans. The pagans killed the leader of my
force and captured one rifle. . . .

July 3, 1918: On Wednesday the 23rd of Ramadhan
I fixed the price of Yerima Baba's horse at 3 slave-girls.

The Diary of Hamman Yaji

JUST A CENTURY AGO, AN illiterate Fulani warlord living in Madagali was
investing some of his time in dictating his diary to a scribe. Madagali
is located just west of the Mandara Mountains in what is now Nigeria
and is only fifty miles (80 km) from Chibok, where in 2014—just one
century later—Boko Haram would kidnap hundreds of schoolgirls.
The warlord's name was Hamman Yaji; his diary consists of a day-
by-day account of his activities, an important part of which involved
the raiding expeditions that he organized and sent into the Mandara
Mountains to attack montagnard communities (Yaji 1995). The spoils

of those raids were grain, clothing, sheep and goats, cattle, and—in entry after entry—human beings, people turned into property, taken to be sold or given away as slaves. The diary is mind-numbing in its juxtaposition of banality and horror: dry recitations of settlement after settlement raided, different numbers of "pagans" (non-Muslim montagnards) killed in different places, enumeration of women and children enslaved.

Hamman Yaji's earliest raids do not seem to have been particularly successful, but he and his forces displayed more acumen from 1913 onward. Over 1,600 slaves are recorded as being taken in the diary between 1912 and 1920, along with many other goods, and well over 150 people are listed as having been killed in the raids (David 2012a), which is probably a gross underestimate. Girls and young women appear throughout the diary as by far the most valued and sought-after slaves—just as, a century later, Boko Haram would threaten to sell the young kidnapped women from Chibok "in the marketplace." The accounts of Hamman Yaji's slave raids are punctuated by other entries that record the workaday preoccupations of a local leader: details of gifts given and taxes taken from the lands he controlled, the scheming and politicking necessary to maintain chiefly status in a very dangerous political environment, and his triumphs and reverses in dealing with the new colonial governments in the region.

Historians don't know precisely why Hamman Yaji kept a diary between 1912 and 1927. This was not something that any other such warlords ever did, as far as we know, and the document thus remains more or less unique in West African history. It does not seem to have been written with any larger audience in mind, nor does it seem to have any obvious religious or political function. By this time, the lands around the Mandara Mountains were being progressively incorporated into the European colonial world, and researchers have suggested that the diary was a kind of aide-mémoire, this warlord's way of rationalizing and formalizing his role and activities in a dramatically changing economic and political environment (David 2012a). In modern parlance, perhaps we would call it a business plan, albeit a business plan of a particularly horrible sort. Although the diary itself is unique, the activity was not. Paul Lovejoy and Jan Hogendorn, in their book *Slow Death for Slavery*, note that enslavement as a legal status ended in the British colony of Nigeria only in 1936, and that slave raids had taken place well into the 1920s (Lovejoy and Hogendorn 1993, 28). Indeed, many people who I interviewed during 1980s field-work in the Mandara Mountains in Cameroon claimed that children had been kidnapped as slaves much more recently, albeit in a more discreet fashion.

There is another aspect of Hamman Yaji and his diary that we need to keep in mind, beyond the clerkish dreadfulness of a day-to-day list of slave raids and deaths in the mountains. Hamman Yaji was very much a frontier warlord, in a number of different ways. The village of Madagali that constituted his base was essentially a preco-lonial border outpost, established on the northern edges of the Fulani Adamawa Emirate and very close to the borders with the Kanuri state of Borno—and thus on an ethnic and religious frontier, as well as a political one. It was located on land taken in the nineteenth century by the Fulani from the Marghi people, who had previously controlled the region. In chapter 3, we saw that Fra Mauro had in the mid-fifteenth century already identified Marghi ("Mergi") people as the occupants of land west of the Wandala ("Mandera"). The Marghi and neighboring communities violently resisted that seizure, which is why Madagali even today sprawls around the base of an inselberg—Fulani rulers, like the Wandala, were not above retreating into defen-sive positions on a hill if threatened. Madagali was close to the most important sources of non-Muslim slaves in the Mandara Mountains to the east, which made the precarity of its location more or less accept-able. It was a dangerous place, with the deaths of at least seventeen of Hamman Yaji's own men recorded in his diary (including one of his sons), but with luck and ruthlessness one could make a living there, and perhaps even better one's fortunes.

Hamman Yaji also benefited greatly from the location of Madagali near a different kind of frontier: the developing borders between European colonies that were just being imposed in the lands around the Lake Chad Basin. In the two decades before Hamman Yaji began his diary in 1912, the British, French, and German colonial empires had scrambled to carve up this part of the continent, primarily for strategic reasons. As we saw in chapter 1, the Lake Chad Basin stands at a crossroads in Central Africa, a point of inflection between des-ert to the north and tropical forest to the south and straddling that great sweep of savanna grassland between the Atlantic and the Nile.

Control over the communications routes that focused on the region, those colonial powers thought, would allow them to build up networks of political domination and wealth extraction on an even larger scale. The frantic land grabs at the end of the nineteenth century resulted in the Northern Nigeria Protectorate becoming a British colony, Niger and Chad becoming French colonies (within Afrique Occidentale Française and Afrique Équatoriale Française, respectively), and most of modern Cameroon being incorporated with the German colony of Kamerun. This helps to explain one of the advantages that Boko Haram enjoys today—the fact that a traveler or a terrorist can cross three international boundaries south of Lake Chad, from Nigeria to Cameroon to Chad, in less than two hours.

Fortunately for Hamman Yaji and unfortunately for his victims, there was a great deal of uncertainty and dispute about which of these colonial powers was actually responsible for his territories around Madagali, located, again, on the borders of the developing colonies of Northern Nigeria and Kamerun. The outbreak of World War I contributed dramatically to that uncertainty: fighting between German colonial forces on the one hand and British and French forces on the other culminated in a siege of German forces in the northeastern Mandara Mountains south of Mora that lasted from September 1914 until March 1916. Colonial officers were too busy with military campaigns to really concern themselves with a local ruler attacking mountain populations that they considered, in any case, to be savages. After the German surrender south of Mora, Madagali passed into French control until 1922, at which point it was incorporated into what became "British Cameroons" under League of Nations mandate (and eventually became part of modern Nigeria). It was only in the early 1920s, after the British took over, that some degree of effective control began to be exerted over the area and Hamman Yaji's slave raids finally ended.

Frontiers, and the dangers and opportunities that exist along frontiers, form a constant theme in the history and modern experience of the Lake Chad Basin. Boko Haram operates in frontier zones, which have also through the twentieth century been areas of smuggling, banditry, and other forms of violence and wealth extraction. In the precolonial past, frontier zones saw similar kinds of violence taking place, and in fact some of the modern lands of Boko Haram were similarly considered dangerous border zones five centuries ago. In this chapter, we will examine the complex histories of precolonial frontiers in this part of Central Africa and look at the kinds of social and political processes that took place on those frontiers. Central among those processes would be enslavement and the unrelenting search for sources of slaves, and in fact such slave-raiding created borderlands as much as it took place in those areas.

As we saw in the last chapter, the settlement of the Mandara Mountains and the subsequent "pulling apart" of mountain and plains identities seems to have been a gradual process, probably beginning in the late first millennium CE and accelerating as states like Kanem-Borno and Baghirmi became increasingly active in the region five hundred years later. Archaeological phenomena like the DGB sites must be understood both as material expressions of montagnard identity, antecedent (but not identical) to the identities of modern mountain people, and as striking cultural statements that would be known to communities within the mountains as well as to those people living in the surrounding plains. However, this was no simple confrontation between two irreconcilable geographical and cultural landscapes; there were intense and continuous interactions across the mountain-plains boundary, and indeed across cultural and political boundaries in the region throughout the whole precolonial period.

To understand those interactions, we have to understand how states worked in the region, because the appearance of states seems to have changed the cultural history of the region in fundamental ways, especially through their involvement with the slave trade. Comprehension of precolonial states in this region is not straightforward, because the constitution and functioning of political units all around the Lake Chad Basin depended on very different understandings of territory and rule than citizens of twenty-first-century nation-states are accustomed to. For present purposes, these understandings particularly involve the ways in which elites made use of resources, landscapes, and ideologies, intimately bound together. In the rest of this chapter, we will first examine how these different aspects of state governance functioned together in the Lake Chad Basin and then look at the specific implications for precolonial populations in the lands of Boko Haram.

Slaves without gold

The international trading systems that enmeshed precolonial West and Central Africa were extremely complex. The exchange of enslaved humans, the "slave trade," dominates our understanding of those systems, as it certainly should, but both the trans-Saharan and the European Atlantic trading system encompassed a whole variety of different kinds of goods that were traded in both directions. We can see this along the West African coast, with the geographical terms that European traders used for different parts of the region: the Pepper Coast in modern Liberia (named for the malagueta peppers that were an important trade commodity in that area); the "Côte d'Ivoire" still memorialized in the name of a modern nation-state; the "Gold Coast," which was until the mid-twentieth century the British colonial name for Ghana; and finally the "Slave Coast," encompassing the modern Bight of Benin in Togo, Benin, and Nigeria. In fact, slaves were taken from all of these areas, but the terms in use vividly evoke the diversity of exports from the West African coast.

The same is true for the trans-Saharan slave trade, which was by far the most important long-distance economic relationship for the Lake Chad Basin.[1] A variety of goods were exported within and across the Sahara from different parts of sub-Saharan Africa, including at different times salt, meat, kola nuts, elephant and hippo ivory, and ostrich feathers, but the most valuable commodities exported from West and Central Africa were gold and enslaved humans, traded into the Mediterranean basin and the Muslim lands of the Middle East. As is the case around the world, gold is a rare commodity, and only certain regions yield significant amounts of the precious metal. In West Africa, the acquisition of gold was historically associated with a limited number of areas: the Bambuk goldfields in eastern Senegal, the Bure fields on the headwaters of the Niger River in Guinea, and the Akan goldfields in modern Ghana.

A huge amount of gold was taken out of these goldfields in ancient times, and gold was the archetypal high-value trade good, hungered after by the peoples of Europe and the Mediterranean basin. The role of West African gold was well understood in the medieval Islamic world from the late eighth century at least, when Muḥammad al-Fazārī called the ancient state of Ghana "the land of gold." West Africa was considered a region extraordinarily rich in gold by Christian Europeans as well, as we can see with the depiction of Mansa Musa, the ruler of the empire of Mali, seated on his throne and holding a nugget of gold in the Catalan Atlas of 1375–1380. Accessing West African gold became increasingly central to European economies from the thirteenth century onward, and the search for gold was a vital impetus for European exploration of West Africa from the fifteenth century onward. All of these gold fields were situated far to the west of the Lake Chad Basin, between Senegal, the Niger Bend, and the Akan area of modern Ghana. Through these areas, rulers and merchants depended on the gold trade as a commercial and political foundation of their regimes.

Further to the east around Lake Chad, equivalent goldfields did not exist, and states like Kanem-Borno, Baghirmi, and later the Sokoto Caliphate had no such access to gold as a basis for trans-Saharan export. Their rulers had to find other commodities that would allow them access to the rare and exotic goods and services that they increasingly needed to represent high status in the wider world and enforce dominion at home: chain mail; weapons and horses (these provided the basis for military domination in the region until the nineteenth century); fine clothing; jewelry and other luxury goods; and eventually the services of scribes, clerics, and scholars. In the area that this book examines, enslaved humans constituted by far the most valuable resource available for obtaining such goods, as well as a vital labor force and commodity in local economies and exchange systems. The very first historical mentions of the Lake Chad Basin by Arab writers like al-Ya'kūbī and al-Muhallabī, in the ninth and tenth centuries, respectively, emphasize that the rulers of Kanem took slaves and sold them, and do not mention other commodities. Indeed, as al-Ya'kūbī says, "The kings of the Sudan sell the Sudan [black people] for no reason, and quite apart from any wars," while al-Muhallabī wrote that the ruler "reduced to slavery those among his subjects whom he wished." At the same time, the Saharan oases north of Lake Chad were already known for their role as transshipment points in the trans-Saharan slave trade (Lange 1988, 451). It seems certain that enslavement and slave export played an important role in the economies of early states around the Lake Chad Basin, and it would continue to be the central element in trans-Saharan trade from the region until well into the nineteenth century.

However, the claims by al-Ya'kūbī and al-Muhallabī that the rulers of Kanem enslaved their own people and sold them deserve careful attention, because this would have been an extremely unusual way for African rulers to obtain slaves for sale—at least if we interpret their words according to modern assumptions. We know a good deal about the circumstances in which people were enslaved and sold in different societies across Africa during the precolonial period, and this almost never involved capricious enslavement and sale of citizens by their own ruler (Lovejoy 2012, 3–8). (We can imagine that such practices would not really endear sovereigns to their subjects, and might result in a sudden and drastic curtailment of their reign.) One of the central features of enslaved people is that they are identified as being outside of society in some way. This is essential to the process in which humans are reduced to the status of property: they must be placed outside the bounds of normal human interaction, beyond appeals to sympathy and fellowship, before such a status can be imposed.

This does not always involve foreigners. In some African societies, enslavement could be imposed as a judicial punishment for crimes like murder or theft. This would often be undertaken with a religious rationale: the Ibinukpabi oracle in the town of Aro Chukwu, in modern southeastern Nigeria, provides an excellent example, even though it is far away from the Lake Chad Basin. This oracle was widely recognized by neighboring communities as the voice of divinity, and it played a vital role in structuring political relationships in the region through the eighteenth and nineteenth centuries. The Ibinukpabi oracle was very frequently directly paid in slaves, or seized people as slaves in the course of its deliberations, and it also supported the slave-trading activities of Aro warriors and merchants (Lovejoy 2012, 82–83). Tens of thousands of enslaved people passed through the hands of the oracle during its period of greatest influence. In extreme cases, people might also place themselves or their family members into slavery voluntarily, if we can call such a desperate act "voluntary," perhaps because of a debt or because of impossible social or economic circumstances. There are historical accounts in parts of the Lake Chad Basin of parents selling one of their children during periods of extreme famine or want in order to gain the means to sustain the rest of their family (Beauvilain 1989, 116–124, 245–249). We can only imagine the hopelessness involved in making a decision of that sort; as we will see at the end of this chapter, the transfer of children during periods of crisis was one of the most persistent forms of servitude known from the lands of Boko Haram, lasting into the middle of the twentieth century.

Even though these forms of slavery did exist, judicial, religious, and voluntary enslavement were not nearly as ubiquitous or numerically as important in Africa as was the violent enslavement of foreigners, whether through warfare, slave-raiding, or kidnapping. This leads us to doubt the descriptions of enslavement provided by al-Ya'kūbī and al-Muhallabī—who were, after all, basing their accounts on second- or thirdhand information. It is far more likely that the rulers of Kanem were raiding into the territories of neighboring ethnic groups for slaves at the time when these accounts were written, rather than simply enslaving and selling their own subjects. As we saw in earlier chapters, the ninth and tenth centuries were also the period when exotic artifacts begin to appear in burial sites south of Lake Chad, and probably when people started to move into the Mandara Mountains. Whether or not Kanem's raids were extending from northeast of Lake Chad into Borno southwest of the lake at that very early date, it does appear that enslaved people were being moved in substantial numbers from Kanem to the oases of the central Sahara by the late first millennium, which if the historical period is any indication also implies that large numbers of slaves were also being held for domestic purposes around Lake Chad itself.

Fields of empire

"States . . . warred to trade and traded to war," as Stephen Reyna says in his magisterial analysis of the precolonial political economy of the Baghirmi state, southeast of Lake Chad (Reyna 1990, 39). Distinctions between the different mechanisms through which outsiders, foreigners, could be enslaved violently—warfare, slave-raiding, kidnapping—may be useful for historians of the slave trade, but they would have little meaning for either those groups involved in taking slaves in Central Africa, or for the unfortunate targets of their attacks. As Reyna says for Baghirmi, and as other authors have documented for other states around Lake Chad, slave-trading and elite identity were closely intertwined across this region, such that war and trade together "drew the other societies [in the region] into the coils of the state" (Reyna 1990, 39). Ruling groups in states across this region had to control commodities and populations, in order to guarantee that consumable and tradable resources could be produced. Sources of revenue had to be identified and exploited; trade routes had to be protected, in great part in order to obtain the means for making war. This was not merely a question of economics. Organized warfare and the capture and ownership of slaves certainly served the economic interests of states, but these activities were also among the defining pursuits of elites in those states. It is likely that the spread of slave-taking and slaveholding had as much to do with efforts by developing elites to become established and accepted among peer groups as it did with economic circumstances.

In the Lake Chad Basin, where that quintessentially valuable trade good, gold, was not available, human populations themselves became the commodity that elites depended on to obtain the goods and services that supported their rule. Other societies had to be drawn "into the coils of the state," most importantly as sources for the enslaved humans whose labor and sale would underpin the economies of the elites. However, those areas that served as reservoirs for enslavement could not be fully incorporated into the state itself, because that would have implied that their inhabitants were not foreigners or outsiders and thus enslavable, but rather subjects of the sovereign. At this point, the paradox becomes obvious, and it extends beyond the Lake Chad Basin: states that depend on an economy of slave-raiding and slave-trading need to establish sources of slaves that are under their control at least temporarily, but where social and cultural identities are quite different. In fact, slave-raiding states in the Lake Chad Basin had a great need for frontier zones, precisely because such zones across the region were the primary area for slave-taking.

It is at this point that we have to detach ourselves from twenty-first-century assumptions about how state control works. In modern nation-states, boundaries are well-demarcated lines on a map and in the landscape. In theory, modern political borders themselves have no width: if you stand at such a border, any step, large or small, that you take can transport you from one nation-state into another. There may be different sorts of border zones between countries—disputed land or maritime borders, demilitarized zones or unmarked frontiers as in

Europe's Schengen Zone, and so on—but an agreed-upon demarcation marks a successful border between successful states. Similarly, modern nation-states are assumed to have jurisdiction over their territory from the capital equally and uniformly to all of the borders. Within the territory, sovereignty and the responsibilities of control go hand in hand, and states theoretically exhibit the characteristics that generations of anthropology professors have taught to their students: centralized political authority, a state bureaucracy, redistribution systems (usually involving taxation), and a monopoly over the legitimate use of coercive force (with a judiciary, police, and/or military forces). States may not be able to control all of their territories: they may be embroiled in warfare, they may be occupied by other states or by representatives of the international community, or they may simply be too weak or find it not in their interests to do so. (We will discuss this latter question further in the next chapter.) If, however, a modern state cannot maintain control over its borders or its territory, it may well be described as a "failed state"—as, for example, Somalia has been described through much of the last thirty years.

On maps, Western researchers usually depict the precolonial African states that we are talking about in the same way as they do modern states, with well-delineated boundaries and without significant international differentiation (Sharpe 1986). On such maps, Wandala could be France or Japan; Kanem could be Jordan (figure 1.3). This certainly does not mean that these authors think of all such states as in every way equivalent to modern nation-states, but it does signal a set of assumptions about control over geographical space, and over social and political differentiation within the state boundaries. This is not how states in the Lake Chad Basin worked—nor, for that matter, is it how many states in Europe functioned before the seventeenth or eighteenth centuries. States in the Lake Chad Basin needed reliable access to areas that served as "reservoirs" of enslavable people, and these areas could not be fully incorporated into the state. This was the case not only for Kanem and later Borno but also for Baghirmi, Wandala, the Adamawa Emirate (with Hamman Yaji at Madagali in the frontier zone) and the broader Sokoto Caliphate, and indeed all of the precolonial states and empire that we will look at in this book.

Rather than using models that are based on modern assumptions, we should again turn to the description of control in Baghirmi by

Stephen Reyna, who in turn uses concepts from a French political scientist, Jacques Le Cornec (Reyna 1990, 67–70). According to Le Cornec and Reyna, we should understand Baghirmi and other states in the region as essentially a series of concentric circles of different kinds of influence: the core, tributary, and predation zones (figure 4.1). The core of the state would be that area under the direct, day-to-day control of the ruler and of the elite; it includes the residence of the ruler, his court, and elements of the state bureaucracy.[2] It would also contain the capital and major population centers, as well as rural areas that recognized the direct sovereignty of the ruler or his vassals and paid taxes to the state. State cores were marked by a common language and a good deal of cultural unity, and probably by some shared historical and ideological understandings about how the world worked. Armed forces from this area, organized around the ruler, members of the elite, and their direct followers, made up the core of any military endeavors that the state might undertake. In this zone, political control might function more or less as we expect in modern states. This core area need not have been particularly large: in Baghirmi, one of the most influential states in the Lake Chad Basin, the core area only seems to have measured about one hundred miles (170 km) across at its maximum extent (Reyna 1990, 68–69). For the much smaller Wandala state north of the Mandara Mountains, the equivalent core probably covered an area of only about thirty by thirty miles (50x50 km) at any one time.

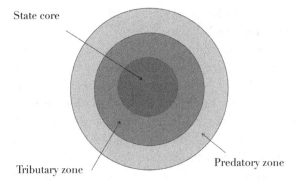

Figure 4.1: Zones of empire

Surrounding this core zone, Le Cornec and Reyna identify a larger "tributary zone." The communities in this zone had long-term relations with the state ruler and with the administration in the core zone; this often involved, for example, having regular representation in the court, paying tribute (instead of taxes) to the state, and furnishing military auxiliaries in time of war and raiding. The relations between core and tributary groups were often justified historically, through stories of common kinship. At the same time, tributary groups managed their own day-to-day affairs without intervention from the state, and often had very distinct ethnic and linguistic identities from the populations that made up the core of the state. State claims of tributary status were often extremely contentious, frequently denied by those communities when they felt they could resist, and only grudgingly acceded to when the state imposed its dominance. In the eighteenth and nineteenth centuries, for example, Wandala claimed as tributaries a number of surrounding communities, some of which vehemently disputed that status, while itself simultaneously trying to evade obligations of tribute that were claimed by its much larger Kanuri neighbor, Borno (Denham and Clapperton 1826, 117–121; Mohammadou 1982, 231; Morrissey 1984).

The "predation zone" was the area beyond the capital and the tributary zones, outside state administration and any kind of regular relations, where state control could only be imposed via military force and then usually only for short periods of time. It was occupied by populations that denied the sovereignty of the state and resisted state presence through force of arms. As we will see in the next chapter, their actions against neighboring states would often be described as banditry, the action of people who were literally "outlaws" and beyond state control. In many cases, these people would see the people living in the state core not merely as strangers but as enemies—and state elites reciprocated, often using the epithet *kirdi*, which labeled people as "savages" and fit to be hunted for slaves. Predation zones were in many (but not all) cases quite distant from state cores and thus difficult and dangerous to access; one of the main functions of communities in the tributary zone would be to furnish a base of operations for state military operations in the predation zones.

At the same time, the predation zone was essential to the functioning of the state and the reproduction of its elite, as it was through raiding and military operations in the predation zone that the state obtained slaves for labor and export. The predation zone was a place of periodic, unpredictable violence: slave raids would only happen at particular times of the year, usually before the agricultural season began, but particular communities in such areas would probably not know exactly where and when the horsemen of the slave-raiders would appear at the edges of their fields or villages. In some cases, the impetus for a slave raid might originate on the other side of the Sahara: rulers in debt to North African traders and worried that their imports might be cut off would sometimes organize a slave raid in order to repay their debts (Cohen 1991).

This concept of core, tributary, and predation zones provides a far more realistic understanding of precolonial states in the Lake Chad Basin than do assumptions taken from modern nation-states. In particular, it gives us a way of understanding how states dealt geographically with the paradox of being dependent on a commodity—enslaved humans—that required significant social distance for its extraction. At the same time, we should not take the image of core, tributary, and predation zones as concentric circles too literally, for two reasons. First, people do not distribute themselves evenly across landscapes, and landscapes offer different advantages and dangers for different groups of people. As slave-raiding proliferated across the Lake Chad Basin through the middle of the second millennium, populations subjected to slave-raiding retreated into areas where they could more successfully defend themselves against the attacks of mounted slave-raiders. That is probably why the Mandara Mountains were settled, as we saw in the last chapter. Similarly, groups ancestral to modern Yedina occupied the islands of Lake Chad, and the people known as Hadjeray live in the Guéra highlands of central Chad in circumstances similar to those of montagnards in the Mandara area, while groups like the Masa and Musgum used the borders and marshes of the Logone and Chari Rivers for protection.

There was thus a great deal of variability in the boundaries of predation zones and in their distance from state cores. In the case of the Wandala state, where rulers situated their capitals at the foot of the Mandara Mountains or neighboring inselbergs for their own defense, those same mountains provided very effective shelter from slave raids for montagnard populations. Just a few miles from the palace of the *tlikse*, the Wandala ruler, were communities of montagnards that were the potential targets of slave raids—groups that could, in retaliation, also make sudden attacks out of the mountains on Wandala towns and villages (MacEachern 1993). The mountains were also sources of other commodities that were vital to the Wandala economy, like iron ore, and montagnard people had need of equally vital commodities like salt that could only be provided by plains populations. This led to extraordinarily complex situations of collaboration between Wandala and montagnard groups, with nearby montagnard communities switching back and forth between tributary status, trading clients, and targets of Wandala slave raids—sometimes within the same year. There is an enormous paradox in the fact that the Wandala traded regularly with peoples who, only a short time later, they might be attacking in the quest for slaves. As one old montagnard man once said to me, "The Wandala are clever. They bought our iron, then used it to make the shackles that they held us with" (MacEachern 1993). This is one reason that the core area of the Wandala state was so small: potential targets for slave raids were located close to hand.

More common would be situations where the predation zones would be perhaps 100–150 miles (150–250 km) from the state core, as was the case for most of the targets of Baghirmi or Borno slave raids (figure 4.2). This raised real logistical challenges in equipping and supporting military forces at such a distance from the core; as noted above, tributary communities often provided a closer base of operations for such slave raids. One natural response to those challenges would be for state elites to encourage tributary populations themselves to act as "subcontractors," raiding into the predation zones and then selling enslaved people back to the dominant state— thus avoiding the hazards and challenges of raiding at long distances. As we saw in the last chapter, this seems

Figure 4.2: Cavalryman in the service of the ruler of Borno

to be how the Wandala first got into the slave-raiding business, acting as subcontractors to Borno and eventually subcontracting out raiding on their own peripheries to populations like the Guiziga in the Diamaré Plain to the southeast. Baghirmi followed a similar course with its tributaries, as did Borno with other subcontractors (Reyna 1990, 144–145). This had the effect of generating similar dynamics of political development among tributary societies, as leaders from such groups would be fitted within state hierarchies at a subordinate level (Forkl 1982; Mohammadou 1982), financing the trappings of authority borrowed from their more "stately" neighbors through the acquisition and sale of slaves. We can see this process at work, for example, through the widespread borrowing of Kanuri and Baghirmi terms for court positions and state officials among societies throughout the southern Lake Chad Basin, even those (like Sukur, west of the Mandara Mountains, for example) that cannot in any real sense be described as states. States thus generated peripheral political systems with similar characteristics, which might later come into competition with them.

The second reason for distrusting any simple image of core, tributary, and predation zones as concentric circles is even more straightforward: the zones of hegemony of different states overlapped, at least in their tributary and predation zones. For the Lake Chad Basin as a whole, we have to imagine coexisting state cores of different sizes, for Kanem-Borno, Baghirmi, Wandala, and so on, in a hugely complex political relationship. These states fought and made treaties with one another, contended for the allegiance of tributary communities—and simultaneously exploited the common frontier zones that lay between their capitals in the search for slaves and other booty. This meant that unfortunate communities in those regions frequently had to deal with attacks and slave raids from the military forces of different states, coming from different directions at different times, making defensible landscapes—mountains, islands, and so on—even more valuable for the small-scale communities that were the targets of such raids.

Sun Kings and Janus-faced sovereigns

These very different understandings of political landscapes had all kinds of historical consequences for the societies of the Lake Chad

Basin. One such consequence is, paradoxically, the production of new social and political forms on the contested frontiers between different states. Stephen Reyna calls those areas "predation zones" in an analysis of warfare, slave-raiding, and wealth creation in Baghirmi—and that is a very useful, albeit fairly negative, way of thinking of them. However, another anthropologist, Igor Kopytoff (1987) described those same kinds of regions as "internal African frontiers" and conceived of them as crucibles of African social and political innovation—a model that has been extremely influential in historical understandings of the continent. Such "internal frontiers" provided havens for refugees, dissidents, and the losers in the interminable political and ideological conflicts that afflicted the region, especially during the periods of religious ferment that we will examine below. They were zones of cultural collision and synthesis: every one of the Mandara montagnard ethnic groups possess oral histories that tell of astonishingly diverse origins of its subgroups, the results of repeated movements by individuals and families looking for new homelands and often fleeing old dangers, people coming from all around the region and making a life together. Other refuge zones are marked by similar diversity.

As such, these internal frontiers were also laboratories for different kinds of social and political arrangements. In Sukur, an extraordinary concentration on iron production allowed montagnards to deemphasize agriculture in favor of iron exports, vital to everyday life in the larger region, in what Nicholas David called a "classless industrial society" (David 1996). The Ningi Mountains of northern Nigeria acted as a refuge for dissident Islamic clerics fleeing the rulers of the Sokoto Caliphate; the polity that resulted blended utopian Islam with local, non-Muslim political calculations and developed into yet another predatory, slave-raiding state (Patton 1987). And, of course, in the northwestern Mandara Mountains, the people who built the DGB sites represented ideology, prestige, and power architecturally, in rather different ways than their neighbors or their descendants did. Not all of these experiments prospered into the modern age, but they do underline the diversity and dynamism of societies existing even within "predation zones."

These political landscapes had significant consequences far away from the frontiers as well. We have already seen how small the "core zones," the areas administered on a day-to-day basis, of many of these political units actually were; one might wonder just how significant a state measuring only a hundred miles across could be. However, this makes perfect sense once we disentangle the functioning of such states in the Lake Chad Basin from our modern assumptions about territory. From the point of view of the state leaders, the primary function of the core zone around the capital was to supply the day-to-day needs of the ruler, his court, and the nobility, and also to supply them with the means to make war (MacEachern 2015; Reyna 1990). By the nineteenth century at least, much of that state production in the southern Lake Chad Basin was undertaken on plantations staffed by slaves (MacEachern 2001b, 197–206; Lovejoy 2012, 196–201). The core zone might produce other goods for export and elite support—iron and cotton for the Wandala, for example—but the chief economic and status preoccupation of state elites continued to be the acquisition of slaves through raiding and warfare, since those slaves could be traded to obtain the goods associated with elite status. This dynamic had the effect of unmooring the state administrative apparatus from territory. The ruler depended not on land for wealth but on people—his own supporters, and the people whom his supporters were able to enslave and sell.

The theme of "wealth in people" has a very long history in African societies, but in complex and multivalent ways (Guyer and Belinga 1995). In agrarian communities across the continent, human labor was the central element in agricultural and other productive activities, and a successful household would be one that could attract and hold the people necessary to carry out domestic tasks through the annual cycle. As societies became more complex, the support of relatives, neighbors, and clients would only become more important in leaders' search for prestige and power. The necessity of holding on to supporters often provided a brake on the free exercise of leaders' ambitions, particularly in those large areas of the continent where population densities were low and disgruntled followers might decide to leave and establish independent households elsewhere. That might not have been a possibility in the densely populated Mandara Mountains around the DGB sites, but it is likely that the labor that built those monuments was coordinated through community ideology and the charisma of local leaders, rather than through the use of force.

The situation would have been quite different in slave-raiding states, where wealth in people would have included people in servile statuses and a trade in humans brought wealth in other forms. Individual enslaved people might attain a significant degree of power and sometimes wealth; in Baghirmi, for example, rulers preferred slave eunuchs in some senior leadership role, as their status and inability to have children would prevent them from founding competing dynasties (Reyna 1990). Most enslaved people would have occupied the very bottom of the social ladder, working in domestic quarters or in the fields, or serving in military forces. In Wandala and the Sokoto Caliphate, entire slave villages were organized in plantations to produce exports like cotton, and a mark of social status was using slaves in the fields, releasing freeborn women from agricultural duties. As we will see in chapter 6, there are significant variations in women's experience of Boko Haram, which in some ways seem to reproduce the precolonial distinction between enslaved and freeborn women.

In many ways, then, what was most significant to the ruler and the nobility in these precolonial states was not governance itself but what we might call "stateliness," the trappings of statehood and especially those high-status and exotic goods noted above: horses, fine clothing and jewelry, weapons (eventually including firearms), and the services of clerics, scribes, and diplomats. Through the second millennium, "stateliness" increasingly involved assuming the symbols and behavior of an orthodox Islamic ruler. "Stateliness" allowed elites to interact, compete, and cooperate with each other across the Lake Chad Basin and beyond. It allowed them to maintain political, social, and economic ties with neighboring states, and more broadly to function within diplomatic and trade networks that extended well beyond the Sudanic zone of Central Africa, across the Sahara and to the Nile and the Mediterranean. From this perspective, the details of state administration, and the degree of control exerted over state territory, might have been somewhat irrelevant. Many European rulers would have understood the principle clearly: what mattered far more than the details of governance were the ruler and the nobility, their dignity and grandeur and the means at hand for them to acquire and protect both. King Louis XIV of France is supposed to have said "L'état, c'est moi" ("I am the state") in the middle of the seventeenth century, when many of the processes described in this chapter were in full development. There is argument about whether the Sun King ever used those exact words, but his contemporaries in the Lake Chad Basin would certainly have understood the sentiment.

This unmooring of the state from territorial control and a preoccupation with external "stateliness" meant that Sudanic leaders in the Lake Chad Basin could be somewhat Janus-faced sovereigns, directing different images of themselves to external and internal audiences. On the one hand, rulers assumed at least some of the trappings of Sudanic "stateliness," and through the second millennium this more and more often involved Islamic norms of behavior. On the other hand, they still needed to interact with traditional systems of governance and ideology, which were most often of far more importance to common people than Islam was. It might be that, as we saw in the last chapter, elites thought of commoners as "grass . . . fodder for horses" (Reyna 1990, 134), but they still needed the support of those commoners in order to exist, to provide grazing for their horses.

Different polities might place more or less emphasis on either side of this opposition between "stateliness" and traditional ideologies, depending on their particular circumstances. At one extreme, the jihadist movements in the eighteenth and nineteenth century that we shall look at in a moment were preoccupied with the imposition of a purified Islam and the eradication of unorthodox practices, by the ruler and by the citizenry. At the other end of the spectrum, small polities like Sukur seem to have been content with the adoption of a few court titles from Borno, within an otherwise entirely local political framework (David and Sterner 2004). Wandala and Baghirmi rulers adopted a middle ground, working to project an image of Islamic orthodoxy outward while tolerating or even participating in non-Muslim ceremonies demanded by their subjects. In some cases, this balancing act was not particularly convincing: as one British colonial officer said, "The 'Mai' [ruler] of Mandara and the bulk of his people profess to be Mohammedans, but their professions are little more than a veneer of respectability over their original paganism" (Tomlinson 1916).

Ideologies

That ruler of Wandala with an image problem was not the only sovereign in the region unable to successfully reconcile these very different public models of royal power and governance. One of the recurring figures of West African Islamic history has for centuries been the apostate king, nominally Muslim but judged by more orthodox followers of Islam to be far too tolerant of traditional religious practices. Sonni Ali Ber, the first ruler of the Songhay Empire along the Niger River in the fifteenth century, was perhaps the most famous of such apostate kings, but later Islamic rulers throughout the region were similarly accused of religious syncretism: tolerance for "pagan" practices was one of the chief accusations directed against Hausa, Kanuri, Bambara, and other rulers by Islamic jihadists from the seventeenth century onward (Loimeier 2013, 109–129; Robinson 2004). A number of medieval Arabic historical sources claim that while the rulers of these African states were Muslims, their subjects were not, or say that not even the rulers were observant Muslims (Levtzion and Hopkins 1981, 76, 87, 174, 179). At the beginning of the nineteenth century, this dispute gave rise to an extraordinary religious debate between Muhammad Bello, the son of the Fulani jihadist leader Usman dan Fodio, who accused the leaders and people of Kanem-Borno of tolerating pagan beliefs (Adeleye 1971), and Shehu Muhammad al-Kanemi, who replied that sin, bad as it might be in an Islamic country, was not unbelief, and that Kanem-Borno had already been an Islamic state for eight hundred years. He combined this theological defense against jihad with a military defense against dan Fodio's allies, thereby ensuring the independence of Borno until the colonial period. We have already seen that one deadly aspect of Boko Haram's history in northern Nigeria is a set of debates with other Islamic groups about this very issue, the conflation of sin and unbelief and how pious Muslims should treat both.

Islam provided an important but ambiguous element in the arsenal of precolonial state rulers around the Lake Chad Basin. As Islam spread through the region and across the Sudanic and Sahelian zones of West and Central Africa more generally from the eleventh century onward, it was adopted first by local elites and only much later by commoners—often being imposed on them. It seems likely that orthodox Islam was not widespread among rural commoner populations of even Islamic states until the seventeenth or eighteenth centuries, during the era of the jihads. The initial medieval adoption of the new religion went along with a great degree of syncretism between Islam and indigenous belief systems, many of which were already very sophisticated. As a state religion, Islam provided a compelling material and behavioral system through which African elite groups could communicate their status regionally, as well as manage their connections to a much wider world. There is no doubt that for many rulers and members of the nobility across the Lake Chad Basin, conversion to Islam was sincere and profoundly important, but it also dramatically increased the possibilities of participation in long-range trading networks controlled by Muslim groups—including the networks of the trans-Saharan slave trade—and in diplomatic contacts with North Africa and the Middle East. This was especially important as elite performance of "stateliness" became ever more cosmopolitan, involving both conversion to Islam and acquisition of the exotic trappings of Islamic rule.

Islam also provided a ready-made justification and demarcation for the process of enslavement. According to Islamic law, freeborn Muslims could not be enslaved, and slaves could only legitimately be acquired through purchase or through warfare—theoretically only in a jihad, although that limitation was widely ignored. Of course, this political and cultural dynamic also provided non-Muslim communities—especially those outside of the refuges of mountains and islands—with a powerful incentive to convert to Islam, as doing so would in theory provide both some degree of protection against enslavement for commoners and increased legitimacy for elites. Important populations in modern northern Cameroon, like the Kotoko communities near Lake Chad and the Guiziga living on the plains east of the Mandara Mountains, were subjected to these processes of Islamization between the eighteenth and twentieth centuries, and are now predominantly Muslim. The Wandala went through the same process, but between one hundred and two hundred years earlier. This ideological and cultural opposition between Muslim and non-Muslim communities has continued into the twenty-first century and forms the basis of that epithet *kirdi*, used to describe montagnards: *kirdi* is originally a Kanuri word meaning "pagans" or "unbelievers." At the same time, the protection of being Muslim would in many cases be only theoretical: kings needed slaves, and if people could avoid enslavement by merely professing Islam, what might a ruler do? And so one constant of Islamic political relations and diplomacy in the Lake Chad Basin (and indeed across West and Central Africa) for the last five hundred years has been perennial disputes about which peoples were or were not really Muslim, and what that might mean.

In such situations, the theological distinction between sin (which, while worthy of condemnation, did not remove the sinner from the *dar al-Islam* and its protections) and apostasy (which made the apostate subject not to merely attack but to enslavement) had real political consequences. Historical accounts and contemporary diplomacy are full of these controversies, and of different attempts at theological reconciliation when the need arose. In Hausa urban society between the sixteenth century and eighteenth century, Muslim elites designated practitioners in indigenous *bori* rituals of spirit possession (which also incorporated some Islamic elements) not as "pagans" but as *maguzawa*—"Magi," or Zoroastrians. Even though *bori* had nothing at all to do with Zoroastrianism, which originated in Iran in the second millennium BCE, this solution contributed to a tolerance of *maguzawa* as a subordinated group within Hausa society. The theological disputes between Muslim clerics in modern northern Nigeria thus exist within a long and important politico-religious tradition in the region.

It would be too easy to leave this discussion at this point, with the confrontation between Islam and indigenous religions in the southern Lake Chad Basin. In this culmination of that process, Christianity would progressively be adopted by non-Muslim communities in the region during the colonial period, as a counterweight to the earlier world religion. However, that would be too facile. Islam in all the diverse forms represented in Central Africa—the Mālikī school of Sunni Islam, Shi'a, the *tariqa* religious brotherhoods with their background in Sufi belief—has always been subject to confrontation and negotiation, as well as devotion, in this part of Africa. It has coexisted with indigenous religious beliefs and continues to do so today, even in the most unlikely of circumstances: witness the protective amulets called gris-gris, widely condemned by orthodox religious leaders as non-Islamic but still widely used by Muslims and regularly recovered from the abandoned camps of Boko Haram fighters. It has been deployed by precolonial and modern states in the region in the service of political struggle, and equally by ethnic groups within those states: Islam has been used as a focus of political resistance by both Kotoko and Guiziga communities against dominant Muslim states, for example, after they had gone through their own process of Islamization. Religion, like resources and landscapes, has been an instrument of cultural and political relations between states, their populations, and their neighbors, and continues to be used that way today.

Making the plains

This is a book about the lands of Boko Haram, about their history and archaeology. How did these processes of enslavement, borders, state violence, and local resistance play out between Lake Chad and the Mandara Mountains—on and in the ground, so to speak? There is rather little archaeological evidence that bears directly on the processes of political elaboration and slave-raiding that I have described in this chapter. This might seem strange, given all of the attention that I paid to archaeology in describing the settlement of the Mandara Mountains in the last chapter. There are a number of reasons for this, beyond the contrast between durable stone architecture in the mountains and more ephemeral mud and mud-brick architecture in the surrounding plains. First, as is the case through most of Africa, the slave trade itself left relatively few identifiable and distinctive material remains. Artifacts that we can identify as being used specifically in the trade are vanishingly rare—although as we saw in the last chapter, there is a fascinating association in oral histories between iron chains, like those found near DGB sites, and communities that interacted with the slave-raiding Wandala. The markets and stockades where slaves would have been kept and sold seem to have been integrated within wider urban settings and were probably built of wood and mud, both materials that disappear in the course of a few decades. The special-purpose stone forts and trading emporia that Europeans built along the West African coast have no equivalent in the Lake Chad Basin, and the slave plantation communities that regional elites assembled for agricultural and export purposes seem to have largely resembled non-slave rural villages and hamlets. This serves as a useful reminder that Central African enslavement, while long-lasting and brutal, was not elaborated and industrialized in the way that slavery was, for example, in the United States.

Second, and in distinct contrast to most of the rest of the world, there has been relatively little research done on the capitals of Lake

Chad Basin states, the places where we might expect these processes of state function to be most evident. Some of these, such as the first capitals of Kanem northeast of Lake Chad and Massenya, the capital of Baghirmi in central Chad, are in areas where political turmoil and logistical challenges have made archaeology impossible over the past four decades. Others, like the successive capitals of Borno at Birni Ngazargamo and (after 1814) at Kukawa, have been visited by archaeologists, but with no substantial fieldwork undertaken. My own excavations at the second Wandala capital at Doulo, and our limited fieldwork around the first capital at Keroua on the Cameroon-Nigeria border, have provided some insights into trade and relations with montagnards for the Wandala state (Jones 2001; MacEachern 1993, 2012b; MacEachern and Garba 1994). However, we were not able to uncover much evidence for the functioning of the state administration itself, in large part because both Doulo and Keroua are still significant Wandala communities and local people were understandably uneasy with the prospect of archaeologists digging up the places associated with their historic rulers.

Archaeology has often been preoccupied with the actions of rulers and powerful people, but on the plains around Lake Chad most of the information obtained from surveys and excavations through the last fifty years concerns common people. We can turn that to our advantage by searching in the general patterning of the archaeological record for the political and cultural processes that I have described and for evidence of changes in these processes over time. This involves an examination of community development and landscape changes in the areas that came to be dominated by states around the Lake Chad Basin. In the last chapter, we saw the ways in which the Mandara Mountains came to be settled and montagnard identities formed in a dynamic relationship with plains communities. Now we will briefly look at what happened to those plains communities themselves, as they were progressively incorporated within the tributary or predation zones of Sudanic states during or after the period of mountain settlement.

When Kanem-Borno first encroached upon the plains south of Lake Chad in the early second millennium, Kanuri elites found the region already occupied by a variety of different groups, descendants of the iron-using communities that had lived there for more than a thousand years and that are described in chapter 2. Those people are still remembered in local legends by a number of names: the most widespread term is "Sao," but around the Mandara Mountains and in the Diamaré Plain to the east they are often called "Maya" or "Zumaya" (Lange 1989; Lebeuf 1962; Seignobos 1986). Sao people are supposed to have been giants, capable of legendary feats of building, but they are described as "pagans"—that is, non-Muslims—in modern oral histories, and they were eventually defeated in their encounters with Muslim states. At the same time, modern communities very frequently say that their own ancestors belonged to these populations: many Kotoko and Kanuri people south of Lake Chad claim or admit to Sao ancestry, and it is not hard to find Wandala living on the plains northeast of the Mandara Mountains who say that their ancestors were Maya. The Zumaya are probably the best known of these earlier groups, as they were defeated by Fulani and destroyed as an ethnic group only in the nineteenth century. There were still a few people who remembered some words of the Zumaya language in the 1980s; it seems to have resembled Chadic languages found along the Logone River to the east, rather than others spoken around the Mandara Mountains, which supports oral histories that say that the Zumaya had immigrated into the region centuries before.

"Sao" is a Kanuri term that might be glossed as "earlier peoples," whatever its actual meaning, and it was applied by the Kanuri invaders to a whole variety of different ethnic groups that would have thought of themselves as quite distinct from one another. There are hints of these cultural distinctions between different Sao groups in the archaeological remains that we excavated from Iron Age archaeological sites scattered across the plains, and especially from the tons of pottery that those sites have yielded. Different locations yield varying proportions of types of ceramic decoration, sometimes with quite striking differences and sometimes with very subtle ones (Langlois 1995; O'Brien, Lin, and MacEachern 2016). As we all know, societies across the globe, in the past and in recent times, express ethnic or social identities through artifacts: clothing, architecture, furniture, and indeed every aspect of humans' material lives. The fact that people do this so ubiquitously is one of the human actions that makes archaeology possible.

These expressions of past identities are often not at all straight-forward for archaeologists to interpret, just as they are not in modern societies, but they offer a fascinating insight into how ancient peoples partitioned their social worlds. Pottery is easy to make, easy to decorate, and long-lasting in the archaeological record; pots may break, but the potsherds themselves do not decay unless they are ground down into dust. If ancient communities used pottery, there is a good chance that that pottery will carry some messages about social identities. In the case of these different Sao sites, virtually all of the pottery we find is broken. However, even broken pottery retains its decoration, and examination and statistical analysis help us detect differences in the distribution of such decorations—painting, incisions, rouletting, and so on—across space and time. For example, there seem to be over-arching contrasts in the pottery produced in Iron Age communities on the plains around the northwestern extremities of the Mandara Mountains (in the area where the Wandala originated) and that from sites around the northeastern massif, about twenty miles (30 km) away (O'Brien, Lin, and MacEachern 2016). We cannot decode the details of what these differences meant to the people who produced and used this pottery, but the fact that it exists still tells us a great deal about these ancient societies.

These archaeological sites are everywhere in the plains around the mountains (figure 4.3). The most striking of them are the Iron Age tell mound sites, accumulations of the material remains of daily life that may include dozens of mounds and cover many acres of land. They are not particularly difficult to find, and in fact the first professional archaeologist to work in the region, Jean-Paul Lebeuf, produced a remarkable map and gazetteer of abandoned sites, spanning Cameroon and Chad and extending into Nigeria (Lebeuf 1969). Local people may give particular names to ancient habitation sites, often characterizing them by the artifacts found scattered thickly on their surface. When in local conversations archaeologists encounter place names that include the terms *dugjé* (like Aissa Dugjé) or *djiddere* (like Mehé Djiddere), we know to pay particular attention: these words mean "garbage mound" in Wandala and Fulani, respectively, and are often applied to archaeological sites.

These tell mounds are daunting places for an archaeologist to discover, because the sheer mass of ancient material accumulated—tons

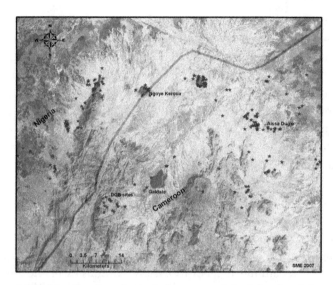

Figure 4.3: Map of archaeological sites around the Mandara Mountains, with the DGB sites

of mud walling, broken pottery, slag from iron smelting, bones, and on and on—mean that a careful investigation of any one of these sites can easily take years to finish (figure 4.4). As we saw in chapter 2, the Aissa Dugjé site yielded some of the earliest horse remains from western Africa, between the sixth and eighth centuries, with all that that implies about social and political dynamics in the region. It covers about forty-five acres (18 ha) and includes over thirty culturally produced mounds; excavations during two field seasons and eight months in 1995 and 1996 barely scratched the surface of this rich and complex site. Radiocarbon dates show that the site was first occupied in the mid-first millennium CE and that occupation continued until sometime after the thirteenth century. Moreover, even in the earliest phase of occupation the site appears to have covered a substantial area, since we have similar radiocarbon dates from three different mounds in two different parts of the site. Statistical analysis of the pottery demonstrates that people living in different parts of the Aissa Dugjé site were, again, making pottery in rather different ways. This may indicate the existence of neighborhoods where members of different social groups lived and made their own styles of pottery—just

Figure 4.4: Excavation at Aissa Dugjé, 1996

as we find in modern communities in the region, and a fascinating glimpse into social complexity a thousand years ago.

These tell mound sites in the plains between the Mandara Mountains and Lake Chad were progressively abandoned through the middle of the second millennium (Gronenborn 1998; Lebeuf 1969; MacEachern 2012a; Marliac, Langlois, and Delneuf 2000). Many of these locations had been occupied by humans for centuries, and some for over a thousand years, but now they lie empty, lost in the bush or incorporated into modern fields or pastures. People pass them every day, on their way to work or school or while traveling from town to town, but they are more or less unremarked, known to be places where giants lived in ancient times but of little relevance to modern lives. They are not entirely forsaken by modern people, though: often as we dig through such sites, we find in the upper levels of our excavations a curious class of artifacts—small, undecorated whole pots, in contrast to the huge amounts of ancient, broken pottery that lies scattered on the surface of these sites and throughout their depths. The fact that these pots are unbroken thus makes them unusual, while their lack of decoration makes them magically dangerous—the decoration on pottery through this region serves to protect the vessels' contents from supernatural attack, as well as acting as a vehicle for signaling social identities. Only pots used for powerful rituals can be undecorated. These undecorated pots were almost certainly buried on mound sites by modern people long after those sites were abandoned, in rituals that in no way conformed to orthodox Islamic beliefs. Mound sites are places of power today, as they would have been to their inhabitants in the past.

It is very difficult to date the end of human occupation of these mound sites, both because most of them have not been adequately dated and because rainstorms and wind have usually stripped away their ancient surfaces and the evidence of their most recent human habitation (Connah 1981; Rosen 1986). Since archaeologists would need datable materials from the most recent occupation levels to identify the time of their abandonment, we are left to estimate the end of occupation by inference from earlier periods of occupation. That is why we can only say, for example, that the Aissa Dugjé mounds were abandoned sometime after the thirteenth century. Nevertheless, the fact that the region is strewn with large archaeological sites that seem to have been thriving villages a thousand years ago but that now lie abandoned, their occupants consigned to myth, is strong evidence of the gradual ending of an agrarian, Iron Age way of life under the steady encroachment of predatory states and their slave raids. When the Kanuri chronicler ibn Fartuwa wrote the *Kirgam ghazawat Barnu* ("Book of the expeditions of Borno") in the late sixteenth century (Lange 1987), describing wars and raids undertaken against Sao populations across the southern Lake Chad Basin, he was describing precisely that process. He also recorded the significant involvement of his patron, the Borno *mai* ("king") Idris Alauma, in the affairs of Wandala: ibn Fartuwa describes the ruler of the Wandala as one of the *mai*'s tributary subjects and tells of how Idris Alauma besieged him on top of Keroua inselberg and ultimately deposed him in favor of a more pliant successor. In a sense, the *Kirgam ghazawat Barnu* describes both trajectories of political development in the region at the time: the building up of slave-raiding middlemen in Borno's tributary zone and the subjugation and often destruction of Sao communities.

Destruction, but not total erasure, because not all of the Sao and Maya settlements south of Lake Chad were abandoned during these times. A number of Kotoko towns south of Lake Chad remained occupied through the historic period and are still inhabited today. The archaeology of these Kotoko settlements is one of the most fascinating

stories in the region, with abundant evidence for political elaboration and participation in long-distance exchange networks by at least
the period 1500–1600 (Holl 2001; Lebeuf et al. 1980). These are
places where indigenous communities adapted to entirely new cultural and political circumstances and survived. Closer to the Mandara
Mountains, communities like Aissa Hardé and Gréa displayed similar
persistence, albeit on a smaller scale. At Aissa Hardé, people say that
they are descended directly from the Maya people who were responsible for the neighboring archaeological site of Aissa Dugjé and claim
that their community was able to survive for a time as an independent
Maya center even with the Wandala capital at Doulo only seven miles
(12 km) away. That claim, if true, vividly illustrates just how small the
core zone of the Wandala state actually was.

At Gréa, on the plains close to the Cameroon-Nigeria border, an
Iron Age settlement that was first occupied more than two thousand
years ago is nestled in a small valley along the edge of a protecting
inselberg. At some point in the ancient past, the settlement acquired
a defensive wall but was eventually overrun and occupied by Wandala
cavalry from Keroua on the modern Nigerian border, which again is
only eight miles (14 km) away. However, although Gréa was incorporated into the Wandala state and the Iron Age settlement was
abandoned, occupation at Gréa continued. More than that, the supernatural powers of the Gréa landscape—which are still important, as
we will see in the next chapter—made the village too dangerous for
its Wandala overlords, who through the entire history of Wandala
dominance from the seventeenth century onward were forced to live
in a village about four miles (6 km) away and try to govern the place
by remote control! As might be suspected, this was not particularly
successful, and Gréa retained considerable local freedom of action
from Wandala through the precolonial period. Today, the ancient site
at Gréa faces the plains to the north and the tracks across which Boko
Haram insurgents move toward villages further to the south, and the
modern village there has itself been attacked by Boko Haram.

In other areas, indigenous populations dealt with the irruption of
slave-raiding states across the plains of the Lake Chad Basin according to a whole variety of different strategies. Some of these—for
example, the construction and maintenance of defensive walls—had
probably been developed in the course of more localized political

conflicts in earlier times, perhaps as long ago as the middle of the first millennium BCE. In some cases, communities banded together in federations to resist the invaders, as early commentators attest. Such strategies were probably sufficient for a time, but eventually the societies that occupied the plains had to make more drastic accommodations to deal with the invaders: retreat into more defensible locations (Mandara communities incorporated immigrants and refugees well into the colonial period); acculturation to the identities of the invaders, as Kanuri, Wandala, or Fulani; and very often adoption of Islam.

The extraordinary complexity of oral histories across this area, which are full of stories of migrations, battles, ruses, and changes of identity, testify to just how complicated these processes would become. Such transformations in identity are often incomplete, or still in progress. If a researcher travels just a few miles away from conversations with the Wandala elite in their last capital at Mora toward rural Wandala settlements like Gréa or Memé, for example, they will find there people who identify strongly as Wandala but who have traditionally followed beliefs and cultural practices very different from those permitted within the more orthodox forms of Islam followed at Mora. It is quite likely that the presence of Boko Haram militants in places like Gréa are destroying such indigenous practices even today, reminding us of the violence and suffering that would have accompanied the incorporation of agrarian societies into slave-raiding states on the plains of the Lake Chad Basin. Many of the archaeological sites that lie quiet and empty today would have been sites of suffering for their last inhabitants, under the violence that states and slave-raiders brought to the region centuries ago. And it is very likely that similar violence accompanied the processes of social transformation that are reflected in the archaeological, linguistic, and genetic data in chapter 2, many thousands of years before that.

Hamman Yaji redux

Hamman Yaji sat dictating his diary to a Madagali scribe a century ago, but there are a multitude of echoes between his words and actions and those of other actors in the history of the region, both in earlier and later times. As we have seen, Hamman Yaji was a border ruler, contributing to and benefitting from the violence and wealth-making potentials of the frontiers between mountains and plains, Borno and Adamawa, and British Nigeria and German Kamerun. Madagali lay in Adamawa's tributary zone, close to the predation zone of the Mandara Mountains.

Hamman Yaji's diary is full of references to slave girls. A century before his rule, the Hausa jihadist Usman dan Fodio discussed the legalities of taking young women as slaves and concubines during jihad; twenty years after he was deposed by the British, French colonial officers would still have to ask themselves whether the practice of placing starving montagnard children under Wandala and Fulani wardship amounted to a continuation of child slavery in another guise, and in 2014 Boko Haram would kidnap hundreds of young women from Chibok and threaten to sell them "as slaves in the marketplace." Local people in the lands of Boko Haram have certainly made the association between the modern terrorist organization and historical experiences of violence and enslavement, whether or not such enslavement has a Kanuri or Fulani accent. Local histories from the Mandara Mountains and its peripheries often merge into an inventory of oppression the different foreign attackers who have raided communities, killed and enslaved people, and tried to impose their will and their rule: French colonial officers; Hamman Yaji; the Mahdist warlord and slaver Rabih az-Zubayr, killed by the French at Kousseri in northern Cameroon in 1900; and even historical figures like *mai* Idris Alauma (although in the latter case, it is likely that written sources have confirmed his importance over 450 years). For people living in the area today, technicalities of identity and chronology do not matter very much; what is important is that violence and slave-raiding are again parts of their lives.

Other historical parallels also exist. States in the southern Lake Chad Basin conducted slave raids into predation zones around state cores, thus addressing the problem of guaranteeing access to a human resource that could not be taken from among their own citizenry. Those predation zones can also be thought of as internal frontiers, incubators of social experimentation and social change. The attraction of such frontier refuges extended beyond societies targeted in slave raids to Muslim reformists as well. Usman dan Fodio, the great jihadist founder of the Sokoto Caliphate, followed a common theme in Islamist reformist movements—the retreat by the virtuous Muslim from the capital of a godless sovereign to the hinterland, where he accumulated his strength before his return to vanquish the apostate king. As we saw in chapter 1, Boko Haram leaders followed this model, retreating from Maiduguri to the borders to gather strength: the lands of Boko Haram, on the borders between Cameroon, Nigeria, Niger, and Chad are thus afflicted by border violence today, as they were in the past. In the next chapter, we will see the linkages between these different historical trajectories, especially in the twentieth century and with different forms of wealth-making to suit different economic and political conditions—particularly smuggling and banditry.

Finally, we leave this chapter as it began, with Hamman Yaji sitting in Madagali. The Fulani warlord undertook no more slave raids after 1921 and the incorporation of his territory into British Nigeria, although he did continue to extract resources from montagnard populations through exploitative taxation systems. He kept his diary up until just before his arrest by the British in 1927. With a twenty-first-century Western lens and an eye toward what we might imagine as justice, we might hope that his arrest and subsequent removal from power was the result of his slave-raiding and all of the misery that he inflicted on surrounding communities. In fact, Hamman Yaji was deposed on European suspicions that he was an Islamic extremist—a follower of the Sudanese religious leader Muhammad Ahmad, who proclaimed himself Mahdi (a Muslim redeemer) and led a revolt against Turco-Egyptian rule in Sudan in the late nineteenth century. Ironically, Hamman Yaji was probably not a Mahdist, at least not in any political or subversive sense, although he was certainly a strict Muslim and heir to the bigotry concerning non-Muslims that was shared by members of the Islamic elite in the region. The English and French authorities who engineered his removal were worried about subversion by Islamist infiltrators from the Nile Valley, decades after the destruction of the Mahdist state; a hundred years later, Western and African governments worry about similar contacts between Boko Haram and foreign militants from the Horn of Africa and across the Sahara. In both cases, their concerns appear to be geopolitics on a large scale, rather than the lives of people daily exposed to these forms of violence.

5

KALASHNIKOVS, CELL PHONES, AND MOTORCYCLES

EARLY IN THE RAINY SEASON in July 1992, I was directing archaeological excavations on the outskirts of the Wandala village of Gréa, which stretches along the flanks of the inselberg of the same name on the plains north of the Mandara Mountains in Cameroon. Gréa lies in a curious right-angled jog of the Cameroon-Nigeria border, which follows the line of local watercourses through the area, and the border is only five miles (9 km) away; Gréa is closer to nearby Nigerian settlements than to those in Cameroon. It was a hard place to get to during the rains, since the trails we used to get there were first turned to mud and then were cut to pieces by smugglers in tractor trailers running gasoline and consumer products along the back roads between the two countries, away from the border posts; we spent a lot of time digging our trucks out of the muck. As we saw in the last chapter, Gréa could be a hard place to get to during the precolonial period as well, when the supernatural powers of the landscape prevented its Wandala overlords from living there, on pain of a horrible death. The *tli-gréa*, the Wandala official traditionally responsible for Gréa, had to live in Kolofata, about four miles (6 km) away, and govern remotely. We were under no such restrictions, we thought, but it still took a lot of effort to get to Gréa every day to dig there.

Early in that field season of 1992, I decided that we needed to place a test excavation close to a prominent rock just at the edge of the Gréa inselberg, where an old red Saharan sand dune from the Last Glacial Maximum, trapped by the prevailing winds against the mountain, gives way to the rocky chaos of the slopes. What I did not know was that that particular large rock was called Dala Nokwé by the people living at Gréa and that it was a powerful supernatural actor in that landscape, with particular influence over the coming of the rains (figure 5.1). As word spread that we were working at Dala Nokwé, people spilled out of the village to warn us away, shouting and gesticulating. In the course of the incident, one of the people who was working with me, an old friend and someone who had worked as a translator for me during my PhD research in the 1980s, took my arm and urged me in French to be cautious, telling me that the circumstances were more dangerous than I appeared to understand: "These people are Gamergu! They are all bandits, they go back and forth across the border, and they all hide knives. They will kill us with knives!"

In fact, the Gréa villagers harbored no hostile intent toward us, but rather concern for our safety and their own welfare. As they told us, if we outsiders—not foreigners, but just people not from Gréa— touched Dala Nokwé, we would simply disappear and never be seen

Figure 5.1: Dala Nokwé at Gréa

again. There might have been some calculated self-interest figuring in their concern as well, since the suspicious disappearance of a half dozen North Americans would certainly have attracted unwelcome attention from the national authorities, as well as cutting off the wages we were paying them as excavators. In any event, we resolved the issue without further trouble, with the sacrifice of a chicken and sorghum beer to Dala Nokwé and a promise that we would not touch the rock or disturb the area around it in any way while we worked, all under the surveillance of our local workmen. The conversation may even have reassured some local people that these ignorant outsiders were ready to recognize the complications of working within a powerful landscape. Our excavations continued, in careful proximity to Dala Nokwé.

A few of the people living at Gréa were indeed Gamergu, or Melgwa, to use their own name for themselves. People from a variety of different ethnic groups dwelt at Gréa, just as they do in almost every modern village in the region: there were Wandala, Mafa, Kanuri, and Shuwa Arab people there, among others. The number of Melgwa at Gréa was actually very small, but their reputation was enough to cause my friend and translator, Michel Kourdapaye, to fear for our safety. Kourdapaye was born and still lives in Adobikwo, a community on the northeastern edge of the Mandara Mountains south of the Wandala capital at Mora, about sixteen miles (25 km) from Gréa—and in this area, that distance can span a variety of cultural worlds. In Gréa, he was interacting with very different people in a border area where banditry and violence were common and well known, and throughout that border area Melgwa have for a long time had the reputation of being dangerous bandits.

In fact, that is what makes Kourdapaye's warning so striking: the first identification of Melgwa as unruly rebels living in violent frontier areas comes in the Kanuri chronicler ibn Fartuwa's account of state raiding into the area around the Mandara Mountains in the 1580s, the "Book of the expeditions of Borno" (Lange 1987, 64–65) mentioned in the last chapter. Descriptions of Melgwa as frontier bandits and robbers reoccur with some frequency over the intervening four hundred years, and indeed at various points through the twentieth century (Barkindo 1989, 94; Rohlfs 1875; Tijani 2010). The continuity of these accounts implies that the two cases that bookend this period, ibn Fartuwa's description in the 1580s and that of my friend in 1992, were not just random or accidental conjunctions: over those four centuries and enormous transformations within Lake Chad Basin societies, a lot of people continued to think that the Melgwa were dangerous and, in particular, dangerous bandits. Why would that be the case? Why would one relatively small ethnic group maintain an identity both as frontier people and as robbers, over centuries and all of the changes in borders through this region? There are today only perhaps ten thousand Melgwa people, mostly in Nigeria and virtually all farmers, which does not sound particularly threatening.

There are a number of ways that we could approach this. Traditionally, Western histories have portrayed African populations as timeless and unchanging; using this assumption, the unwary reader might simply accept that that was how the Melgwa had always been and leave it at that. However, we have seen how societies have transformed in the Lake Chad Basin across centuries, and it is very unlikely that, among all of that change, the Melgwa have remained more or less static in their banditry. Instead, we should probably examine more closely the circumstances that have defined the Melgwa ethnic group for indications about why they have traditionally been feared in the area. This involves some issues specific to the Melgwa, but there are also broader implications for our understanding of modern frontiers and their associations with violence.

We first need to realize that the Melgwa speak a language related very closely to that of the Wandala—in fact, linguists often identify Melgwa as a dialect of Wandala, rather than as a distinct language. More than that, there is a good deal of overlap between the territories historically associated with the Wandala and the Melgwa (Lohr 2003; Tijani 2010); if the Wandala dominated the plains directly adjacent to the Mandara Mountains, with their successive capitals at Keroua, Doulo, and Mora, the Melgwa were to be found only slightly further to the northwest, along the Bama Ridge and around modern Maiduguri. Melgwa are supposed to have originated at a place called Muna, now abandoned but just outside Maiduguri, and their oral histories share significant elements with the earliest histories of the Wandala. In some ways, the Melgwa are the earliest named society to occupy the heartland of Boko Haram, although modern Melgwa people have not joined that organization in any numbers; given the location of their settlements today, between Maiduguri and the mountains, they have on the contrary suffered disproportionately under Boko Haram attacks.

Traditionally, Melgwa people were identified by Kanuri as non-Muslims until the nineteenth century, although many of them have converted to Islam in the last hundred years. Given their positioning on the plains and on the edges of powerful Islamic states, their conversion is probably not surprising—although it has to be said that, even today, Muslims in the region remain suspicious of the sincerity of Melgwa conversion to Islam (Tijani 2010). In this, we can see a specific case of some of the processes described at the end of the last chapter, with the Melgwa as one of the plains agrarian populations that lasted long enough to escape being subsumed under the general terms "Sao" and "Maya" that Islamic states used to memorialize their vanished predecessors. For Wandala elites and for colonial administrators, the Melgwa were an ambiguous and somewhat disturbing group, often identified as part of a proto-Wandala population of the mid-second millennium that did not become incorporated into the Wandala state and that only tardily accepted Islam. One element of this persisting Melgwa identity, then, is that they are distinctively "non-Wandala," closely related to but existing in open or tacit opposition to the developing Wandala state. Even today, though, at places like Gréa there is less cultural distance between Melgwa and rural Muslim Wandala than there would be in the capital at Mora (as, for example, in their mutual belief in the supernatural potency of the Dala Nokwé rock). The Melgwa have perhaps reminded Wandala elites of who they once had been, which would have been an embarrassment for an enterprising Islamic state on its way up.

There is, however, a larger issue at play here, because Melgwa territory has been a frontier zone for a very long time. As the Kanuri state of Borno extended its control across the plains south of Lake Chad in the fifteenth century, it came into contact with a variety of Chadic-speaking populations, and, as we saw in the last chapter, the trajectories of accommodation or resistance to Borno dominance varied dramatically. When ibn Fartuwa was writing about the exploits of the *mai* Idris Alauma of Borno in the late sixteenth century, the state was in full expansion against these Chadic communities. Some of these groups were already making use of the inselbergs and heights around the Mandara Mountains for defensive purposes, while others, like the Melgwa, were forced to defend themselves in fortified settlements on the plains. They were described as "bandits" by the Kanuri, then as in later times. As the Wandala progressively took on the role of expansionistic slave-raiders around the Mandara Mountains, exporting those slaves to Borno, populations like the Melgwa found themselves again living in an internal frontier zone between the two states, caught on the plains between Keroua and Birni Ngazargamo through the seventeenth and eighteenth centuries—with, it appears, periodic raids from as far away as Baghirmi to the east. The period of jihads at the end of the eighteenth century only added to the complex geography of domination in what is now the Chad-Cameroon border area, with Fulani forces from Adamawa pushing up the western edge of the Mandara Mountains toward Madagali—where Hamman Yaji would eventually rule—and toward the Diamaré Plain to the east. Through all of the precolonial period, Melgwa communities seem to have been caught at the edges of and between expanding states.

That situation would continue. When European colonial powers began to take an interest in the southern Lake Chad Basin in the late 1880s, they found themselves becoming involved in a region in turmoil. At that point, much of the area was under the occupation of a warlord and slave trader named Rabih az-Zubayr from Sudan, who had taken advantage of repeating rifles and the chaos associated with the Mahdist rebellion along the Nile to instigate a reign of terror between that river and Lake Chad. In the early 1890s, he successively defeated the rulers of Baghirmi, Wandala, and then Borno, killing the descendants of Shehu al-Kanemi, who had ruled the latter state for the previous century, and installing himself as ruler of the region between 1893 and 1900.

When Rabih marched against Wandala in 1895, the Wandala reacted as they had in earlier times and with earlier opponents, moving their court and treasury up into the Mandara Mountains south of Mora, where they had previously made alliances with montagnard communities. Eventually, though, Wandala forces sallied out of the mountains to confront Rabih and were summarily defeated; the *tlikse* and many of his relations were taken back to Dikwa in captivity, where the males (including the *tlikse*) were eventually put to death and the females entered into slavery. Refugees from the attack fled to the massif, where in cooperation with montagnards communities they successfully resisted attacks by Rabih's forces over many months, relying on supplies bought with money from the Wandala treasury.

Rabih was certainly influenced by the Mahdi in Sudan and claimed to fight on his behalf (Mohamed 2010)—one reason why the colonial powers were so concerned with the question of Islamist infiltration into the Lake Chad Basin in the early twentieth century, and why Hamman Yaji would be deposed from his rule at Madagali in the mid-1920s. There is no particular evidence, however, that Rabih ruled Borno as a Mahdist state himself: in fact, he left most of Borno's preexisting state apparatus in place, seemingly only concerned with extracting as much money and as many slaves from the territory as possible. In 1900, Rabih was killed by a combined French military expedition at the site of the modern Cameroonian town of Kousseri, across the Chari River from the capital of Chad at N'Djamena, his head displayed on a spear by a colonial rifleman. The European powers had theoretically carved up the entire Lake Chad Basin into different colonial spheres of influence ten years earlier, but without any effective power on the ground and usually in profound ignorance of the political and cultural situations in the regions they now claimed to control.

Those first boundaries—between what would eventually become the colonies and then nations of Niger, Nigeria, and Cameroon—were simply straight lines drawn on a map (figure 5.2), bisecting states and communities without any reference to facts on the ground (Hiribarren 2012, 97).

When the European powers actually entered the area and took up control after 1900, their jockeying for position and

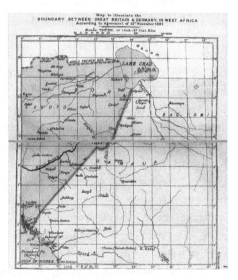

Figure 5.2: Map of British and German boundaries south of Lake Chad, 1896

attempts to find local allies led to some adjustment in those borders. (As an Atlantic Canadian, I appreciate the fact that, in the signing of the Entente Cordiale between Great Britain and France in 1904, some minor adjustments of Lake Chad Basin borders in France's favor were compensated by France giving up fishing rights around Newfoundland. Such were the days of global empire.) The negotiations between Britain and Germany on the frontier between their colonies lopped off the eastern tributary zone of Borno, as constituted in precolonial times, and made it part of German Kamerun, while Borno's heartland was incorporated within Nigeria. This again left Melgwa territory poised along the border between the two colonial powers, roughly between Maiduguri, Dikwa, and Keroua, and that situation would continue as those borders became permanent, into the postcolonial period and to the present day.

In essence, then, Melgwa really have been border populations for centuries, marginal to states in both a spatial and a political sense. They have lived variably in the tributary and predation zones of those states, at different times making alliances and waging war according to the demands on the situation. It is there as well that we see the continuing association of Melgwa communities not merely with borders but with border violence. In chapter 4, we examined the roles of states along their frontiers, particularly with the deep involvement of state violence in the expansion and sustainment of large-scale slave trades. Slave-raiding and trading were potential sources of wealth, both for state elites in capitals and for ruthless and determined people living on state borders. Some of the latter would have been people like Hamman Yaji, who held a recognized place in the administrative apparatus of larger states—in his case, both the Fulani jihadist state of Adamawa and the different colonial powers who successively claimed to control the area around Madagali.

However, many of the peoples living in these frontier regions were not state officials and were never fully assimilated within the control of centralized states. Some were people like the Melgwa. Because of their marginal status, in every sense of the word, and their lack of incorporation into states, the activities of Melgwa and people like them would not be described in the language of diplomacy by writers in state courts and capitals. Rather, they would be called robbers and bandits, as the Melgwa were from ibn Fartuwa onward. Through the nineteenth and early twentieth century, Melgwa communities were widely known as centers of banditry, in the area between Maiduguri and approximately the modern Cameroon-Nigeria border. This involved both raids on Hausa and Kanuri merchants moving between the markets of the region and robbery of Shuwa Arab cattle pastoralists, whose herds represented a great deal of wealth on the hoof (Tijani 2010, 48, 89–90). As we will see below, these activities parallel other forms of banditry that would take place in the Lake Chad Basin through the twentieth century.

The long-standing reputation of Melgwa as frontier bandits begins to illuminate some broader issues of non-legal activities (sometimes violent ones) in the Lake Chad Basin through the twentieth century and of the involvement of state elites in those activities. The fact that we call these activities "non-legal" indicates that, unlike precolonial slave-raiding, they are placed beyond the legal boundaries of legitimacy and control by states and their elites, and they signal very different kinds of relationships with states more generally—whether precolonial Islamic polities, European colonies, or modern nation-states. At the same time, such activities may not necessarily be seen as illicit or illegitimate within society as a whole, and the distinction between non-legal and illicit activities has been an important focus of anthropological work in this area (Roitman 2006). I will examine these issues through the rest of this chapter, with particular attention to the implications of two sets of non-legal activities that have in various ways affected the conduct of my own research in the region through the last thirty years: banditry and smuggling.

The question here is not whether the Melgwa are particularly associated with these activities today—by all accounts they are not—but rather the ways in which non-legal activities have taken place around state frontiers over time and how states, their elites, and their citizens have conceptualized and made use of those activities. If the last chapter focused on the view outward from precolonial state capitals, on elites and the wealth that they created for themselves (particularly through the slave trade), this chapter focuses on very different forms of wealth accumulation in more recent times—that of "lawless" people, on the roads, in the bush, and particularly on the borders. At the same time, it examines how those "lawless" activities articulate with the state, and more particularly with the elites who control the state. My understanding of these issues has been greatly enriched by the seminal research on states, violence, and economic activity undertaken by a number of investigators working in this area.

Zoua-zoua and *coupeurs de route*

The roads out to Gréa caused us endless trouble when we were working around that inselberg in 1992, mostly because of the rains but also because of the smugglers. Our trucks could usually deal with the mud itself, but we would often meet overloaded tractor-trailer trucks slowly navigating those same backwoods trails, always coming from the general direction of the Nigerian border. Those trucks would slip, slide, and spin their way across the countryside during the rains, and the ruts that their tires would rip into muddy trackways were awesome to behold. They would get stuck constantly; when that happened, they needed to be excavated, sometimes using even larger trucks or bulldozers and sometimes by entire hamlets hired to dig them out by hand. That in turn would force everyone else traveling along the same route to detour around the site, creating new, subsidiary routes, and the holes left after they were dug out would often last for months. Those hazards to navigation were not limited to the area around Gréa, either: we would encounter such trucks, and the marks they left on the landscape, all throughout the Cameroon-Nigeria border area north of the Mandara Mountains.

We would rarely see them on the same tracks heading back to Nigeria. If we had worked in that area in the early 2000s, they would probably have been smuggling subsidized Cameroonian cotton and rice on the return trips, but that trade was not so important ten years before that (Bolak Funteh 2014). They were moving a whole variety of goods from Nigeria into Cameroon, and indeed across the Lake Chad Basin—consumer goods, clothing, foodstuffs, or building material—taking advantage of different systems of tariffs and price controls in the various countries of the region, and once their cargoes were discharged, they could move back across the borders relatively easily. Others smuggled less benign goods as well, albeit more discreetly: firearms, illegal drugs, and stolen cars. Stories circulate in the region about the Cameroonian government official who encountered his stolen Mercedes SUV being driven by one of his counterparts in the Chadian government in N'Djamena. Smuggling has been a hugely significant force in the regional economies of the Lake Chad Basin over the past decades, although it is now—as we will see—somewhat diminished by the activities of Boko Haram and the actions that national governments have taken to fight terrorism.

In many cases, the vehicles we saw around Gréa and elsewhere were tanker trucks carrying gasoline, because illegally imported Nigerian gasoline, universally known as *zoua-zoua*, was and remains the fuel of choice for any kind of transport in northern Cameroon. If a traveler ever needs gasoline, to journey to the lands of Boko Haram, for example, *zoua-zoua* is always available in the smallest village market or roadside stop, in reused plastic vegetable oil bottles sized for motorcycles and in jerrycans for cars and trucks. It is often dirty and adulterated, and can be very hard on automobile engines—we sometimes strained twigs out of it when we had to use it—but *zoua-zoua* has through the last thirty years been extremely cheap, for quite straightforward and elementary economic reasons, and thus it is very popular in Cameroon. Nigeria has extraordinarily large oil reserves (perhaps the tenth largest in the world) and is a member of the Organization of the Petroleum Exporting Countries (OPEC), and in order to maintain good relations with its citizens, the Nigerian government provides subsidies that minimize the cost of gasoline. In late 2016, gasoline in Nigeria cost about US $1.85/gallon ($0.50/l), and about twice that in Cameroon. In the mid-1990s, before Nigeria relaxed some of its price controls, gasoline cost three to four times as much in Cameroon as in Nigeria. Unsurprisingly, that price differential led to a huge trade in smuggled gasoline from Nigeria into Cameroon, such that until very recently perhaps two-thirds of the gasoline consumed in northern Cameroon came from Nigeria (Bolak Funteh 2014)—thus the tanker trucks rolling back and forth across the tracks around Gréa. They would be sent through a complex network of illicit exchange centered on the northern provincial capitals of Cameroon, Maroua and Garoua, as well as a number of other trading hubs, and from there gasoline would be distributed to the smaller villages and hamlets throughout the region.

At other times, when the roads were too bad for the trucks or when the national governments decided that they had to make a show of enforcement along the frontiers, *zoua-zoua* would be moved by very different methods. Groups of young men would strap four or five forty-liter plastic jerrycans of gasoline on small Japanese or Chinese motorcycles and then set off in fleets across the border, using the backcountry trails that tanker trucks would attempt in better times or even smaller and more obscure routes. This would sometimes involve moving across tracks in the Mandara Mountains themselves; the journey described at the beginning of chapter 1 was a popular route, going in reverse from Nigeria via Itéré and Koza to the town of Mokolo in Cameroon. If a few of these motorcycles were stopped by the border authorities, the vast majority would probably still get through. They would come together on the paved roads well beyond the frontier and its checkpoints, and so periodically our archaeological field crews would encounter long lines of heavily laden motorcycles, all with their identical cargoes of gasoline, trundling into the provincial capital of Maroua (figure 5.3). Smuggling *zoua-zoua* this way was brutally hard and extremely dangerous work. The amount of gasoline that these small motorcycles carried would weigh between two hundred and three hundred pounds (100–136 kg) in total, making them very hard to control; drivers often carried jerrycans of gasoline on their laps, and even a minor accident—with ruptured plastic containers spilling gasoline over a hot two-stroke engine—frequently resulted in a conflagration. In certain circumstances, even bicycles would be loaded down with containers of gasoline and sent across the border, especially through the mountains, although their range and speed was such that they could not make the entire trip on their own; bicycles were more often used for local distribution.

Figure 5.3: Gasoline smuggling in Cameroon

The young men who piloted those motorcycles across the border, relying on their strength and courage and their knowledge of the back trails, saw themselves as both operating outside the law and sustaining the economy of the region, in circumstances where they had no other way of making a living. The economy in Cameroon is largely moribund after more than thirty years of one-man rule under President Paul Biya. Advancement in Cameroonian society depends largely on connections and patronage, and these young men, known locally as *cascadeurs* ("stuntmen") or *attaquants* ("attackers"), had no such connections and no particularly hopeful futures. They would usually have graduated from jobs running motorcycle-taxis in rural and urban areas. These moto-taxis are called *clandos* in Cameroon, as those in northeastern Nigeria are called *achaba*. *Clandos* are not given that name because they are particularly clandestine but because they were traditionally unlicensed and more or less unregulated. *Clando* drivers would often move on to the more prestigious, and much more dangerous, job of smuggling gasoline and other goods as *cascadeurs*. They adopted a tough, swaggering persona, often chemically enhanced through the consumption of locally produced amphetamines and opiates to help them deal with the rigors of their trips across the border. In North America, we might call them "bikers," with the Hells Angels association to the word; in the southern Lake Chad Basin, *cascadeur* has more or less the same connotation.

Smuggling—and especially the activities of the *cascadeurs*—is also related to the modern practice of another form of illicit activity along international borders throughout the Lake Chad Basin: banditry. In African French, such bandits have long been called *coupeurs de route*, literally "cutters of the road," for their habit of setting up blockades across roads and robbing travelers. In areas that are generally very poor, static wealth will be concentrated in places that are fairly well defended—banks in towns, for example. But money must travel too, especially when banks are unreliable and much of the day-to-day economy runs on cash: people have to buy and sell, and merchants have to transact their business, and in many cases that means moving around the countryside. A bus shuttling between towns will be packed with farmers, traders, housewives; individually they may have little money, but the collective payoff for bandits may still be lucrative. A merchant traveling after having sold a herd of cattle, or a rich man's car, or a four-by-four full of European tourists would be much more rewarding—albeit also generating more complications, especially with responses by authorities. If robbery does not yield enough ready cash, then travelers can be kidnapped and held for ransom. In late 2016, the mayor of the town of Lagdo in northern Cameroon, along with more than a dozen other people, was released after a year in captivity, having been taken by bandits while traveling and held for ransom across the border in the northwestern part of the Central African Republic. It is unclear at this point whether a ransom was actually paid for their release, although one was certainly demanded.

Like smugglers, *coupeurs de route* have been a ubiquitous presence in the social and economic worlds of the southern Lake Chad Basin, and in the imaginations of voyagers in all of the countries of the region. Because of its violence, banditry is a relatively invisible activity, unlike the smuggling that generally goes on in front of people's faces. It usually takes place in relatively unpopulated areas, where the robbers can carry out their activities with little interference, and ideally in close proximity to international borders, which allows a rapid escape into another country if the robbers are pursued. For the majority of people, *coupeurs de route* exist only in conversation and in the tightness in one's stomach while traveling through a dangerous area, but for some there will be a dreadful moment when, rounding a corner on a road with brush close on both sides, they see the line of armed men strung across the road, and then the others moving out of the bush behind their vehicles to cut off their retreat. As we shall see, such bandits occupy an equivocal position in Lake Chad Basin communities. On the one hand, their activities are often recognized as licit even if non-legal—banditry is seen as a legitimate form of economic extraction from states and elites that have no concern for common people (Roitman 2006). On the other hand, bandits are widely recognized as being violent and pitiless: people have been not just kidnapped but also raped and killed in the course of holdups along the roads.

The history of modern banditry in the southern Lake Chad Basin is complex, with a whole variety of factors affecting the intensity of banditry at different times in recent decades. Rural banditry has a long history in the region, particularly involving the theft of cattle (as we have seen for the Melgwa above), but this was quite localized and relatively small in scale. During the colonial period, the activities of *coupeurs de route* were recognized by the colonial authorities in all of the countries of the region, as was their use of borders—although, as in earlier periods, the distinction between a robber operating at the edges of society and the leader of a nascent community that might ultimately be accorded legitimacy was often quite blurred (Issa 2010; Roitman 2005, 140–146).

One of the initial impulses that dramatically increased banditry in recent times was the vicious fighting in Chad in the 1970s and 1980s, which saw various factions competing for power within the country, an invasion of northern Chad by Libya, and then a near-constant state of armed internal conflict in one part of the country or another—a situation that still exists today. The Lake Chad Basin as a whole was awash in small arms through this period (and remains so) and full of demobilized Chadian fighters who were ready to try almost any other kind of activity to find a way to support themselves. The French political scientist Marielle Debos's book *Living by the Gun in Chad* explores the lives of Chadian men who follow the *métier des armes*, the "ordinary job of weapons," in their navigation of various forms of armed work, transitioning fairly seamlessly between the statuses of soldier, rebel, bandit, and customs inspector (Debos 2016, 3–5; see also Issa 2007). They do so within a political environment where armed conflict is always taking place in some area of the country, where the relations between different factions are endlessly mutable, and where the president of Chad is the strongest of the "politico-military entrepreneurs" (to use Debos's term), directing the most powerful such faction with the largest military force—that is, the Armée Nationale Tchadienne, the Chadian military.

During the 1990s, the most important area of operations for such bandits was that area south of Lake Chad where the borders of Nigeria, Cameroon, and Chad converge, and especially in Cameroon's Waza National Park, a huge game reserve on the *firki* clay plains north of the Bama Ridge (Issa 2007, 2004, 2010). The road connecting the N'Djamena, the Chadian capital, to the cities of Cameroon ran north-south through Waza, and the traffic along that road was a lucrative target for robbers. The fact that no settlements existed in the park meant that *coupeurs de route* could undertake their activities there in relative security, and they could also use their spare time for killing animals in the game park for meat and ivory. (It is not at all surprising that this is also a region where Boko Haram has operated since early 2013 at least.) Banditry was sufficiently well established in the area and the zone of operations for the Waza bandits sufficiently well known to local people that we were able to excavate the site of Aissa Dugjé in 1995 and 1996, even though that site was only about six miles (9 km) from the edge of the danger zone.[1]

By the time we were excavating at Aissa Dugjé, travelers could only use the road through Waza in convoys of buses, accompanied by military vehicles. This situation was more or less intolerable to the governments of both Cameroon and Chad. The initial response to banditry was local: it involved the mobilization of "vigilance communities," associations of hunters dispersed through villages and hamlets, to fight the *coupeurs de route*. In many of the communities of the region, both Muslim and non-Muslim, hunters had traditionally acted as scouts in times of war and as the enforcement mechanism for community decisions in times of peace. They did so because hunters had experience in dealing with powerful supernatural forces, both the spirits of the bush in which they worked and the powers of the gris-gris that covered their clothing, amulets containing Koranic verses or charms blessed by practitioners of highly syncretistic local forms of Islam that are often lumped together under the old French colonial term *maraboutage*. Hunters crossed international borders about as easily as bandits, so that Nigerian traditional hunters often cooperated with their Cameroonian colleagues. They played an important role in the struggle against banditry throughout the southern Lake Chad Basin, fighting the Kalashnikovs of the *coupeurs de route* with their bows, spears, and Dane guns.[2] As we will see in the next chapter, they continue to play an ambiguous role in the violence associated with Boko Haram.

The Cameroonian government finally mobilized national resources to fight banditry in the northern part of the country, first through deployment of units of the Gendarmerie and ultimately with the deployment of elite army units, especially the Bataillon d'Intervention Rapide (BIR, "Rapid Intervention Battalion"), which in 2017 remains the primary Cameroonian military unit fighting Boko Haram. Banditry throughout the region around Waza was suppressed with great savagery, a good deal of which was directed at innocent civilians. Bandits certainly did rely on informants living in market towns and roadside communities for news of movements, and to some degree on local leaders for logistical support, and the "anti-gang" units (as the Gendarmerie unit fighting the bandits are called in Cameroon) and BIR do not seem to have been particularly interested in the finer points of guilt and innocence in the course of their summary executions. Their violence was also ethnically based, and particularly directed at Shuwa Arab communities that were assumed to be more closely associated with Chad and its fighters (Issa 2007).

Over this period, the *coupeurs de route* shifted the focus of their activities further to the south, and especially to the territory around the Mbéré River valley where the borders of Cameroon, Chad, and the Central African Republic come together (Seignobos 2011). As in the Waza area further to the north, this meant that bandits could retreat from one country into an entirely different one after their attacks, thereby escaping the security forces pursuing them. While I was working on an archaeological project associated with an Exxon oil pipeline around the Mbéré, in the southwest of Chad in 1999–2001 and about five miles from the border with the Central African Republic, I had to survey for ancient sites accompanied by a group of bodyguards because of bandit attacks along the roads in the region. This was, not coincidentally, also very close to one of the regional emporia for international trade—and smuggling, to a major degree—at Touboro on the Cameroon-Chad border; as already

mentioned, *coupeurs de route* are attracted to the presence of people who have to travel with large amounts of cash. My bodyguards were a piratical-looking group, dressed in combinations of military fatigues of various ages and origins and armed with a great diversity of weapons—different varieties of AK-47s, an American M-14, even an ancient Stoner AR-10 rifle that must have originally come from across the border in Sudan, after being shipped there from the United States in the late 1950s (figure 5.4). I sometimes wondered what they did in their off hours.

Figure 5.4: Guards on oil pipeline survey, Chad 1999

Through the last twenty-five years, the composition and techniques of these bandit gangs have changed, but many of the broader characteristics of banditry itself have remained the same. Demobilized soldiers, deserters, and militants from the many different factions involved in the wars in Chad continue to be an important constituent of those bandit gangs, after having "entered the bush" to join the illicit world (Debos 2011). They bring significant military expertise to the *coupeurs de route*: witnesses often describe the tactical proficiency with which these gangs work. As we will see below, one vital question is the extent to which actual soldiers and police—that is, serving officers of the state—are also involved in these activities. Over the past fifteen years, the Central African Republic has also been racked by political conflict and inter-group warfare, and those disruptions have also added their quotas of destitute and desperate young men to bandit gangs. Cattle-herding communities, especially those of Mbororo Fulani people, have been subjected to particular pressures through this period. Mbororo traditional migration patterns have been interrupted by political borders and wildlife refuges, and they were subjected to a terrible series of kidnappings at the beginning of the 1990s, where children would be kidnapped and the herders forced to sell their valuable cattle to pay the ransoms (Issa 2006; Seignobos 2011). This led to a breakdown of economic systems and the authority of elders, and paradoxically to Mbororo youths joining bandit gangs. In the words of one author, "This very early delinquency explains the traveler's surprise at being robbed by Mbororo who are only 14–15 years old, Kalashnikovs in hand, stuffed with Tramol [Tramadol—an opiate manufactured in Nigeria], totally uninhibited and laughing" (Seignobos 2011, 239).

The *coupeurs de route* have also drawn a steady flow of young men from more urban settings, from the expanding towns and cities across the region who have not been able to find more conventional work; they may not be as used to the rigors of life in the bush as ex-soldiers and herdsmen are, but they bring connections and intelligence from the towns, vital in planning bandit attacks. This population of young men overlaps significantly with the *cascadeurs* who smuggle gasoline across the border from Nigeria on motorcycles. It is difficult to say how many young men actively participate in both activities, and perhaps more likely that the leaders of the gangs—significantly more shadowy figures, with ties to the political and social elites that we will examine below—would also be involved in directing smuggling activities, with more expendable young men working for them in these different capacities (Roitman 2006).

The success of *coupeurs de route* across the Lake Chad Basin during the last twenty-five years has involved three transformative technologies: Kalashnikov assault rifles (the AK-47 and its innumerable variants and descendants), cell phones, and those motorcycles (Seignobos 2014). All are now widely available, and—just as importantly—all are cheap consumer goods. Kalashnikovs were widely dispersed throughout the area during the Chad wars, and more recently the conflict in Darfur and the collapse of the Gadhafi regime in Libya have made such weapons even cheaper and more abundant. Cell phones have enormously changed the lives of people throughout sub-Saharan Africa over the last twenty years, allowing quick and ubiquitous communication even in remote areas—a vast change from the 1980s when I first started working in the region, with landlines scarce and extremely unreliable.[3] Local people use them in all kinds of ways: families communicate with their children in faraway cities; farmers and merchants use them to arrange meetings and to check market prices; bandits use them to collect information from informants and coordinate attacks.

Cheap imported Chinese motorcycles replaced more expensive Japanese versions at the end of the 1990s, becoming a much more ubiquitous consumer good in all of the countries around Lake Chad. People of comparatively modest means, especially in urban areas, might be able to afford a Chinese motorcycle. They quickly proliferated among *coupeurs de route* as well, where their utility was obvious, allowing gang members to assemble and disperse quickly. The increased mobility that they conferred allow bandits to operate further from their frontier sanctuaries, since they can return to those sanctuaries relatively quickly and easily; in this sense, "the border" is a flexible concept, one defined by technological change as much as by geography. Over time, motorcycles made bandits less dependent on isolated camps in unpopulated places like the Waza game park and better able to blend into urban environments, where they could pursue a more normal life and enjoy the fruits of their "labor." As we will see in the next chapter, these three technologies—Kalashnikovs, cell phones, and motorcycles—have been central to the success of Boko

Haram as well, allowing that terrorist organization a great deal of flexibility in its guerrilla warfare against the militaries of the region.

"The man in the car"

To this point, I have described two different aspects of illegality and violence in the Lake Chad Basin. They appear at first glance dissimilar: What does the Melgwa's local and historical reputation for robbery—now more or less undeserved—have to do with the very real and often violent practices of smuggling and banditry that take place across the region in the twenty-first century? There are, however, a set of important factors that connect these two cases. First, as I have noted, they are both characterized by violence that takes place in border regions. Melgwa are "border people" par excellence on the plains south of Lake Chad, and smugglers and bandits both require the wealth-making potentials of borders in order to make a living: smugglers for the differentials in availability and price in different national markets, and bandits for a sanctuary against pursuit. Motorized transport means that these border zones have expanded geographically, compared to the precolonial period, when violence came on horseback or by foot, but the necessity of borderlands as places between jurisdictions, and as places of violence and wealth creation, remains.

Secondly, and equally as important, all of these border activities implicate the state and state elites in different ways. These different kinds of border transgression—in an exact analogy to the structured violence associated with the slave trade—are not simply activities that happen beyond the control and understanding of the state. They take place because the state itself, or at least principal actors in state functioning along with some element of the populace, has an interest in retaining places and times where the state's own control is not exerted. We have already seen in the preceding chapter that this was the norm in the southern Lake Chad Basin in precolonial times, when the predation zones of slave-raiding states existed as places outside of state administration, but as places essential to state functioning *precisely because of that fact*. It was outside the core zones of state administration that elites were able to deploy violence in order to obtain the commodity—human bodies—whose possession and sale made elite lifestyles possible. But how does this work in the twenty-first century, with nation-states that are supposed to run according to very different models?

The attentive reader might have wondered, in this description of smuggling around Gréa and in other parts of the Lake Chad Basin: Where is the government in all of this? It is not as if there were many precautions being made to keep the activities of the smugglers discreet. Tractor-trailer trucks and gasoline tankers are easy to spot, especially when they are off-road, and the destruction they wrought on roads and trackways was a major impediment to travel in the area, not just for archaeologists but for local people as well. The routes that they took around border control points were well known to people in the area. Even the *cascadeurs* running gasoline across the border would then reform into convoys on the paved roads and arrive in the provincial capital together, fleets of motorcycles trundling along the highway piled high with jerrycans of illegal fuel. Smuggling was not merely indiscreet; it was blatant. Encounters with smugglers were a fairly common occurrence, even far beyond settlements in the trackless countryside. On one occasion while conducting an archaeological survey out on the plains east of Gréa, we literally ran into a smuggler's truck while cresting a hill. We joined forces with the people in the truck to disentangle our bumpers, exchanged pleasantries, and went on our way. It is notable that there was never any particular feeling of threat involved in these sorts of encounters with smugglers; they were simply a part of daily life, like the boys herding cattle and goats along the road, the farmers in their fields, or the men and women going to markets.

One would expect that such obvious smuggling would be easy to stop, especially since the representatives of the state were also ubiquitous through the region, in every country. Over the period that I have worked in the southern Lake Chad Basin, I have spent literally hundreds of hours at roadblocks and control posts, operated by the police, by paramilitaries like the Cameroonian Gendarmerie, or by soldiers. Some of these are at international borders, but many are thrown across roads at even the most obscure locations. The security forces deployed at those control points would have easily been sufficient to prevent the massive amounts of smuggling that go on—if that was a priority for the forces of order involved, or for the members of the administration who directed them. But that is not the case.

As we saw in chapter 4, the assumption is that in modern nation-states, sovereignty runs undifferentiated from the capital to the borders. States that cannot enforce that sovereignty risk being labeled as "failed states," with all of the implications for governance that that term implies. The nations of the Lake Chad Basin are certainly not "failed states," according to this definition, although Chad may have come close during the civil wars of the 1980s and early 1990s. These states have often demonstrated ample power for control over their territory, such as by the quashing of political dissent or rebellion. Both Nigeria and Chad have survived a variety of civil wars and regional insurrections since independence, and the government of Cameroon successfully suppressed a significant pro-democracy movement that spread across the country in the 1990s—the *villes mortes*, or "ghost town" campaign. These countries can exert control when they need to, but what if exerting control over territory is not in the best interest of the people who are actually running the state?

When I worked in the area south of Lake Chad, it was common knowledge that government officials and rich merchants were heavily involved in the smuggling networks that extended through all the different countries of the region. This was merely a fact of life, accepted by everyone. It was those people who had the resources to make the kinds of investments that underlay illicit trade: tractor trailers and gasoline tankers are hugely expensive investments, far beyond the means of an ordinary person, and even the motorcycles used to smuggle *zoua-zoua* were often bought by investors and then provided to the *cascadeurs*, who worked on commission. It takes both wealth and significant political and economic connections in multiple countries to identify and buy the materials that can profitably be smuggled, make the arrangements to get those goods across international borders, and then ensure that they can be distributed in the most efficient way in the recipient markets. Wealth and connections were also needed to make sure that transporters were not unduly harassed by customs or police officials during their trips; this would usually involve provision of a standard amount of money in bribes (often called "taxes" or "duties" in this context) where it was necessary to navigate through roadblocks.

The involvement of government officials seems to have been greatest around the border emporia that served as redistribution points for consumer goods into regional economies. These were locations like the neighboring villages of Banki, Limani, and Amchidé, seven and a half miles (12 km) north of Gréa on the Cameroon-Nigeria border; Fotokol-Gambaru, further north on the same border and closer to Lake Chad; or Touboro, on the Chad-Cameroon border to the southeast. Kousseri, in Cameroon and across the Chari River from N'Djamena, the Chadian capital, served a similar role. In their heyday in the 1980s and 1990s, these were sprawling, bustling market towns, where it seemed possible to find any sort of consumer goods under the sun: I remember seeing a number of exercise bicycles in Banki in the early 1990s, utterly incongruous for that part of Central Africa. These border emporia had official status as transshipment points for legal trade between the different countries, but that status did not really disguise the diversity of negotiations and avoidances that went on there. Trade that actually went through these towns and their border points depended on a complicated web of inside knowledge and bribes and payoffs to officials, such that even "legal" economic transactions involved a great deal of non-legal activity. Meanwhile, more dedicated smugglers simply bypassed these border emporia entirely, making use of the paved roads that governments had built to support legal trade to get as close to the border as possible before going off-road to avoid customs controls.

It is perhaps no surprise that contraband has been so important in the regional economy, nor that local elites and government officials have been so heavily involved in those activities. Economic exchange in this area long predates the imposition of colonial and national borders, which in any case were drawn with very little attention to preexisting socioeconomic or ethnic relations. We found fish bones that seem to have come from Lake Chad on Iron Age sites near the Mandara Mountains, and by at least three thousand years ago, stone from sources close to the mountains was exported across the stoneless *firki* clay plains of the region. Economic flows across this region have been central to cultural and political developments ever since that time. In the late nineteenth century, tensions over taxation on imported goods and tax evasion by merchants were important elements in a reorganization of the Wandala state's administration (Morrissey 1984). In recent decades, both Cameroon and Nigeria have been ruled from the south, with national economic policies that have tended to disadvantage populations in the Lake Chad Basin—because those parts of the two countries are to a great extent seen as national backwaters. Under these circumstances, we might certainly expect that smuggling would be an important constituent of the regional economy and that, given its scale, rich men, government employees, and politicians would be heavily involved in it.

However, members of regional elites also appear to be heavily involved in banditry, the other realm of non-legal activity that I have described in this region—and this would seem to be considerably more surprising, given the fear and violence that the *coupeurs de route* inflict on the regions where they operate. Smuggling may be accepted as part of the socioeconomic order, but that is a very different state of affairs from the upheavals associated with banditry. We have seen the different groups from which bandit gangs drew their membership: ex-soldiers, often from Chad; disaffected and rootless young men from Mbororo pastoralist communities; urban youth without any prospects. The leaders of these gangs are, however, much more ambiguous and shadowy figures in accounts of how banditry works. They often appear to have different origins from other members of the gang, and their functions are also different: they coordinate information on the movement of travelers and the security forces; they supply the money, equipment (weapons, automobiles, motorcycles), and logistics for their attacks, and dispose of that equipment afterward; they pick up the proceeds of banditry and divide it among the gang members—all the while keeping a substantial proportion for themselves. The resources that are needed to support bandit gangs can be extremely substantial in some cases. I noted above the kidnapping of the mayor of Lagdo, along with over a dozen other people, in mid-2015. Those people were moved across the border into the Central African Republic and held there for ransom for a year, which certainly implies significant resources on the part of the gang that held them.

Janet Roitman and Saïbou Issa, researchers in the region who interviewed a whole variety of people associated with the world of the *coupeurs de route* in the southern Lake Chad Basin, strikingly describe the figure of the "man in the car"—a faceless person, unknown to the people they talked to who actually carried out the attacks (Roitman 2006, 2005). The "man in the car" never participated in attacks himself, although his money, support, and information made them possible; the leader of the gang in the bush in turn reported to the "man in the car," who was associated with the city and not the rural areas where attacks actually took place. In some cases, the weapons used in the attacks would come from the trunk of the car and would vanish back into it afterward, while in other cases they would be found at a particular point in the bush and would be left there again. This allowed the bandits themselves to more easily integrate into normal society, as they did not have to possess such incriminating weapons themselves.

It is not merely ex-bandits speaking anonymously to researchers who make such claims. When they meet each other in the markets and beer halls, along the streets and on buses, people discuss the involvement of government officials, policemen, and soldiers in banditry through the whole region. The names and activities of these individuals may be obscure, subject to gossip and speculation, but the involvement of officials in such activities is never doubted. At one point during our fieldwork on the DGB sites in 2011, word spread in the region that a high-ranking member of the Gendarmerie, the paramilitary national police force of Cameroon, had been killed during an "anti-gang" ambush on *coupeurs de route* operating in the vicinity of Keroua, close to the border with Nigeria and now at the epicenter of Boko Haram violence in the region. Inconveniently, however, he had been killed in plainclothes, as a member of the gang. Local gossip at the time reflected no particular surprise that a government official would also have been a *coupeur de route*; what astonished people was the breakdown in communications that had led to a raid on the gang without advance warning being given to the gendarme who was killed.

Occasionally, northern Cameroonians would use the term *douaniers-combattants* to describe government representatives who played such roles in the non-legal economy, although I never heard the phrase used in Cameroon outside of Maroua and Kousseri; it seems to be more of a Chadian usage than a French one, and is fairly common in N'Djamena (Debos 2016, 207–210, 247; Roitman 2005, 18). This extraordinary term in French can perhaps best be translated as "fighting customs officials," and it designates social and political leaders who are able to use their associations with violence to work within both the "normal" economy and the world of smugglers and *coupeurs de route*. These soldiers, ex-soldiers, and state bureaucrats may also lead bandit gangs in their off hours, making use of their expertise in economic extraction and military control for both themselves and their state patrons, in border areas where these kinds of activities take place. Their roles overlap with those of the "politico-military entrepreneurs" described by Marielle Debos, leaders of armed factions who also play a role in government; although the term is used in a Chadian context, similar figures exist in the other countries south of Lake Chad, albeit with less military freedom of action in most cases. The success of *douaniers-combattants* depends to a great degree on the patronage of these more powerful political figures.

The borders of social life

The "man in the car" might be a gendarme or a *douanier-combattant*—or he might not be. One of the most important characteristics of these forms of non-legal activity in the southern Lake Chad Basin is their obscurity, and that is a characteristic that they share with many of the activities undertaken by states in the region as well. The countries of the region are largely controlled by autocrats and strongmen, and those forms of control ramify down to the regional level as well. Under those circumstances, where public mechanisms of state oversight are weak or nonexistent and where state resources may mysteriously appear, shift, or disappear entirely, citizens have little information on and less control over what their government officials are doing. This generates an immense amount of uncertainty about whether a particular individual is acting in an official capacity at any particular moment, and if so what that capacity is—especially when the structures of legal and non-legal activity interpenetrate as much as they do.

Witnesses have often said that the *coupeurs de route* who held them up were dressed in police and military uniforms, and their weapons and actions demonstrated their military expertise. In fact, one widely recognized problem for travelers in the region has been establishing whether an unexpected blockade across a road was a temporary checkpoint set up by the security forces or a holdup by *coupeurs de route*. In such cases, it would be difficult to say whether uniformed robbers were actually serving members of the police, military, or gendarmerie; ex-members of those forces still wearing their old uniforms; or common thugs wearing clothes supplied by the "man in the car."

At frontier trading emporia, on the bridges between Kousseri and N'Djamena, or at Banki-Limani-Amchidé on the Cameroon-Nigeria border, it can be equally hard to tell who is acting as an official agent of the state and who is a *douanier-combattant*; experienced traders may know—that is their business—but ordinary people will find it much more difficult to tell one from the other. In fact, it may make little difference (Debos 2016). On a day-to-day basis, bribes extorted at roadblocks and control points are routinely presented as "fines" or "taxes"—and the magnitude of those bribes is unendingly negotiable. In order to navigate that world without being cheated, one must have specialized knowledge and political connections, unavailable to the great majority of people.

These daily indignities and uncertainties imposed on common people are paralleled by their quite realistic evaluations of how social and political life are actually organized more generally. The national societies of the modern Lake Chad Basin are characterized by extreme differences in wealth and power and by very hierarchical social structures, and in all of these countries the state appears to work primarily for the benefit of the wealthy and powerful: the poor remain "grass" in the twenty-first century, still fodder for the horses of the nobility, as that old praise song from Borno said. Social advancement depends to a significant degree on patronage and connections, and ordinary people have access to little of that. This is not to say that honest and hardworking people do not exist in the government and in other organizations of power in these countries; they certainly do, often laboring under burdens that would drive Western officials from their jobs. I have been helped by many of them. But ordinary citizens cannot depend on encountering such people when they are in need, nor on structures of governance that would discourage those who want to prey on them.

In those circumstances, people may well evaluate the legality of particular activities in moral and ethical terms that take account of the social and economic exigencies that define their lives. In these cases, smuggling and even banditry can be judged to be *licit* activities to some degree, even though they are widely acknowledged as *non-legal*. They are accepted as a normal part of the world, and even an aspect of what it takes to live successfully in that world. The anthropologist Janet Roitman has written an extraordinary book, *Fiscal Disobedience*, that describes the relations between northern Cameroonian citizens and the state in the late twentieth century, especially as they involve fiscal structures, taxation, and the provision of state services (Roitman 2005). She convincingly argues that there exist in this area fundamental differences of interpretation about the legitimacy of different kinds of economic activity; those different interpretations are closely connected to debates about the regulatory power of the state and its right to turn private wealth into public wealth through taxation and duties.

In circumstances where the state does not provide agreed-upon services—services as basic as provision of utilities, health care, transportation infrastructure, or even the salaries owed to state employees, for example—informed citizens increasingly doubt the right of the state to demarcate legitimate economic activity and to generate national wealth through control of that activity, when national wealth is either routinely misused by elites or funneled back to the rich Western world as payments for international debts. (Many Cameroonians say that such debt repayments are another form of misuse of national wealth by elites.) Smuggling and banditry may in that case be accorded some social legitimacy by ordinary citizens, because these are activities that allow people to function as independent economic actors. In the case of smuggling, this even allows lawbreakers to contribute to the regional economy—both through the goods being smuggled across borders and the "taxes" (established bribes) that smugglers would transfer to ill-paid officials en route. People may argue, indeed, that smuggling is a form of democratization, because it allows common people access to markets, work, and the possibility of wealth on the frontiers, forms of economic autonomy that they would not have otherwise. Sometimes these debates about the legitimacy of state regulation themselves involve the specter of violence. Even that smuggled Nigerian gasoline, *zoua-zoua*, can confer the potential for resistance to the impositions of the state—not merely because of the economic autonomy that it confers but because of the implied threat that tyrannical, grasping public officials could be burned alive using that gasoline, in their homes or in their cars. "We have *zoua-zoua*; it's the public's fire" (Roitman 2005, 31).

One of the great strengths of Janet Roitman's research on the structure of state regulation in modern northern Cameroon is that it places contemporary debates about the legitimacy of that regulation in a historical context. Her work provides us with an avenue for connecting the day-to-day lived experiences in the southern Lake Chad Basin with archaeological and ethnohistorical research. She does so in part through an examination of the colonial period and of French colonial preoccupations with fixing people in place, stabilizing ethnic and "racial" identities and local political hierarchies. It was absolutely vital for the French to have well-defined censuses of communities and maps of their boundaries throughout the newly conquered colony of Cameroun, in order to be able to govern people most efficiently—and especially to be able to tax them, in order to contribute to the profitability of these new possessions for their European masters. This was in fact true through the entire region, for all of the colonial powers (MacEachern 2001a).

Under these circumstances, the populations previously incorporated within precolonial states—Borno, Wandala, the Sokoto Caliphate, and so on—posed little problem: administrative hierarchies already existed to deal with those people, and their chiefs and rulers were largely left in place under the different systems of indirect rule that all of the colonial powers used in the region. Those peoples that were not incorporated within preexisting political hierarchies, on the other hand, constituted a real challenge for their new colonial overlords: Who were those people; how many of them were there; and how could they be settled in one place, counted, and (especially) taxed? Such populations certainly included the montagnard groups inhabiting the Mandara Mountains, groups like the Yedina on the islands of Lake Chad, pastoral communities like the Mbororo, and the Melgwa people that I discussed at the beginning of this chapter. It also included a host of other individuals and groups that were not so well defined historically, some of them certainly refugees from communities shattered by the violence of the region, the jihads and the wars of Rabih az-Zubayr, through the late nineteenth century. It is not just the twenty-first century that produces refugees.

Colonial records routinely refer to these different populations as bandits and robbers, or with a whole variety of similar terms—"rebels" who were "unruly," "uncivilized," "turbulent," and so on—that are used almost interchangeably for the different groups in question. German, French, and British colonial officers routinely used the contemptuous epithet *kirdi*, borrowed from their new Muslim subjects, to refer to montagnard people en masse—and indeed to all populations not explicitly incorporated into states. In many cases, it does not seem to have particularly mattered who the people in question actually were; they were *kirdi*, living on the margins of the colonial state, and that was all that mattered. European colonial officers were often encouraged in these attitudes by the vanquished elites of precolonial states, now incorporated within the new colonies but with continuing authority over their own people.

To such elites, the nobility of Wandala, Borno, Sokoto, and the other states in the region, European conquest offered opportunities, once the humiliation of military defeat had passed: if they could manipulate European ignorance of the sociopolitical structures of the region, they could potentially make use of European military and administrative power for their own ends. To do this, members of local elites offered their services as guides and interpreters to the new colonial administrators, in order to control the information about local conditions that reached them. One colonial officer used the term *l'écran Mandara* ("the Wandala screen") to refer to the Wandala nobility's filter over his knowledge of montagnard populations, for example (Lembezat 1949). In many cases, Muslim elites claimed sovereignty over areas where it had certainly not existed before the arrival of Europeans and then appealed to the colonial government for military assistance in such areas under their control. Very frequently this aid was granted, and expansionism by the rump nobilities of precolonial states was supported in this new dispensation by European firepower, in punitive expeditions to enforce "traditional" state rights.

It is with the assumptions and actions of these colonial officers that we see a point of inflection between the precolonial sociopolitical relations that I described in the last chapter and the twentieth- and twenty-first-century conditions of life in the southern Lake Chad Basin that I have described in this one. In theory, European colonialism brought with it a dramatic reformulation of the characteristics of the state in the region, in contrast to those largely Islamic states that had existed there for centuries. The colonial powers imported the forms of nation-states—themselves largely eighteenth- and nineteenth-century creations, born in the crucible of Europe's internecine struggles—to sub-Saharan Africa, and tried to reconcile those creations with models of human "tribes" that were equally artificial and Eurocentric and that drastically underestimated the dynamism of precolonial African societies. According to European models, boundaries between colonies (as between European states) should be precisely demarcated, territorial control should extend equally across all of the land of the colony, and colonial subjects should be uniformly incorporated within fixed administrative units. If that model had actually been applied to the region, it would have transformed life in the region in a myriad of different ways.

In reality, that is not what happened. The European colonial interlude in the lands around Lake Chad wrought huge changes on the region in the relatively short period from 1900 to independence in the 1960s. Colonialism introduced new technologies, new forms of economic articulation on a global scale, a significant expansion of urbanism, and a new world religion, Christianity, that offered a potent alternative and counterweight to Islam. Colonialism, and the nationalist response it inspired, certainly introduced new forms of thinking about statehood and citizenship, as was the case throughout Africa, and the implications of those innovations ring down to the present day. What colonialism did not do was erase the wealth-making potentials of borderlands, although it did much to change the nature of the wealth that could be made along borders. Nor did the colonial project obliterate earlier structures of relationship between individuals, communities, and the state that were conditioned by the potentialities of those borders. The colonial powers were never willing to invest the resources necessary to actually transport European systems of territorial control to the Lake Chad Basin; there were never enough administrators or enough resources for that. Throughout the colonial period, European officials wrote constantly about the impossibility of satisfactorily enumerating mobile communities, of controlling transborder movement of people seeking work or profit, and of eradicating the "bandits" (whatever that term meant in the different accounts) who used the frontiers as refuges and as worksites (see, among many others, Beauvilain 1989; Kelly 2013; Lembezat 1949, 1950; Stewart 1970). Their preoccupations were somewhat different than those of elites in the precolonial states that colonialism assimilated, but some of their challenges were quite similar.

This emphatically does not mean that the sociopolitical world of the southern Lake Chad Basin in the twentieth and twenty-first centuries is simply a continuation of the precolonial condition, carried over into a new millennium. That is certainly not the case. Twenty-first-century states, in Africa and across the globe, have vastly greater potential to control space and people than their precolonial antecedents did, just as motorized transport expands the geographical extent of border zones—and that is without taking into account all of the different issues and conflicts that globalization focuses into this relatively small zone of Central Africa. All of the countries around Lake Chad are implicated in resource extraction projects, mostly but not all involving oil, that make the area significant to the West in economic terms (Soares de Oliveira 2007). In a different realm, the Cameroonians interviewed in Janet Roitman's *Fiscal Disobedience* questioned their own condition as citizens, taxpayers, and consumers within a nation called the Republic of Cameroon, comparing their situation to their hopes and expectations for such a condition. Their evaluation of their circumstances would certainly have been historically conditioned, as it is for every human, but the *villes mortes* campaign of civil disobedience did not advocate for a return to life within a precolonial state, Islamic or otherwise. As we will see in the next chapter, that might not be true in all cases if Roitman's book were written today. The conditions of life have changed for the people of the region over the last century, but some of the themes remain the same.

Melgwa and banditry

Much of chapter 4 was devoted to an account of the actions of states and frontier zones in wealth creation in the precolonial Lake Chad Basin. This wealth creation was directed toward the maintenance of state elites and to a great extent involved the capture and sale of enslaved people. The people living within the predation zones of these states had no opportunity to record their own understandings of their cultural worlds and their relations to predatory states. To understand the lives of those people, we have only the accounts written by literate members of state elites themselves—in which frontier populations are typically dismissed as uncivilized savages, *kirdi*, and bandits—and the mute testimony of the archaeological record.

This is supplemented for the late nineteenth and early twentieth centuries by ethnohistorical accounts recorded by anthropologists and historians, but even those cover only the twilight of precolonial states and are usually secondhand stories handed down from older people. Our historical understanding of frontier processes in the region is almost entirely state-centric.

In this chapter, I have tried to present another perspective on the relations between frontier people and states in the modern Lake Chad Basin. Some of these frontier people may seem more comfortable topics for anthropological research than others. The Melgwa, after all, are an ethnic group, what through much of the twentieth century was called a "tribe": they are recognized as a distinct group of people by their neighbors, by the states that they have interacted with— Borno, the European colonial empires, Nigeria, and Cameroon—and by anthropologists. Historical sources referring to the Melgwa (as Gamergu) extend back more than four hundred years. It might seem incongruous to juxtapose the Melgwa, now mostly farmers, against today's floating population of *cascadeurs* and *coupeurs de route* and the violence and illegality that accompany modern smuggling and banditry. However, there are common elements here that we can use, not to condemn the Melgwa through invidious comparisons to lawbreakers but to help us think about the social and political worlds that both groups have inhabited.

First, we can understand the continuity of groups like the Melgwa in the historical record as a border phenomenon. It is not that the essential character of the Melgwa as bandits has remained unchanged for centuries, but rather that populations occupying a particular frontier area, taking advantage of the opportunities that such a situation involves, have been identified and identify themselves as Melgwa over the long term. There is no purity, no essentialism, in that identity: Melgwa, like other peoples in the region, recognize diverse origins within their own communities. Questions of Melgwa identity, which tie the present to archaeologically and politically significant periods in the history of the southern Lake Chad Basin, may usefully be refigured as questions about frontiers, where frontiers sit, and what kinds of contacts they mediate and encourage (Tijani 2010). But the same is also true of other kinds of bandit groups. If state elites describe different people as "bandits," that description is as much about their status as about their activities, given that banditry involves the *non-legal* deployment of violence in wealth creation on the frontiers. We have recourse to the full meaning of the term "out-law" here: people may cease to be bandits if their activities are recognized as becoming legal, as when they settle down and start behaving in ways that state elites find more comprehensible. When frontiers become state centers, banditry sometimes transforms into the proper business of kings; when states fall, rulers may become fugitives and bandits.

We have historical examples of this from the region. In the mid-nineteenth century, a Fulani chief named Hursu was a thorn in the side of the Wandala state, raiding for cattle and hostages on its north-eastern frontier. He was a "bandit" from the point of view of the Wandala administration, and there were sporadic attempts to bring him to book as such. However, the situation changed completely when Hursu established a town at Pété on the Bama Ridge, one that still exists, and began to gather to himself the trappings of an Islamic mini-state; in his eyes, state building was probably his objective all along. At that point, the Wandala recognized a qualitatively different kind of threat from Hursu and took military action to eliminate him as a state threat—not as a bandit (Morrissey 1984, 114–116). In a wonderful reprise to this incident, one of the most important smugglers in northern Cameroon over the last two decades, a man named Hamadou Bouba (universally known in the region as Bouba Pété, after the place where he was born) is now mayor of his hometown, and a pillar of society and supporter of the national government (Tilouine 2016b). Hursu would have understood completely. There are larger parallels here between the *douaniers-combattants* and bandit leaders of today and the "Janus-faced sovereigns" that I discussed in chapter 4, both holding on to power and wealth by navigating very different cultural and political worlds, each with its own definitions of legal and non-legal, licit and illicit behavior.

Second, we have to remember that frontiers are not only places where kings—or the modern "man in the car"—can become wealthy and powerful. Such places hold possibilities for common people as well. Every Hamman Yaji or Bouba Pété has been the chief or patron of many more humble people, seeking to find their way through the borders to some other end: soldiers, servants, slave-raiders, *cascadeurs, coupeurs de route*. There would be other individuals or groups as well, existing outside of such networks of power or patronage but engaged in the same kinds of quest. Common people may hope to find wealth on the borders, or their goals may be more modest: economic autonomy, the means to become a recognized adult, respect from their community. These latter goals seem to be among the hopes of today's *cascadeurs*, for example, poor young men shut out of conventional trajectories to respectable adulthood but also immersed in images of wealth and ease from Western and African media (Roitman 2005, 34–36). In societies that offer few means for social or economic advancement, the fluidity of border circumstances presents the possibility of success to common people who are courageous, ruthless, and lucky. Frontiers in the Lake Chad Basin are profoundly ambivalent places, zones of violence and of wealth accumulation, spaces of danger but also spaces where excluded people may gain access to opportunities otherwise denied them in rigid sociopolitical structures—places where the marginalized can become wealthy and where the wealthy and powerful can become even more so. They continue to exist as internal frontiers, spaces of cultural creation and the formation of new sociopolitical forms. Sometimes we may not like the innovations that are brewed in such places.

6

PLACING BOKO HARAM

THERE IS A RECENT IMAGE from the fighting in the Lake Chad Basin that preoccupies me more than one might think reasonable. It's a photograph released by the Nigerian military on its Twitter account in the summer of 2016, showing the aftermath of an encounter between Nigerian soldiers and two men, claimed to be Boko Haram militants, who were driving a motorcycle south of Maiduguri (figure 6.1) (Nigerian Army 2016). Other images show the torn bodies of the men, but this one shows their weapons, two AK-47s with two magazines each (not really the weapons load of fighters, enough for perhaps a minute of firing for each weapon) neatly laid out on the ground, arranged beside the goods that they were carrying on their motorcycle. These were utterly banal, instantly identifiable to anyone who has ever spent time in a small village market in this part of the southern Lake Chad Basin: bags of Maggi bouillon cubes, flour, black sachets of salt or sugar, sacks of candy, cheap plastic Chinese sandals still in the bags they were sold in, brown bricks of laundry soap. They are the results of a shopping trip.

This particular picture makes me wonder: Just how do terrorists go to market in this area today? Do they hide their weapons somewhere and then stroll into town, and if so, does anyone suspect or care who they are? Do they need to hide their identities when they buy things—and do they pay for them in the first place? The assortment of

Figure 6.1: Goods recovered from insurgents

cheap market items in that photograph doesn't look like the fruits of pillage; it looks like the items you'd find on a grocery list.[1] Were these men selling those everyday consumer goods themselves, or perhaps smuggling them across the border into or from Cameroon for a little money? Instead of being about Boko Haram, as the Nigerian military claims, does this picture simply show the ubiquity of Kalashnikovs in the region today, perhaps carried by young men of some village defense organization on the way home from market? What are the boundaries of terrorism in this region, and how easy is it to separate such terror from the more routine violence that has afflicted people living for so long in the lands of Boko Haram? And where does this terrorist organization fit within the larger historical and cultural contexts within this part of Central Africa?

Terror in the name of God

In mid-2017, Boko Haram is continuing its bloody attacks on communities throughout the southern Lake Chad Basin. The forms of that terror and the military situation of Boko Haram vis-à-vis the national governments of Nigeria, Cameroon, Chad, and Niger have changed significantly since Boko Haram's insurgency began, and indeed during the months that it has taken me to write this book. If you listen to recent Western news reports, the situation has been transformed for the better, with the militaries of these four countries having united to push Boko Haram out of much of the territory that it held in northeastern Nigeria—in particular, from the town of Gwoza west of the Mandara Mountains, where the terrorist organization had established the capital of its "caliphate." With these successes and the assumption that the organization has been more or less defeated, Boko Haram has to some degree fallen out of the consciousness of the Western news media and general publics, with only sporadic news reports reminding the outside world that they still exist. It was particularly easy to have that happen, given that Westerners knew relatively little about the conflict in the first place, except that it was African, "remote," and "savage" the three terms still being more or less synonyms in the West, and that it had involved a kidnapping of young women—mostly Christian, but with some Muslims among them—from the town of Chibok, which attracted Michelle Obama's public attention.

In fact, much less has changed than those news reports would suggest. The Nigerian military's hold on Gwoza itself continues to be extremely tenuous, because Boko Haram still controls significant areas of the Mandara Mountains, which loom above the outskirts of Gwoza town, and the plains close to the Cameroon-Nigeria border, southwest of the border town of Keroua. Boko Haram has controlled that area for more than three years, and some of the people living in the region have joined the organization, as we will see below. Beyond that region, Boko Haram has lost continuous control over much of its territory, but its ability to instill terror has not diminished. From refuges in and around the Mandara Mountains and, it appears, from isolated bush camps throughout the whole region, Boko Haram still carries out sporadic attacks on villages and travelers, lays land mines on roads, and sends suicide bombers—often girls and young women—into village markets. People throughout the southern Lake Chad Basin live in fear of Boko Haram terror attacks, while people from montagnard communities who have not joined the group have spent long periods hidden in caves and refuges, without reliable access to food or water. Disruptions to daily life have meant that, in many communities around the northwestern Mandara Mountains in Nigeria, crops have not been planted or harvested effectively in the last three years, and so famine has become endemic.

Boko Haram terrorists still kidnap people in the course of their attacks; although only the mass kidnapping of schoolgirls from Chibok in 2014 really attracted the attention of the Western media, this was a Boko Haram tactic from considerably before the Chibok attack and continues to be used today. The fate of most of the people kidnapped is unknown; in many cases, their relatives can only hope that their bodies will eventually be returned to their home communities. Tens of thousands of people have been driven from their homes in Nigeria entirely, so that they have become domestic refugees, living in the most tenuous of circumstances as internally displaced persons (IDPs) in camps that often suffer from appalling deficiencies in food, water, housing, and sanitation. Tens of thousands of others have fled across the border into Cameroon, to live in refugee camps there.

People in the region suffer from the attentions of their governments, as well. Nigerian, Cameroonian, and Chadian military and security personnel have been accused of atrocities against local communities and against detainees and people suspected of being Boko Haram members or sympathizers (see among many others Amnesty International 2016, 2015; Nossiter 2015; H. Umar 2016). In the Nigerian case, this has involved massacres of civilians, as in the town of Baga close to Lake Chad in 2013, and credible reports of security forces beheading Boko Haram suspects, in apparent retribution for such atrocities perpetrated by Boko Haram. Airstrikes and attacks by helicopter gunships and artillery have frequently been indiscriminate; these have possibly included the Nigerian use of cluster bombs, which are banned in many parts of the world. Nigerian civilians in the area have frequently said that they had more to fear from attacks from their own military than from those from Boko Haram. The Nigerian government has hired South African mercenaries to assist its soldiers in fighting against Boko Haram. Some of these men are veterans of Koevoet, a notorious counterinsurgency force that operated in what is now Namibia during the brutal apartheid wars of the 1980s, and it is quite unlikely that they are much concerned with collateral damage or civilian casualties. Civilians often appear to be caught between opposing armed forces, sometimes quite difficult to tell apart and all of them ready to use dreadfulness and weapons of fear in the prosecution of warfare.

Under these circumstances, my attempts to place the violence and brutality associated with Boko Haram in any kind of historical or cultural context may seem perverse to some readers of this book, an excuse for justifying or rationalizing that violence or for diluting it with the abstractions of detached analysis. These are today's events, after all, not ancient history. I obviously disagree with that position, for a number of reasons. In the first place, I think that we can better understand what Boko Haram insurgents have done in the past, and what they might do in the future, by looking at the historical worlds within which their violence has developed. Terrorists in this region, as across the globe, do not simply generate random violence de novo, without any reference to what has gone on before them; rather, such violence—and all of the daily activity that goes along with it and supports it—has to be comprehensible to them, if not always to their victims (for a cogent introduction to these issues, see Asad 2007). The historical resonances of terrorist violence will certainly be different in different places and times, but such resonances will exist. Second, an examination of earlier contexts of violence in the region may yield a better sense of the resilience and vulnerabilities of populations faced with such violence today, providing clues to the cultural models that they have available to them to cope with terror. And third, and perhaps more self-interestedly, looking at processes of violence that occur today may help researchers, other archaeologists and historians and even me, to better comprehend similar kinds of violence in the past. In this chapter, I will point out some parallels between the modern situation in the lands of Boko Haram and the historical processes (some of them very recent) that I have described in the earlier chapters of this book.

Ethnicity and ethnic relations

The Minawao refugee camp is just a few kilometers off that paved road leading into the Mandara Mountains that I described at the beginning of chapter 1. In 2015, the American ambassador to the United Nations took this road from Maroua to visit the Minawao refugee camp, and her convoy of speeding SUVs killed a little boy in the roadway at Mokong (Cooper 2016). The camp holds around sixty thousand people—a population far larger than that of the nearby mountain town of Mokolo and perhaps a third the size of the provincial capital of Cameroon's Extreme North Province at Maroua, out on the plains to the east. That mass of people has accumulated within three years, housed within a regimented grid of tents imposed on the brushland at the edge of the Mandara massif. Minawao shows up like a beacon on satellite images, utterly unlike the densely packed houses of Cameroonian and Nigerian towns in the region (figure 6.2). Conditions at the camp are perhaps somewhat better than those in the shambolic IDP camps in Nigeria, but people there have no idea when they can go home again. The refugees at Minawao are people from societies throughout the Mandara Mountains—from the Glavda, Chinene, and Mafa communities—and from the plains of the southern Lake Chad Basin: Kanuri, Shuwa Arab, Hausa, Fulani (United Nations High Commissioner for Refugees 2016). The diversity of people living at the camp is a testament to the impact of the Boko Haram insurgency across the region; no one—Muslim, Christian, or otherwise; rural or urban; rich or poor—has been spared, and people from every ethnic group have been forced to flee terrorist attacks. Given what we have seen of the history of ethnic relations in the southern Lake Chad Basin, what does this imply about ethnicity and Boko Haram?

Figure 6.2: The Minawao refugee camp

Boko Haram certainly began as a Kanuri phenomenon with the "Nigerian Taleban," involving primarily young urban Kanuri, some from upper-class families in Maiduguri. The successive leaders of Boko Haram, Mohammed Yusuf and Abubakar Shekau, are both Kanuri, and a competitor to Shekau who emerged in mid-2016 is named Abu Musab al-Barnawi. "Al-Barnawi" can be translated as "the one from Borno" and is certainly a Kanuri name, whether or not he is, as sometimes claimed, the son of Mohammed Yusuf. The leader of the Boko Haram splinter group Ansaru, Khalid al-Barnawi (now in Nigerian custody) is also Kanuri, although he is not (as far as anyone knows) related to Abu Musab al-Barnawi. From all accounts, a large proportion of Boko Haram's fighters continue to be drawn from Kanuri communities, especially those in and around Maiduguri, and references to the history of Borno and the Sokoto Caliphate have been a central theme of Mohammed Yusuf's teachings. One element sustaining Kanuri membership in Boko Haram is probably the hostility engendered toward Nigeria's security forces after their brutal and indiscriminate crackdown on the group in Maiduguri in 2009, in which members of the group as well as innocent bystanders were killed. That hostility was heightened by the fact that many of the security forces involved in those massacres came from outside the area and included Christians from the south of the country (Pérouse de Montclos 2014, 150–151). There is also some evidence that preference has been given to Kanuri members of Boko Haram at different times, as with claims that non-Kanuri were periodically designated to carry out suicide bombing missions.

In some cases, long-term Kanuri ethnic hostilities seem to be playing out in the violence associated with Boko Haram. We first have to remember their repeated, savage attacks on non-Kanuri populations around the region, which have caused a great deal of destruction and damage. Many of those groups, including montagnards, were historical targets of slave raids, and we can place those Boko Haram attacks in a historical sequence that extends back more or less continuously to the Kanuri slave-raiding expeditions of five centuries ago. In his threat to sell kidnapped Chibok girls and young women in the market place, Abubakar Shekau explicitly harked back to the period and practice of slave-raiding, and the sexual abuse and forced marriage that freed women have documented was also characteristic of the processes of enslavement, as Hamman Yaji's diary and many other historical sources detail. Hamman Yaji and other precolonial slavers seem to have avoided destroying communities where they operated, probably so they could take more slaves later, while Boko Haram has taken a more scorched-earth approach to the villages they attack. That is probably due in large part to a lack of the long-term experience with slave-raiding characteristic of the nineteenth century. Some people in Mandara communities certainly understand the depredations of Boko Haram in these historical terms, as just the latest in the series of predatory forces from the plains that have sought to enslave them—at the same time as they realize the distinctive features of this new threat. It is quite likely that Shekau will join Hamman Yaji, Usman dan Fodio, and other oppressors from the plains in the oral histories of future generations of montagnard people.

There are other cases where ethnically based violence seems to be part of Boko Haram activities as well. In fighting close to Lake Chad in mid-2015, Boko Haram militants sought out and killed Shuwa Arab civilians while sparing their Kanuri neighbors in the same villages, apparently in reprisal for attacks on the militants and on local communities by predominantly Shuwa Chadian Army units (Fonka Mutta 2015). We do not know whether the Chadian military's original decision to send units made up mostly of Shuwa soldiers to fight Boko Haram was also ethnically inspired, or when this deadly tit-for-tat began. Although Shuwa communities were allied with the kings of Borno two centuries ago, at the time of Shehu Muhammad al-Kanemi, they subsequently allied themselves with Rabih az-Zubayr at the end of the nineteenth century, and there have been continuing conflicts between Shuwa and other ethnic groups on the plains south of Lake Chad—especially Kanuri and Kotoko people—ever since (Issa 2007). It is hard not to see some historical resonance in that pattern of attacks.

But we should not draw this historical equivalence too far. Boko Haram broadcasts many of its news reports in Hausa, the region's Chadic lingua franca, which is far more widely understood than Kanuri, albeit sometimes in a Kanuri-inflected Hausa that can be hard for Hausa-speaking people themselves to understand. It preaches an Islamist gospel that is not itself centered on Kanuri identity, and both Mohammed Yusuf and Abubakar Shekau have expressed admiration for Usman dan Fodio, the Fulani founder of the Sokoto Caliphate two centuries ago, while simultaneously criticizing dan Fodio's Kanuri contemporary Shehu Muhammad al-Kanemi (Pieri and Zenn 2016; Zenn 2016). They appear to have done so because dan Fodio's support for jihad and his rigid interpretations of Islamic law suited their own understanding of the place of Islam in the region, while al-Kanemi defended the Kanuri elite against accusations of apostasy by Muhammad Bello, dan Fodio's son. Paradoxically, this may also have to do with the origins of Boko Haram in Maiduguri, where a descendant of al-Kanemi still reigns as the *shehu*, the traditional ruler of Borno, and is closely associated with the state government (Harnischfeger 2014; M. Umar 2012).

Boko Haram has incorporated many non-Kanuri fighters into its ranks. In Nigeria itself, most of these people have probably been Hausa and Fulani. In northern Cameroon, it seems that many of the recruits to Boko Haram are not from local Kanuri communities but rather are young Wandala men—although this does, of course, reflect the fact that the Wandala have also been Muslims for a long time and perhaps also echoes their own history as slave-raiders and state-builders close to the Mandara Mountains. On the shorelines and islands of Lake Chad, Boko Haram has made common alliance with Yedina communities, the population that has been most closely associated with the lake for more than five hundred years. Cooperation between Boko Haram and Yedina communities is significantly associated with the dramatic ecological changes that Lake Chad has undergone since the middle of the twentieth century. Yedina people have been marginalized and exploited in their historical homeland by the great immigration of people from across the Lake Chad Basin to the shores of the shrinking lake, which has opened up new areas for commercial activities, especially fishing and grazing. The population of the area has tripled in the last thirty years—a powerful indication of how environmental changes may have unforeseen results (Seignobos 2015). Over that period, Hausa traders and fisherman from diverse groups have established their own communities and monopolized trade, particularly in dried fish, around the southern part of the lake. In this case, it appears that some Yedina leaders see in Boko Haram a mechanism for regaining control of their territory, while for Boko Haram Yedina guides can help them navigate the maze of islands and marshes distributed across the shallow lake, especially in the event that the insurgents lose control of their bases in the plains and mountains to the south.

The most striking case of non-Kanuri joining Boko Haram, however, is probably the case of some people from the Mandara Mountains, especially from originally Christian montagnard communities in the massif east of Gwoza. This is particularly the case for the Dghwede ethnic group, which occupies the heights directly above Gwoza and is one of the most populous montagnard groups in the area. One of the most important Boko Haram leaders under Abubakar Shekau was a Dghwede man, Ibrahim Tada Ngalyike, who has since been killed by Nigerian security forces, and the cooperation of Dghwede people is certainly one of the main reasons that Boko Haram has been able to hold out in the mountains long after Nigerian and allied military forces retook the town of Gwoza, only a mile or two away on the plains below. Dghwede is not the only montagnard society to have contributed fighters to Boko Haram: some of their Chikide and Guduf neighbors have joined as well, as have small numbers of men from other montagnard groups in the region (Gerhard Muller-Kosack, March 19, 2015; Matfess 2016).

There are many conflicting stories about which particular people joined Boko Haram voluntarily and which were coerced into joining the organization; their violence toward communities through the region and survivor accounts leave no doubt that some unwilling people have been forced to join Boko Haram. However, there is equally no doubt that they have received significant manpower and support from at least a few montagnard communities. With Dghwede, this cooperation was preceded in the 2000s by significant conversion to Islam from Christianity and indigenous religious beliefs. It was probably led by young people who had gone to Maiduguri looking for work and fed by widespread grievances against the population of the town of Gwoza, who Dghwede people felt took advantage of and looked down on them (Walker 2016, 158–159). In this, there are similarities with the alliances that Boko Haram has built up with Yedina people on Lake Chad, as noted above. It is also true, however, that significant Islamic conversion has taken place within the last twenty years in a number of montagnard societies that have taken no part in Boko Haram, including Kapsiki and Mafa (van Beek 2012). In other cases, individual Christian montagnards appear to have converted to Islam and subsequently joined Boko Haram; this probably accounts for persistent reports in Nigeria of "Christian Boko Haram."

It might seem very strange, on the face of it, that members of any montagnard ethnic groups would willingly join Boko Haram, given the savage attacks that the organization has carried out in the mountains and their great hostility to the non-Muslim groups that they still denigrate with the epithet *kirdi*. In a whole variety of ways, however, this is not nearly as surprising as it might be. Boko Haram has deliberately honed its appeal to poor and marginalized people, both urban and rural, young men—and some young women (Matfess 2016)—who have little hope for advancement as it is and who are thus open to ideologies that promise the possibility of better things, either in this life or in the hereafter. The montagnards who have joined Boko Haram come from some of the poorest and most marginalized communities in the southern Lake Chad Basin today; the mountains themselves are extraordinary products of human ingenuity and labor, but they have been largely ignored by the colonial and post-independence governments in both Nigeria and Cameroon. Why should they not be attracted by the Islamist preaching of Boko Haram?

There are other political factors, local to the mountains, at play here as well. Although Mandara communities share a whole variety of cultural elements, most notably their use of Chadic languages, they have never in any sense been unified politically. In fact, political conflict and warfare has been endemic through the mountains, only gradually lessening since the 1950s; when I began working in the region in the mid-1980s, montagnard men would routinely bring weapons to markets on the edge of the mountains. There has historically been no real sense of "montagnard solidarity" among these communities, and in the past, specific montagnards groups often did ally with plains states when such alliances were useful. As we have seen in the previous chapters, it is not as if there was a great gulf forever fixed between the peoples in the mountains and those in the plains, even after the different populations drew apart culturally and politically more than five centuries ago. There are well-known historical analogies for the assistance provided by Dghwede and other communities to Boko Haram, such as when montagnards around Mora sheltered the Wandala elite in the mountains in the face of attacks by Rabih az-Zubayr in 1895. In that case, some Wandala women stayed up in the mountains and eventually married montagnard men. Less than twenty years after that, Vamé and Dumwa montagnard communities again made alliance with and supported German forces in the mountains during the early years of World War I. Only the assistance that those Vamé and Dumwa people rendered to the Germans allowed them to sustain an eighteen-month siege by British and French forces in the northeastern Mandara Mountains, in conditions of extreme deprivation (Damis 1929).

As we saw in chapter 3, one significant element in the development of the DGB sites in the massif seems to have been their positioning close to the margins of mountains and plains and to the contemporary Wandala capital at Keroua, now well within the lands of Boko Haram. To the extent that was the case, the DGB sites would likely have functioned in the power relationships associated with the developing Wandala state. The DGB sites remain charged with power and menace, and to some degree continue to be associated with the "eating of people" and enslavement, that quintessential source of wealth born out of border violence. Mountain communities did more than offer shelter to plainsmen in times of crisis; they have often allied with plains groups against other montagnard people as well, even to the point of cooperating in enslavement. The present case is somewhat different, because it involves significant changes in ideology among montagnard populations like the Dghwede, but of course conversion to Islam has been an important dynamic within societies across the wider region for the last three hundred years at least. Populations like the Wandala did not begin as Muslims, but rather found advantages in converting to Islam, first elites and then ordinary people in a process that extended over more than two centuries. In an era of continuing globalization, there is no reason to think that such processes today will lap up against the edges of the massif and then stop.

In thinking about such alliances, we also need to remember that political upheavals in this part of Central Africa—as in many other parts of the world—have historically led to the amalgamation of hitherto unrelated or even hostile peoples and the formation of new kinds of ethnic identities in the crucible of such encounters. There are many such cases known from throughout Africa: the social breakdown associated with the Atlantic slave trade, for example, disrupted communities and led to new ones across the continent, and these were often made up of amalgamations of refugees, soldiers, and other hangers-on. Such processes frequently involved ideological movements like Boko Haram, which aim to overturn preexisting social and economic orders and usher in a new world of human relations. The most recent historical example in the Lake Chad Basin would be, again, the jihad of Usman dan Fodio, which led to the formation of the Sokoto Caliphate in Nigeria two centuries ago. This was to a significant degree a multiethnic social and military movement, albeit one with a Fulani core. The school of Islamic scholarship that gave rise to this and the other West African jihads of the time, the Torodbe, incorporated clerics from a variety of different ethnic groups, and dan Fodio's supporters included a whole range of poor and marginalized people, including Hausa peasants, pagan Fulani pastoralists, and even freed slaves and people still enslaved. To a great extent, his jihad was a revolt of the powerless, those mocked as "grass" and thought only fit to be grazed on by the horses of nobles in that old Borno praise song. The millenarian aspect of dan Fodio's jihad, the image it provided of a future world more just and more godly than the present one, was evidently attractive to such marginalized groups. That is still the case today.

In the course of dan Fodio's jihad, significant groups of people of different origins appear to have adopted Fulani identities, as those identities were most closely associated with the core group of jihadists (Salamone 1985; Smith 1997). Indeed, we can see traces of this in the genetics of modern populations in the region today, since Nigerian Fulani people seem to be more closely related to other neighboring Nigerian populations than they are to Fulani people living in other areas of West and Central Africa (MacEachern 2000; Tishkoff et al. 2009). This genetic relationship seems to be much more recent than the one between Chadic- and Nilo-Saharan-speaking populations in the Lake Chad Basin that I discussed in chapter 2 and fits well with the historical data of population amalgamation two centuries ago. We might in fact use the jihad of Usman dan Fodio as a way of thinking about the sociopolitical upheavals that led or forced Nilo-Saharan-speaking communities in the Lake Chad Basin to adopt Chadic languages six thousand years ago or more. As in the past, modern cultural identities are not fixed over the long term, although they may seem to us to be so, in our limited timescales of years and decades. Whether or not the activities of Boko Haram will actually lead to substantial changes in the way that people identify themselves and are identified by others, in the Mandara Mountains and elsewhere, remains to be seen.

Borders, wealth, and status

Whatever combination of force and persuasion that Boko Haram has used to dominate different areas in and around the Mandara Mountains (and this is likely to have varied depending on where the group has operated), there is no question that they have made good use of the potentials of these landscapes in carrying out their operations. In mid-2017, they still seem to dominate parts of the northwestern Mandara Mountains and the plains between the mountains and the Cameroon border to the east. In a military sense, these mountains play more or less the same role for Boko Haram today that they have for montagnard populations for the last five hundred years or more. I can attest that climbing up those steep mountain slopes is hard; attacking up them would be much harder. The rocky hillsides and crests of the massif provide extraordinarily strong defensive positions without a great deal of preparation, and they negate many of the technological advantages that states in the region have historically relied on, whether that advantage involved horses and firearms up to the early twentieth century or the heavy armor and airpower that the Nigerian government in particular has relied on more recently. Artillery can certainly be used, but as the British and French found while besieging German forces south of Mora in World War I, it can be extremely difficult to spot people and movement in the jumble of granite boulders on the slopes, especially when they are overgrown with bushes and trees. It is extremely likely that many more civilians than Boko Haram militants have been killed in artillery fire, as was the case a century ago during World War I. At this point, state forces seem incapable of definitively rooting Boko Haram insurgents out of their mountain hideouts, as long as they have some degree of support—coerced, grudging, enthusiastic, or otherwise—from people living in the mountains.

However, landscapes are not just configurations of terrain, good for impeding military movements and providing refuge against artillery. The potentials of landscapes also depend critically on the knowledge

that people deploy to make use of them and the historical understandings that people have about the meaning of such landscapes. We
have to think again about how the landscapes of plains and mountains
have been used through time, in order to understand how they are
used today. To do so, we need to look at this area through two different historical lenses simultaneously, one involving the recent exploitation of the Cameroon-Nigeria border region for illicit activities and
the other much longer-term, involving Islamic religious conceptions
about how virtuous Muslims deal with corrupt rulers. Both can help
us think about how the people who make up Boko Haram think about
frontier landscapes in the mountains and plains and on the islands of
Lake Chad and about their possibilities.

As we saw in chapter 5, frontier zones throughout this region are
interlaced with trails and pathways that have been used for smuggling
and banditry for a very long time. These activities have taken different forms, from the rural cattle-raiding and hold-up of merchants
that the Melgwa and other groups undertook in the nineteenth century and earlier to the more organized undertakings of *cascadeurs* and
coupeurs de route during the last three decades. The common themes
in all of these cases are that these activities take place on state borders
and that they are non-licit forms of economic activity from the perspective of state centers—they are smuggling and banditry and not
trade and warfare, precisely because they are illicit.

What could such illegal economic activities have to do with the
actions of a modern terrorist organization like Boko Haram, which presumably has very different objectives? In fact, the day-to-day activities of Boko Haram on the Cameroon-Nigeria frontier have a great
deal in common with the activities of smugglers and bandits during
the last few decades, in part because there seems to be a lot of overlap
between these two groups. As the geographer Christian Seignobos has
documented, the cheap Chinese motorcycles used by smugglers and
bandits in the 1990s and 2000s have in the last few years become the
vehicle of choice for Boko Haram attacks, their jerrycans of Nigerian
gasoline replaced by spotters and gunmen with Kalashnikovs
(figure 6.3) who make a column of such vehicles a very mobile and
quite formidable striking force (Seignobos 2014)—especially against
isolated villages or security posts.[2] The drivers of these motorcycles
use the same footpaths and backcountry ways as did the *cascadeurs* of

Figure 6.3: Boko Haram motorcycles (courtesy Christian Seignobos)

ten or twenty years ago, in both mountains and plains, and they seem to be equally adept at avoiding the national military forces of any of the countries in the region when the need arises. That sort of expertise is not acquired quickly or easily: remember that Boko Haram in Maiduguri originally drew many of its foot soldiers—if that is the right term in the circumstances—from the *achabas*, the helmetless moto-taxi drivers who in both Cameroon and Nigeria sometimes graduate to smuggling. It is virtually certain that many of the insurgents who use those back ways across the frontier today learned about them first-hand in the past, while carrying more lucrative cargo.

Or perhaps not necessarily more lucrative. One recurring theme in Nigerian reports about Boko Haram is that insurgents are relatively well paid for their activities, certainly earning far more money than they would have as farmers, *clando* drivers, or laborers. The emphasis on religious violence in the activities of Boko Haram should not obscure the fact that its fighters often receive recompense in this world, before their eternal reward in Paradise. Of course, that raises the question of where this wealth is coming from: pillage and banditry, surreptitious support from high government officials, the sale of young women as slaves, smuggling? We do not have a clear idea of the answer to this question, but that is precisely the point. Border wealth is subterranean, originating in obscure sources and flowing through channels and for purposes undetectable by ordinary people.

The fragmentary evidence available after the kidnapping of young women in Chibok in 2014 indicates that some were probably moved across the border into Cameroon quite quickly, almost certainly along the same routes used by smugglers and insurgents. In the 1980s, people on the eastern side of the Mandara Mountains in Cameroon said that children would still occasionally be stolen while going to school or tending fields at the foot of the mountains, to be spirited across the border into Nigeria, far from their homes and any possibility of rescue (MacEachern 2011), a wicked echo of the slave trade of fifty years before that. Boko Haram seems to have used the same approach in the other direction, making use of smugglers' expertise to move kidnapped girls from Chibok into Cameroon, where at least some were made available to insurgents as "wives"—in essentially the same status as enslaved young girls in the early twentieth century and beforehand. Both Hamman Yaji and the leaders of Boko Haram have thus distributed captured young women to their followers, and those young women seem to have played similar roles in both cases: as sexually enslaved subjects ("partners" is an inappropriate term in such cases), as labor, and potentially as the involuntary nucleus of families that undergird male status in Lake Chad Basin communities.

At the same time, other women say that they married Boko Haram members willingly, whether out of religious conviction or because they seemed to be relatively well-off and make suitable husbands. Such women may say that their Boko Haram husbands have been generous, paying allowances to their new wives, giving them their own substantial bride price at marriage (instead of giving it to their fathers), and exempting them from work in the fields (Matfess 2016). These different accounts, where captive young women are forced into sexual enslavement and menial labor while other women who marry Boko Haram husbands are rewarded with gifts and freedom from such labor, parallel the different destinies that would await enslaved and free women during the period of the slave trade. As I mentioned in chapter 1, women now identified as "Boko Haram's wives" slip across the border to markets like Kolofata in Cameroon, where they sell their goods—goods pillaged in the course of insurgent attacks on other communities—cheaply for food (Tilouine 2016a). We must ask ourselves, what motivates women to remain in relations with Boko Haram members, in contexts of fear and violence? It may well be indoctrination in some cases, but the experience of some "Boko

Haram wives" argues that some have been able to make the choice to join the insurgency.

Boko Haram insurgents are certainly continuing to exploit the wealth-making potentials of border regions in the same way as did their slave-raiding predecessors, as they obtain young women as "wives" when they would not otherwise have the wherewithal for marriage. As Janet Roitman makes clear in her book *Fiscal Disobedience*, smuggling and banditry were intimately bound up with ideas about manhood and adult male identity in the region, with family life as an important element in that identity. Full manhood makes one a *baaba saare*—in Fulani, "master of the house"—while the failure to achieve that status dooms a man to the status of permanent social adolescence (for a Cameroonian example outside the Lake Chad Basin, see Argenti 2008). (For reference, a successful bandit is known as a *baaba ladde*, "master of the bush," a term which is also often applied to a lion [Issa 2010, 230].) In these circumstances of border violence, women play a paradoxical role, as both a source of wealth that can be deployed to attain the status of a grown man and also one of the central indicators of that station via marriage.

Other activities by Boko Haram also indicate its parallels with earlier forms of illicit activity. The first actions claimed by Boko Haram in Cameroon were quite unlike the groups' undertakings in Nigeria at the same time. In 2013 and early 2014, at a time when Boko Haram was engaged in a whole series of bombings and killings in Nigeria (and not only in the northeast of the country), they also carried out a series of kidnappings of foreigners in northern Cameroon: a family of French tourists in Waza National Park, a French priest in Koza at the edge of the Mandara Mountains, a Canadian nun and two Italian priests near Maroua, Chinese engineers again from near Waza. Sometimes the kidnappers are said to have spoken French, which would have been extremely unusual for Nigerian Boko Haram at the time. In all of those cases, the hostages were held for a significant amount of time, and substantial ransoms were demanded and in most cases probably paid (Zenn 2014), at which point they were released—kidnapping as a profit-making activity. This certainly was done in the cause of Boko Haram, probably in cooperation with its offshoot Ansaru, and a number of the hostages were eventually released in Nigeria, after having been smuggled across the border at some point during their captivity. But it seems to have had very little to do with how Boko Haram was behaving in Nigeria at the time.

These kidnappings involved exactly the modus operandi used by the *coupeurs de route* who had been operating in Cameroon over the previous decades, and who were quite happy to kidnap people for profit. Such activities still go on in other parts of the north of the country, as the unfortunate mayor of Lagdo discovered in 2015. The conversations that I had with Cameroonians when I was in the north in 2014 returned to the same theme: that these kidnappings, especially those around Waza, were directly related to the activities of the gangs of *coupeurs de route* active in the area in the 1990s and 2000s. People argued about whether past *coupeurs de route* were now simply calling themselves Boko Haram in order to increase the level of threat in their extortions or whether they were acting as subcontractors, kidnapping foreigners, moving them across the border in time-honored fashion, and then selling them on to Boko Haram itself. In fact, the distinction hardly mattered: in 2014 those northern Cameroonians saw the violence associated with Boko Haram in their country as simply a continuation of the border violence that had already afflicted the region for more than twenty years, involving both well-connected outlaws and the inevitable government reprisals.

Local people see other continuities in the modern situation in northern Cameroon as well. The areas around the border trading emporia of Banki-Limani-Amchidé and Fotokol-Gambaru have seen ferocious fighting between Boko Haram and the militaries of Cameroon, Nigeria, and Chad since 2013. The damage inflicted on these communities and the formal closures of trading and movement along the border have devastated "legitimate" trade at those locations, leading to a dramatic worsening of the economic situation across northern Cameroon. At the same time, however, cross-border smuggling has continued throughout the region, and smuggled Nigerian gasoline, *zoua-zoua*, is still available more or less everywhere in northern Cameroon. Its price has increased dramatically, to the point where it is often now more expensive than "super," the legitimately imported gasoline that comes up from southern Cameroon or Chad and that is sold in service stations—but there are only a few service stations in the region, whereas *zoua-zoua* can be bought in even the smallest villages. Its continuing availability at a time when borders are theoretically closed obviously raises questions in the minds of Cameroonians: How is this gasoline getting across the frontier?

To a great degree, the routes for moving *zoua-zoua* have shifted south, to the region around Garoua about one hundred miles (160 km) south of Maroua as the crow flies; Cameroonian drivers say that they can tell Borno gasoline from gasoline originating further south in Nigeria by its color, and more *zoua-zoua* is southern gasoline today. However, that is still well within the frontier area affected by Boko Haram, and there are persistent reports that the insurgency has some role in controlling the movement of *zoua-zoua* from Nigeria into Cameroon (Légaré-Tremblay 2016; Tilouine 2016a). That would not be at all surprising, given the locations of smuggling routes and the relations between *cascadeurs* and Boko Haram insurgents that I have noted above.[3] As the historian Saïbou Issa noted, "Smuggling is at the heart of this war. . . . Boko Haram is also a for-profit criminal enterprise that incorporates many smugglers, and which depends on crime and violence that generate significant income in an environment of socio-economic distress" (Tilouine 2016a). Local people around Maroua assume that the continued availability of *zoua-zoua* means that powerful people, bureaucrats, merchants, or politicians, have some means of dealing with Boko Haram, either actively cooperating with them in moving gasoline across the border or paying them to allow the shipments to pass unmolested—the same "taxes" that were paid in bribes to police and customs officials in previous decades, now simply being paid to the new guardians of the frontier. Obviously, the obscurity that shrouds the activities of powerful state and nonstate actors in all the countries of the Lake Chad Basin contributes to citizens' evaluations of Boko Haram. Why should it not? They have a great deal of prior evidence that the hidden machinations of powerful people affect their daily lives and no indication that things have changed in recent years.

Boko Haram seems to have inherited networks of illegal activities and moneymaking that have existed around the frontiers of the Lake Chad Basin for decades, if not centuries—but we should not make the mistake of assuming that Boko Haram is simply a gang of criminals disguising their activities under the banner of jihad. This is primarily a religious and social movement, one that originated in proselytization and vehement disputation between Islamic religious leaders in places like Maiduguri and in the hopelessness of its followers. It exists in great part because it offers a vision of a better life, the raising up of good Muslims and their triumph over the wicked, to people who see no prospect of a decent or fulfilling life in their present circumstances. Western observers may quite rightly condemn the savage atrocities that members of Boko Haram have carried out, the terror that they have sown all over the Lake Chad Basin, but they are largely religious fanatics by origin, not criminals or lunatics. We also need to remember, while condemning those atrocities, that the West has tolerated and indeed enabled the development of extraordinarily repressive economic and political systems in this region. These are systems in which poor and marginalized people continue to be treated essentially as human detritus, of no interest to rich outsiders except as objects of pity in disaster-porn documentaries or objects of fear when, as "economic refugees," they try to reach the West. That pretty much remains the case in 2017. Such an understanding does not excuse the actions of Boko Haram militants, but it may render those actions more comprehensible.

In addition to looking at the connections between Boko Haram and frontier smuggling and banditry, we thus need to examine the religious reasons for the group's association with frontier zones. As I noted above, one of the paradoxes of Boko Haram's appeals to regional history is its Kanuri leadership's veneration of Usman dan Fodio, the Fulani leader of the jihads that gave rise to the Sokoto Caliphate, while being relatively dismissive of dan Fodio's Kanuri contemporary and rival Shehu Muhammad al-Kanemi. Dan Fodio's long dispute with the established Hausa rulers at the end of the eighteenth century, and especially with the ruler and elites of the Hausa state of Gobir, is a central part of the history of his jihad. As disputes worsened between the two groups, an attempt was ultimately made on dan Fodio's life, after which he led his followers on a *hijra*, an emigration away from the capital of Gobir to the state's borders in 1804. This was a political statement as well as a migration, a rejection of the ruler of Gobir as wicked and an apostate. It was also an action with a great deal of significance within Islam itself, connecting dan Fodio with Muhammad and his *hijra* from Mecca to Medina in 622, a turning point of the history of that religion.

In undertaking this emigration to the *dar al-hijra*, "the land of exile," faithful Muslims like dan Fodio and his followers removed themselves from the snares and temptations of the ruler's court to the borders of the country. They did so, however, not to dwell in virtuous exile but rather to gather their forces to retake the capital and the ruler's palace, thus transforming insurgents into a government and remaking society as a whole (Hiskett 1973; Last 1989). Dan Fodio did this successfully, using his time in exile to build his forces; ultimately, he and his lieutenants defeated the forces that the existing rulers sent against them and seized control of the different Hausa city-states, amalgamating them into the (still somewhat decentralized) Sokoto Caliphate. This was not the only such case. The same religious ferment existed across West Africa at that time and spawned jihads large and small, and as we might expect, this religious fervor was not easy to control once it was unleashed, so that subsequent religious leaders rejected the rule of dan Fodio's successors and moved away onto the frontiers in turn (Patton 1987). Some returned from the borders; others did not.

This pattern of religiously inspired retreat to the frontiers very closely fits the actions of Boko Haram, as described in chapter 1—the initial retreat of the Nigerian Taleban to the frontier of Niger at Kanama in 2003–2004, which seems to have been explicitly patterned on dan Fodio's example, and their subsequent movements into the Mandara Mountains and the shorelines of Lake Chad in 2004 and again after 2009. It may well be the case that the Dghwede montagnards east of Gwoza who converted to Islam, and the moto-taxi drivers and smugglers who were an important component of Boko Haram's strength in Maiduguri, played a leading role in the latter move: both groups would have known the regions around the Mandara Mountains very well indeed, and the various kinds of potentials that existed there. Even the virtual siege that Boko Haram conducted against Maiduguri in 2013 and 2014, while the city swelled with refuges and the insurgents were conducting audacious attacks on military and government installations in the heart of the state capital, fits this model. After they established the caliphate on the frontier at Gwoza, it always seems to have been the goal of the insurgency to return and conquer the capital itself, just as dan Fodio had done, in order to seize power and remake the wider society. They failed in that, of course, but there are many historical examples of West Africa jihads that went on much longer than the seven or eight years that Boko Haram has been in armed rebellion against the state.

Frontiers in this area of Central Africa and across the continent have been important places in a number of different ways. They are often places of violence. They are arenas for advancement, perhaps first economically but ultimately socially, spaces where ruthless and lucky people might find a future for themselves or improve their lot in the present day. Collectively, they can function as laboratories for different kinds of social experiments, landscapes where individuals and groups can escape the limitations imposed on them in established societies and where they can dream about creating new worlds. For Boko Haram, the frontier zones around the modern Nigerian state of Borno have functioned in both realms. They are places where Boko Haram's leaders can work to establish their caliphate, in regions around the Mandara Mountains and the shorelines of Lake Chad that have remained beyond the ambit of states for centuries. Furthermore, they are places already intimately familiar to Boko Haram's foot soldiers, who have honed their skills of mobility, evasion, and violence in contact with state power and state elites along the borders for decades. There is even some evidence that they have taken part in the illicit networks of economic exchange and exploitation that already existed there, as so many people share the identity of jihadist with that of *cascadeur* and *coupeurs de route*. All of these impulses, religious, economic, and political, will probably make the frontiers of the Lake Chad Basin arenas of violence for some years to come.

Gris-gris and kingmakers

There are other kinds of identities implicated in the actions of Boko Haram as well, sometimes in unexpected ways. As I described in the last chapter, "vigilance committees" made up of traditional hunters had organized themselves to fight bandits throughout the Lake Chad Basin in the 1990s and 2000s. For centuries, those specialists have developed the knowledge to work in the world of the bush, confronting both dangerous animals and different kinds of supernatural forces, and their Dane guns, bows, and magical amulets have often acted as an unexpectedly potent counterweight to the Kalashnikovs carried by the *coupeurs de route*. Today, these vigilance committees continue to act as local militias fighting against Boko Haram on the Cameroonian side of the border, while in Nigeria hunters are incorporated within the Civilian Joint Task Forces (CJTF), with much the same roles but under greater state control. They act as trackers and scouts, gather information about the communities that they know so well, and sometimes fight the insurgents directly. In some cases, they have been implicated in atrocities against suspected members of Boko Haram. These hunters' activities have a significant regional precedent: groups of traditional hunters have intervened in a number of recent civil wars in West and Central Africa, most famously with the Kamajor hunters who fought in their thousands against insurgents during the wars in Sierra Leone in the 1990s (Ferme and Hoffman 2004). Hunters played such military roles in the precolonial period, and they continue to do so today.

Hunters against terrorists: perhaps it sounds appropriate or even uplifting to some degree, "traditional" society aligned against the forces that seek to remake that society according to different models. But the picture is not as neat as that, because tradition and modernity overlap in different ways. Nigerian forces have overrun Boko Haram camps and hideouts at various times over the last two years, and the accounting of the goods seized in such raids includes unexpected juxtapositions. They have found Kalashnikovs, RPGs, and cell phones, certainly, all the accoutrements of modern insurgency in Africa, but also the Dane guns, bows, and even the magical amulets—the gris-gris—associated with earlier forms of warfare and hunting. It is difficult to know what to make of such discoveries. Are some groups of hunters allied with Boko Haram, at the same time that others fight them as CJTF—or perhaps some hunters act on both sides simultaneously? Are these weapons associated with village self-defense committees, and if so, what does this imply about our assumptions about how Boko Haram imposes itself on or allies itself with local communities? It is also possible that Boko Haram simply does not have enough modern firearms to supply all of its members. Certainly in some videos of Boko Haram attacks, there are participants who appear to be more or less unarmed; they may be running toward the fighting and ready to pick up a weapon if it is dropped. More fundamentally, why would Boko Haram adherents who seek to eliminate paganism and unbelief drape themselves with magical amulets that are supposed to protect against bullets but that have been specifically condemned as un-Islamic in the preaching of Mohammed Yusuf? Kamajor fighters in Sierra Leone festooned themselves with gris-gris, as do the Christian "anti-balaka" militias operating against Muslim "séléka" forces in the civil wars in the Central African Republic. These kinds of discoveries suggest that the motivations and cultural loyalties of Boko Haram fighters are more diverse, and in some cases more rooted in historical and regional models of conflict, than our stereotypes of Islamist terrorism might indicate. It is as if, along with the committed Islamists, the group includes and tolerates fighters who go to war as their ancestors did in the days before jihad and as their non-Muslim neighbors do in other parts of Africa today, against magical powers and hostile spirits as much as against apostates and unbelievers.

There are other identities that play equally ambiguous roles within the phenomenon of Boko Haram, very different than the roles that may be played by hunters or those people who put their faith in gris-gris for protection. The *coupeurs de route*, the bandits who have particularly afflicted the region since the 1990s, are associated with the figure of "the man in the car," the shadowy individual who coordinates bandit activities, provides information and equipment, and takes a hefty share of the loot for himself. Even theoretically illegal activity in the borderlands of the Lake Chad Basin has historically depended on relations with the state and its leaders, who take on themselves the right to map the limits of legality and illegality, and who decide where wealth can be produced and who will reap the benefits. As we have seen, states in this region are not weak, but their leaders may choose not to govern in particular places if the advantages to be gained through such state absence are sufficient. As Cameroonians and Chadians expect that there are elite patrons for the *douaniers-combattants* and *coupeurs de route* who periodically afflict their lives, many Nigerians believe that Boko Haram has its patrons in the highest levels of government and society.

Like the violence associated with the *coupeurs de route*, the violence associated with Boko Haram has involved ambiguous and sometimes subterranean relations with the state, for the most part with the Federal Republic of Nigeria, and within that federation particularly with the northeastern state of Borno. In chapter 1, I noted that the predecessors of Boko Haram, the so-called Nigerian Taleban, counted as members a number of young people from wealthy and well-connected Kanuri families from northeastern Nigeria. These included the nephew of the governor of the neighboring Yobe State, the son of a high-ranking official in Borno State government, and five sons of Alhaji Kambar Adam, a wealthy contractor in Borno, one of whom ultimately became a high-ranking leader of Boko Haram (Mohammed 2014, 12–13). These young men were not *achaba*, impoverished moto-taxi drivers, or poor farmers. The origins of Boko Haram are not to be found among such marginalized or powerless individuals, although as we have seen, by the late 2000s it certainly appealed to such people in and around Maiduguri, in large part because of the preaching of Mohammed Yusuf. The movement had important connections with the upper strata of Nigerian society from the beginning.

The involvement of Nigerian politicians and government officials with Boko Haram goes significantly beyond the religious activities of wealthy young scions of prominent Kanuri families, however. The primary impetus for the adoption of sharia, Islamic secular and religious law, in northern Nigeria between 1999 and 2001 was not the religious devotion of governors and politicians, most of whom do not seem to have been particularly observant Muslims. Rather, those politicians saw support for sharia as a way to curry favor with electorates that were predominantly Muslim and with the clerics of different Islamic persuasions who preached fidelity to sharia to listeners in mosques, in the street, and over the airwaves (Harnischfeger 2014). In the brawling world of Nigerian politics, such tactical alliances between politicians and religious or ethnic leaders are necessary elements in assembling coalitions and winning elections. The constitutionality of sharia's introduction does not seem to have been an important issue to the politicians involved.

Boko Haram's original leader, Mohammed Yusuf, was heavily engaged in state politics in Borno between 2000 and his death in 2009, and through him Boko Haram was implicated as well. In 2003, he supported a wealthy Kanuri politician, Ali Modu Sheriff, in elections for state governor, in exchange for Sheriff's pledge to push for a greater implementation of sharia. Then and in the subsequent election in 2007, in which Sheriff was re-elected, Mohammed Yusuf sent Boko Haram supporters into the streets in his support. In return,

Sheriff had prominent Boko Haram leaders released from jail and placed the group's supporters in government positions. Sheriff proved to be as thoroughly corrupt and kleptocratic as most of his associates in other states across Nigeria have been, but that made little difference. Through most of the 2000s, Mohammed Yusuf was preaching about the corruption of Nigerian government and Borno society, at the same time as he was deploying his organization to help a powerful Nigerian politician win gubernatorial elections in the state. This does not, of course, sound much like the behavior of an Usman dan Fodio, but even that Islamic reformer engaged with the rulers of pre-existing states as he sought to change them. Mohammed Yusuf's actions may merely be an indication of what Usman dan Fodio's maneuverings looked like in practice.

The cooperation between Yusuf and Ali Modu Sheriff even continued through the increasingly violent period in Maiduguri between 2007 and 2009, as police and Boko Haram members shot each other in the streets, and even when Yusuf publically condemned the governor as *taghut*, an idolater (Pérouse de Montclos 2014; Roelofs 2014). Their long-standing cooperation, however, did not save Mohammed Yusuf when he was arrested and extrajudicially executed by the police during the crackdown of July 2009. The alliance between Mohammed Yusuf and Sheriff—who remains an important Nigerian politician in 2017—was in no way unprecedented in the country, where the common factor connecting politicians and religious and community leaders often seems to be their determination to extract personal wealth and power from public finances. Even the lethal falling-out between Yusuf and Sheriff in 2009 had its precedents in other states at different times. The great difference is that most similar relationships between different strains of power-hungry individuals in Nigeria have not generated long-term insurgencies that result in tens of thousands of deaths and untold suffering and destruction.[4]

In Nigeria itself, one perennial point of debate since 2009 has been the degree of continuing involvement between politicians and Boko Haram, at both the state and national level. There are an extraordinary number of claims in Nigeria about these relationships, some of them coming from senior political and military figures in the country, and they routinely implicate other senior officials—often the political opponents of the people making the accusations in the first place. It has been claimed that Ali Modu Sheriff continued to support Boko Haram as a platform for his political ambitions after the death of Mohammed Yusuf. A number of other northern governors have been accused of supporting Boko Haram, sometimes financially and sometimes rhetorically. In 2014, the current governor of Kaduna State and the chief of the army staff accused each other of being backers of Boko Haram (Omonobi 2014). Other allegations abound: that Boko Haram is a creation of either of the two largest Nigerian national political parties (Pérouse de Montclos 2014); that it is an instrument developed by northern Muslim politicians to eliminate Christians from that part of the country; that it has been supported by southern Christian politicians in order to depress voting during elections in the Muslim north. This last claim was in fact central to debates during the Nigerian national elections in 2015, in which the southern Christian incumbent Goodluck Jonathan was suspected of failing to prosecute the campaign against Boko Haram in order to further his chances of being elected president. If that is true, his strategy failed: he was replaced by Muhammadu Buhari, who promised more support for the campaign against the insurgency.

Such allegations of conspiracy and treachery circulate in a Nigerian political culture that is even more deeply divided than those in most West African countries, which is saying a lot. The *oga*, kingmakers and oligarchs whose power is closely tied to oil wealth, operate as patrons of politicians, businessmen, and soldiers across Nigerian public life, and it is accepted that elites will do almost anything behind the scenes for their benefit and that of their *oga* (Campbell 2013, 26–33). Communal violence is widespread and frequently deadly, reflecting the tensions generated by long-standing ethnic grievances and perceptions—often accurate—of elite favoritism of some communities over others. This is, after all, a country where members of Christian churches have carried out attacks on rival churches in central and northern Nigeria while claiming to be members of Boko Haram, conveniently settling their own scores and mobilizing national and international opinion against Muslims at the same time (International Crisis Group 2012, 15; Mohammed 2014, 20). Ordinary Nigerians both expect and deplore this level of obscurity and ambiguity in public life, just as their French-speaking neighbors in Cameroon and Chad do.[5]

The widespread belief that Boko Haram is supported by elements of the Nigerian establishment manifests itself in various ways,
besides accusations by and about one or another politician at the state
or national level. One very common theme in reports about Boko
Haram attacks, particularly between 2010 and 2015, has been the difficulty in distinguishing insurgents from members of the Nigerian
security forces. Insurgents frequently claim to be members of the
Nigerian Army or police forces in order to gain the trust of civilians,
as they apparently did during the mass kidnapping of young women
in Chibok in early 2014. However, there are also frequent reports that
Boko Haram attacks were carried out by men in uniform who carried
weapons and acted as if they were members of the military. In other
cases, such attacks are said to have been directed by those men in
uniform, even when most of the attackers were dressed in civilian
clothing.

There are probably a number of factors behind such claims. Raids
by the Nigerian security forces and their CJTF auxiliaries on suspected Boko Haram locations and sympathizers have been sufficiently indiscriminate that some such operations have likely been
mistaken for terrorist raids; we can certainly expect some degree of
confusion when communities are attacked suddenly and without
warning. Boko Haram also uses a great deal of captured Nigerian military equipment, from small arms and uniforms to tanks and armored
personnel carriers, which would add to the difficulty of telling one
side from another. However, there have also been much more specific
accusations of cooperation between members of the security forces
and Boko Haram. These have included sales of military equipment
to Boko Haram, as well as cases where members of the security forces
have been caught moonlighting as insurgents. Whether these cases
stem from ideological commitment or the desire for financial gain
remains very difficult to say. The extraordinarily poor showing of the
security forces against Boko Haram until 2015 also led to widespread
suspicion that intelligence and direct assistance were flowing from
the military to the insurgency, possibly for political ends. For many
Nigerians, military successes from that time onward were due to the
election of a new national government that was actually committed
to Boko Haram's defeat, as well as to the increasing involvement of

foreign forces (especially the Chadian military and South African mercenaries) in the conflict.

As with the "man in the car" who directs banditry and smuggling in Cameroon and Chad, Nigerian understandings of Boko Haram and its activities are haunted by the specter of the "man in uniform"—a representative of the state who also engages in violence during illegal activities. In all of these countries, the magnitude of those proceedings and the circumstances in which state officials may moonlight as smugglers, bandits, or terrorists remains very difficult to evaluate. However, that is a vital element in these undertakings, which exist along the frontiers between licit and illicit behavior just as they so frequently take place along national frontiers. In the Nigerian case, there is probably more direct evidence for elite complicity with Boko Haram than there is for elite complicity with bandits and smugglers in Cameroon. Such complicity in Nigeria may be political in most cases, but there is no reason to think that political exigency is the only factor involved. Some such cooperation may be ideological: over time, after all, Boko Haram has proven its appeal to members of very different strata in Nigerian society, both rich and poor. There are almost certainly financial considerations at work as well, with innumerable reports from Nigeria about graft in the provision of services to the military and more recently to IDP camps across the northern part of the country. In addition, the smuggling networks that continue to move *zoua-zoua* and other goods into northern Cameroon and throughout the region must have contacts at both ends: money continues to be made from smuggling in Nigeria as well as Cameroon.

In many ways, Boko Haram provides an even more striking illustration of the paradoxical relations between society, the state, and its borders than we saw with the bandits and smugglers who have roamed northern Cameroon for decades. On the one hand, the history of the organization is full of instances when representatives of the Nigerian state seem to have found advantages in refusing to fully exert the state's control over its territory, either in Maiduguri when Boko Haram was cooperating with a sitting governor while engaged in clashes with security forces, or more recently on the borders, where the terrorist organization was able to carve out its "caliphate" around the Mandara Mountains and where it still seems to have considerable freedom of action in the mountains and closer to Lake Chad. On the other hand, the Nigerian state has also demonstrated that it has the capacity to exercise control over its territory when circumstances require; indeed, Boko Haram's 2014 declaration of a territorial "caliphate" centered at Gwoza seems to have largely motivated Nigeria's first effective response to the insurgency. Nigeria is not a "failed state" but rather one where powerful individuals appear at times to have found convincing political and financial reasons to allow lawlessness to flourish on the frontiers, and at other times to suppress such lawlessness.

Putting Boko Haram in context

Boko Haram is a terrorist organization operating in a globalized twenty-first century, and it needs to be recognized as such. It is not a movement that could have developed a millennium or even a century ago, embedded as it is within a world of nation-states and developing in a context of Westernization, urbanism, and other Islamist movements on other continents. At the same time, it is a movement anchored in a particular region of Central Africa, and now especially in the landscapes of plains, mountains, and lakeshores around Lake Chad. The histories of those landscapes and the cultural understandings of human action that are generated by those histories account for some of Boko Haram's particular features. As I noted at the beginning of this chapter, even terrorism must be more than simply a spasmodic, directionless eruption of violence; it has to make some kind of sense to its perpetrators, if not to its victims. As a collective activity undertaken by a group of people, terrorist violence has to fit into some kind of structured, shared understanding of the world. It may be exceedingly difficult for outsiders to fathom the logics of these kinds of violence, and even perpetrators of terrorist violence may struggle to articulate their intentions after the world has changed and the impulses that led them to terrorism no longer seem relevant (Zucker 2013). Boko Haram is no different. We thus need to examine the activities of this religiously based insurgency from different perspectives simultaneously, because no individual or group of people is capable of seeing the world exclusively through the lens of religion—or for that matter of politics or of economic deprivation.

Boko Haram continues to operate along the international borders of the southern Lake Chad Basin for a number of different reasons. It does so because of the religious and historical resonances of Usman dan Fodio's *hijra* of two centuries ago, but also because of the advantages that those frontier regions confer on insurgents, especially on modern insurgents familiar with the terrain and its possibilities through their experiences as smugglers and bandits through the last two decades. As in precolonial times, border violence continues to offer the potential for wealth and status for Boko Haram foot soldiers and leaders operating in regions beyond state control, through the group's revival of slave-raiding (at Chibok and in other places) and general pillage, and probably through continued involvement in smuggling and banditry. Boko Haram members are not simply repurposed bandits, however, and there is no reason to doubt that such mercenary motives coexist with a hunger for a more godly world today—according to their own definitions—and an afterlife in paradise.

The effects of Boko Haram's activities and state responses on local communities have been horrific, with many thousands of people killed and millions of people displaced by the conflict, and with the survivors afflicted by famine and continuing violence. The experiences of these people closely parallel those of the historical populations that existed in the extensive predation zones of precolonial states throughout the region. At the same time, some of these people have tried to adapt to these dangerous frontier conditions by engaging with new cultural forms that Boko Haram has introduced, such as its "caliphate" in Gwoza or the more haphazard alliances between Boko Haram and local individuals and communities from the Mandara Mountains to the shore of Lake Chad. In the past, Nigeria and Cameroon displayed a good deal of ambivalence in cracking down on Boko Haram, probably in part because of a recognition of the local popularity of some of the organization's goals. That ambivalence seems to have disappeared as the group became more threatening and began to seize territory in 2014–2015—as we saw in the last chapter, Lake Chad Basin states become uneasy when bandits begin to set themselves up as competitors—and it seems unlikely that these alliances between some local communities and Boko Haram will survive over the long term. The discovery of local hunters' equipment in Boko Haram camps, including amulets used for magical protection, is a vivid reminder of how little we understand the diversity of motivations within the organization. That discovery suggests that there are significant disconnects between the strict forms of Islam that the group preaches and the actual beliefs and actions of some of its followers.

We know very little about how Boko Haram forces have interacted with local communities, beyond the gruesome attacks they have perpetrated across the region. There is no doubt that Boko Haram interacts regularly with local economies, if only because the existence of large numbers of militants living in the countryside over periods of months and years virtually requires such interactions. Even terrorists need to be supplied with food and other necessities, but thinking about terrorists integrating into local systems of economic and social interchange remains very challenging for Westerners, since it implies the normalization of such activities. The area of northern Cameroon east of Keroua where Boko Haram camps are supposed to have existed in 2013–2014 is quite heavily populated; it is more or less inconceivable that such camps existed without some degree of local knowledge and even cooperation. This brings us back to the photograph that I discussed at the beginning of this chapter. It is entirely possible that the Nigerian military is correct when it described the two men killed on their motorcycle as Boko Haram terrorists. However, that description does not in itself bring us any closer to understanding the motivations behind the terrorist activities carried out by members of the group, nor about the ways that they continue to live in the region in 2017. An examination of the historical contexts of border violence at least affords us a different way of thinking about the actions of Boko Haram insurgents.

7

PASTS, PARALLELS, AND THE FUTURE

THERE IS NOTHING REMOTE OR inaccessible about the lands of Boko Haram, either geographically or in terms of the cultural and political developments that take place there. They are a part of our modern world. The tracks and roads and airline routes that a traveler can follow to reach the dusty frontier lands of the Lake Chad Basin are one manifestation of a globally connected planet, as are the flows of information that help determine how we think about such places. When Western commentators talk about Boko Haram in 2017, one possibility they often discuss is the question of whether links exist between that terrorist organization and similar groups in other parts of the world, like al-Qaeda or ISIS—whether terrorism, like so much of modern culture, is also becoming globalized. Those linkages seem to be primarily rhetorical in the case of Boko Haram, which remains largely a regional movement based in the Lake Chad Basin. Unlike ISIS, it has not attracted adherents from beyond the African continent; Western countries do not have to question themselves over Boko Haram, for fear of the young people who may come back home bearing its ideology. Or at least, that has not happened yet.

These global connections manifest themselves in other ways as well, of course. They exist in the flows of material culture that archaeologists are trained to look for in prehistory but that are just as characteristic of our modern world. One aspect of such flows involves the technological innovations and economies of scale that make certain kinds of violence or wealth-making activities feasible, today or in the past. Centuries ago, horses, camels, and sailing ships, and the institutions that deployed them, made possible the transatlantic and trans-Saharan slave trades. We saw in chapters 5 and 6 how the troika of Kalashnikovs, cell phones, and motorcycles revolutionized smuggling and banditry south of Lake Chad from the 1990s onward and has enabled terrorist attacks more recently. What made those different technological advances important was not merely their availability but also their pairing with the ambitions and desperation of the young men who raided for slaves in the past, and who have become *cascadeurs*, *coupeurs de route*, and Boko Haram insurgents more recently.

It is equally possible to track the diplomatic and military maneuvering of the nations involved in the conflict with Boko Haram, through other forms of material culture—the weapons that they use, for example. The appearance of Israeli Tavor assault rifles and Negev machine guns in the hands of security forces in Chad and Cameroon and the South African Ratel armored vehicles now used by the Nigerian Army tells observers about the allies that these different countries are finding in their struggle. Sometimes these webs of material connection take particularly terrible forms. Young women, perhaps including some of those kidnapped in 2014 by Boko Haram in Chibok, walk into markets in northern Cameroon to blow themselves up as suicide bombers (Peccavi 2016). Their explosive belts occasionally include repurposed GR 66-EG bomblets from French Belouga cluster bombs (figure 7.1), air-dropped weapons sold by France to the Nigerian military in the 1980s to be deployed from European-made jet aircraft against Nigeria's enemies. None of the explanations for Boko Haram's access to French-made cluster bombs are particularly convincing; did they steal those Belouga cluster bombs, which weigh about 650 pounds (290 kg) apiece, during attacks on military installations in order to extract the bomblets, or did they salvage them from Nigerian military disposal sites? Did they buy the bomblets from members of the Nigerian military, or has the Nigerian Air Force been using cluster bombs on its own civilian population in northern Nigeria—allowing Boko Haram to salvage that proportion of the bomblets that did not explode? We do not know how they obtained these munitions, but the

Figure 7.1: Boko Haram suicide bomb munitions

juxtaposition of kidnapped young women and repurposed Western military technology is particularly horrific.

These kinds of flows of materials, ideology, and wealth have existed for a very long time in the Lake Chad Basin. We can trace the deep roots of such flows, and of globalization more generally, back to the late first millennium CE, when rulers in Kanem were first exposed to Islam and traded slaves across the Sahara, while artifacts from those faraway places began to appear as grave goods south of Lake Chad. Two centuries ago, European abolitionism changed the demographics of enslavement in the Lake Chad Basin, as the decline of the trans-Atlantic slave trade led to the rise of slave-based plantation exports in the Sokoto Caliphate. In more recent times—only a century ago— European colonial officers were preoccupied with the threat of subversion and rebellion by Mahdist infiltrators from the Nile valley, just as their successors in both national governments and America's Africa Command worry about the spread of Islamist terrorism today. Any understanding of the area has to deal with the balance of internal and external influences on social and political developments, and with the timescales over which such developments have taken place.

Reprise: Timescales

This is a book about the lands of Boko Haram and about the violence associated with that terrorist insurgency. It argues that we can understand aspects of that violence as a manifestation of historical processes that have played out in the southern Lake Chad Basin over long periods of time—centuries or, in some cases, millennia. This is certainly not the only way to look at the upheavals that Boko Haram has wrought, but examining the historical background of this terrorist insurgency brings into focus parts of its story that might otherwise remain puzzling. The historical processes that we have observed in this book involve a number of different elements, including both changes in the natural environments of the region and changes in the social and political relationships between different groups of people.

I have argued that one productive way to understand these different aspects of the history of the Lake Chad Basin is by looking at how human landscapes have developed there. People living in the lands of Boko Haram, like others around the world, imbue the physical and environmental features of their world with cultural meanings, through processes of naming, memory, and personification, and then they put those meanings to use in their own lives. We are continuously immersed within culturally constructed landscapes of great complexity and diversity. Some of these are as intimately familiar to us as the streets where we walk our dogs and go to work, while others, more exotic, may exist largely within our imaginations—the foreign places that we dream of visiting on vacation or that we fear as lands of violence and savagery. All such landscapes help make us who we are, providing an essential framework for our lives as we dwell within them; they form us, even as we define them.

Thinking about landscapes helps us to integrate our conceptions of nature and culture, and that is particularly important in Africa. Westerners still often assume that the continent is quintessentially the space of untamed nature, where human activity is secondary and takes place only in a timeless moment beyond history. In archaeology and historical research, our choices of topics and concepts are always political to some degree, and I have taken this landscape approach in part to make this particular region of Africa—so often described as remote and unknowable to Westerners—feel less exotic and less timeless to readers of this book. The Lake Chad Basin has a long history of human occupation and cultural development, stretching back to the end of the last Ice Age and with roots that go even deeper into time than that. That history has been an intensely dynamic one, and the landscapes that people inhabit there today are products of incredible transformations in human life: long-distance migrations, the coming of farming and settled life, political violence and the rise of elites, slavery and state formation, the occupation of the Mandara Mountains and the islands of Lake Chad, urbanism, long-distance trade, colonialism and its ending, globalization. This region, like much of the rest of Africa, has if anything suffered from too much history over recent centuries, not from any lack of historical experience.

Frontiers are one of the most important categories of landscapes for an understanding of historical conditions in the Lake Chad Basin. Frontier zones are by definition places of encounter, and they often imply confrontations between different groups of people, different systems of thought and ideology, and different political forms. Such frontiers may be formalized by boundary markers and exact delineations in space, but that is not necessarily true in all cases—in fact, such expectations of frontier zones may simply be a product of a particular moment in the history of Western nation-states. Frontier zones are very frequently areas of both danger and opportunity, and they can themselves play a central role in the self-imaginings of a group of people—as they do, for example, for many Americans in the national story of the opening up of the "American frontier" or the "American West" in the eighteenth and nineteenth centuries. Other people (Native Americans, for example, or Hispanic people living along the border with Mexico) may have very different understandings of that process, which illustrates the degree to which the idea of a frontier is primarily a cultural construction, and often a contested one. Frontier zones have been equally charged with meanings in the lands that we have examined in this book, but, as on the American frontier, different groups of people have very different appraisals of what life may be like in such frontier zones, and what the dangers and opportunities of such places may be.

We have looked at the development of frontier landscapes in the Lake Chad Basin from a variety of different historical scales and using different types of data, which in turn affects the historical narratives that can be created by those processes. The initial human settlement of the region after the last Ice Age, and subsequent encounters between different populations there, can be examined by using data from archaeology, genetics, and linguistics. Through these disciplines, we can learn a great deal about the economic and technological adaptations that settlers used to make their homes in new and rapidly changing environments, as Lake Mega-Chad shrank and the Green Sahara withered away. Juxtaposing different data sources shows us that encounters between different groups of people in the middle of the Holocene were so momentous that some indigenous communities changed their identities in vital ways, adopting the language—and almost certainly many other cultural elements—of later immigrants. There are a number of historical cases that let us contextualize the impact of such encounters, as with the changes in language and cultural identity that accompanied the jihads of Usman dan Fodio and his successors in this part of West/Central Africa at the end of the eighteenth century.

In general, the coarse chronological resolution available in these disciplines, where we can rarely distinguish events that happened even a century apart, and the simple lack of fieldwork in an area that is larger than Germany mean that our reconstructions of prehistoric events in the southern Lake Chad Basin are rather abstract, especially for periods up to about 1000 CE. It is difficult to understand how many of the large-scale processes evident in the archaeological record—the coming of iron technology, for example, or the changes in settlement that led to the accumulation of tell mound habitation sites—actually played out in terms of everyday lived human experience. Paradoxically, it is often the intensity of ancient human activity that makes it hard for researchers to identify individual episodes of human action: such traces are broken up, dispersed by the weight of everyday life through centuries of occupation on tell sites or the constant refurbishment of terraces in the Mandara Mountains. About a thousand years ago, we see the first historical accounts that mention the region, and it is this "entry into history" that introduces us to themes that dominate the historical narratives of succeeding centuries: the rise and expansion of states, human migrations, violence and slavery, the sheer cultural and political complexity of the Lake Chad Basin as a whole.

History. Narrative. It sometimes seems as if humans only appear in the past when they are spoken or written about by other people, that only then do human goals, motivations, satisfaction, and suffering become accessible to us. This reinforces the notion that there is a conceptual gulf between history and prehistory and between the roles of chroniclers and archaeologists, in the Lake Chad Basin and across the world. Of course, no such gulf exists: humans were humans before they were being written about, and it is the challenge of archaeologists and other researchers to translate our investigations into accounts that recognize and take account of the humanity of prehistoric peoples.

It is particularly important to study those earlier periods in this area, for two reasons. First, they set the stage for many of the processes that occur in later times and even into the present. The climate changes that altered the extent and the human potentials of Lake Chad and its surroundings five thousand years ago were also implicated in the shift of the Kanuri state to Borno five or six centuries ago, and such climate changes affect the region's population today—the fact that such climate change is now significantly affected by human actions does not lessen its consequences. The original encounters between Nilo-Saharan and Chadic people that we saw in chapter 2 and the cultural transformations that resulted prefigured the much later transformation of the Mandara Mountains into a human landscape and the gradual pulling apart of montagnard and plains-dweller identities that still dominate the region today. In the same way, the large settlement sites that appear in the area by 2,500 years ago, like Zilum with its protective ditches, were early precursors to the sociopolitical complexity and violence that would dominate the region in succeeding millennia.

Second, the coarse-grained, centuries-long social processes that we glimpse through archaeology and related research are real and important, even if they are hard to correlate with human experiences at the scale of years or a lifetime. In the long run, we don't know how Boko Haram's insurgency will fit into the history of the region, but the variety and density of historical connections that it evokes—echoes of the slave trade and Kanuri identity, of Usman dan Fodio and the Maitatsine—suggest that this particular episode of violence is a manifestation of long-term cultural processes that will continue into the future. One particularly important element in the region's history through the last millennium has involved the progressive incorporation of communities with profound local identities into ever-larger cultural and ideological systems: states in different forms, world religions like Islam and Christianity, and an expanding web of continental and intercontinental networks. Dala Nokwé, the rock at Gréa that I wrote about at the beginning of chapter 5, is a powerful supernatural force in that particular landscape, and such "spirits of place" exist through the whole area, providing a vital, unseen element to human landscapes there. However, such "spirits of place" have little relevance beyond the local communities that interact with them. It seems unlikely that Dala Nokwé will have deterred Boko Haram fighters in the way that it deterred precolonial Wandala officials, who shared the local contexts of such beliefs. Such local references, whatever their power, are being increasingly superseded by global symbols and associations that may mutate dramatically on the journey from their origins to the Lake Chad Basin, but that can still have great significance there.

Reprise: States, people, and violence

The relationship between states and their elites and the communities that existed around such states has been central to this region for centuries. It is a complex relationship, in part because of the way it has changed over time. A thousand years ago, states were not dominant political forms in the area, although the existence of walls around ancient towns and villages and horses at the site of Aissa Dugjé imply that structures of political hierarchy and military power were already developing during the first millennium. The last thousand years has seen a steady encroachment of the rule of states into the Lake Chad Basin and the accommodations that preexisting communities have been forced to make to these new and aggressive political systems.

For archaeologists and anthropologists, considerations of force and violence are fundamental to the definition of states, because state rulers and elites claim the right to decide when the use of violence is legitimate and who it can be directed against. In the lands of Boko Haram, however, state rule has historically been associated with violence in an even more intimate way. Lake Chad Basin states were not only exuberantly hierarchical and exploitative of their own citizens— the poor "like grass," to be grazed on by the horses of the nobility— but they also depended on the exploitation and sale of enslaved humans to obtain the material and ideological trappings of elite status. Rulers and elites signaled their "stateliness" through the possession and display of exotic goods and services, in many cases originating in trade and exchange with North Africa, the Mediterranean world and the Middle East. Such exotic elements—luxury goods, armor and firearms, clerics and chroniclers, and so on—demonstrated the power, cosmopolitanism, and civilized status of rulers in their dealings with one another and with the wider world. Through the second millennium, such demonstrations were increasingly couched in the language of Islamic kingship and culture. In the Lake Chad Basin, they were largely paid for through the traffic in enslaved people.

States have frontiers by definition, but the pressures of enslavement and of the slave trade made state frontiers particularly important and particularly violent places in the Lake Chad Basin. Such frontier areas were the predation zones of slave-raiding states, the regions where elite wealth and power were created through the violent taking of humans into slavery, with more general pillage contributing to the profits for leaders and fighters alike. In parallel with the expansion of states, new landscapes of refuge and resistance were created in places where state military activity was most difficult: the Mandara Mountains, the shorelines and islands of Lake Chad, the marshes along the Chari and Logone Rivers. During the last millennium, the Mandara Mountains have been transformed into a densely settled human landscape, one of the most diverse and complex such landscapes in West or Central Africa. In that process, the mountains became a true "internal frontier," with all of the hazards and possibilities that that term implies. Mountain communities situated within the predation zone of multiple plains states were subject to attacks from those states, but at the same time the area saw the flowering of a vibrant montagnard culture, one that built on a common Chadic linguistic and cultural base into a variety of different political and social arrangements. Mountain communities existed in a violent and creative tension with the plains societies with which they shared an Iron Age ancestry, trading and fighting with plains states and among themselves as circumstances and opportunity warranted. Other such refuge areas developed their own distinctive adaptations, as for example with the Yedina communities on the islands and along the shorelines of Lake Chad.

This situation did not end with the colonial takeover of the region at the end of the nineteenth and during the early twentieth century, although the terms of engagement may have shifted. Slave-taking and then enslavement itself were gradually outlawed in the new European colonies, although such prohibitions were often subordinated to the exigencies of colonial rule and the placating of preexisting state elites. As we saw in the case of Hamman Yaji, colonial administrations often had rather little idea and perhaps even less interest about what went on in their frontier zones, except when it involved border duties or when the threat of Mahdist subversion became important. The colonial interregnum of the early/mid-twentieth century did not transform the day-to-day realities of state governance as fundamentally as Westerners might assume. It is certainly true that new European languages and new administrative structures were imposed on the region and on much larger areas that by the early 1960s were being recognized as newly independent states. It is equally true that these new nation-states brought with them new forms of life and new contexts of citizenship: the dramatic expansion of urbanism, a new world religion in competition with Islam, the (very uneven) spread of Western education, different forms of media, nationalism. At the same time, the regional realities of state functioning did not change that greatly in the Lake Chad Basin. Through this period, states continued to be run for the benefit of their elites, while ordinary people, the citizens of those states, continued to be treated as "grass"—although today perhaps as grass under the tires of luxury cars or SUVs, rather than as fodder for the horses of the nobility.

The colonial powers in practice do not seem to have treated frontier zones much differently than their predecessors did, in part because they never really had the resources to do so. This meant that the essential tension between states and the people living on their borders—the fluid frontier zones that endured on the ground, rather than the artificial borders newly drawn on European maps—persisted through the colonial and independence periods, with border populations continuing to be described as "bandits" because of their depredations on state representatives or state lands. The language of state raiding into the predation zones similarly shifted, with such raiding now described by state forces as "pacification" or "reprisals" for bandit raids. However, the relationship between states and border regions continued to be essentially exploitative. One of the charms of terms like "bandit" or "smuggler" is that they are situationally variable, in an African context and elsewhere. When the borderlands of states are arenas for wealth production and extraction, then the status of illicit activity in such areas becomes fluid—because wealth is the origin and the province of elites, who make state laws. In such a circumstance, the actions of "bandits" and "smugglers" are more and more difficult to distinguish from more legitimate forms of wealth creation. Banditry, if undertaken by a sufficiently powerful person, becomes impossible to differentiate from policy.

This, then, is the puzzle that ordinary people in the Lake Chad Basin faced through the late twentieth century, and still face today: What is the relationship between legitimate economic activity and the regulatory power of the state, and how do economic actors use the mechanisms of the state for their own ends? The *cascadeurs* and *coupeurs de route* who helped sustain the regional economy through their smuggling and made travel hazardous through their banditry acted as the foot soldiers for much more powerful individuals, far more closely integrated into the function of legitimate commerce and the administrative and judicial apparatus of the states of the region. Even the terminology of "legitimate commerce" carries the freight of history and violence in this part of Africa: "legitimate commerce" was the language of European abolitionists and merchants in the nineteenth century, content to accept the fruits of enslaved labor in commodity exports to Europe as long as the slaves were kept laboring on plantations in Africa itself, safely out of sight and mind.

Reprise: Boko Haram on the borders

The regimes of wealth creation and violence that exist in the lands of Boko Haram during the late twentieth and early twenty-first centuries are thus not very different than those that had existed there in earlier centuries, although the focus of wealth creation had—temporarily, perhaps—shifted from people to gasoline and holdups. As chapters 5 and 6 demonstrate, there are further continuities between the *cascadeurs* and *coupeurs de route* and today's Boko Haram insurgents. Some of these continuities exist because the actors are the same in both cases, with former smugglers and bandits wielding their expertise with guns, motorcycles, and backcountry trails in the service of Boko Haram. Boko Haram kidnappings of Westerners in Cameroon look very much like the activities of earlier bandits and seem to have been similarly carried out for the sake of profit; some were quite likely perpetrated by the old bandits of the 1990s under new slogans. Other continuities appear to exist because of more occult connections between state elites and illegal activities, as in the smuggling of illicit gasoline that continues when borders are supposedly closed because of terrorism, or the different kinds of claims that are made about the government relations of Boko Haram leaders.

Beyond this, it is necessary to understand the activities of Boko Haram itself as a continuation of the pursuit of wealth on the frontiers. This seems incongruous if we identify Boko Haram as only an Islamist insurgency, one that is exclusively concerned with jihad on Earth and Paradise thereafter. There is no reason to doubt that Boko Haram is an authentic Islamist religious movement, the most recent in a long line of revitalization movements that have accompanied the spread of Islamic states in West and Central Africa. Boko Haram models itself on the historical jihads of Usman dan Fodio and other Muslim religious leaders and sees itself as a modern remedy to the excesses of a sinful and apostate state apparatus. It appears to make use of the religious potential of frontier zones as those earlier movements did, with the retreat to the *dar al-hijra*, "the land of exile" on the borders, and an ultimate aim of returning to conquer the capital. The factional splits within Boko Haram mirror the theological disagreements between jihadists that we examined in earlier chapters. Boko Haram's foot soldiers have real political and economic grievances, even if its leaders have been cynical manipulators often ready to cooperate with the states that they condemn as ungodly.

At the same time, the terrorists fighting for Boko Haram are still engaged in the wealth-making activities associated with frontiers in the history of this region. They seem to be comparatively well paid for their activities with Boko Haram in dangerous border areas, they pillage settlements in those areas, and in some ways they have reproduced the slave-raiding for young women that was characteristic of the region in the precolonial and early colonial periods. Such dangerous activities have been closely connected to the challenges that ordinary young men face in their lives in this part of Africa, if they do not command the wealth or the social and political connections that are necessary for advancement in their communities. If they fail to surmount such challenges, they remain stuck in a status of perpetual adolescence, powerless and patronized—in every sense—by their

superiors. We must remember that there has always been a fundamental gendered asymmetry in the historical experience of frontier
zones of the Lake Chad Basin: the possibilities for wealth creation
and social advancement have largely been the province of men,
while the violence that accompanies those possibilities has very often
been sexual violence and sexual exploitation suffered by women,
and perhaps especially by young women. That remains true in the
region today.

Songs of smugglers and bandits

[Border raids in northern Mexico] were not pre-political
acts of banditry: many raiding parties were made up of
multi-ethnic peoples, Indians, Africans, Europeans, and
mestizos, with complex internal hierarchies and elaborate
espionage networks. Nor did they sabotage commodity
flows: raiding parties systematically sold their loot to rival
European buyers.

Jeremy Adelman and Stephen Aron,
"From Borderlands to Borders"

Even if we appreciate the complexities and dynamism of societies in
the Lake Chad Basin, historically and in the twenty-first century, the
human experiences and cultural logics that I have described in this
book may still seem quite foreign and even exotic. Peoples' experience of life in this part of Africa might appear entirely irrelevant to
readers immersed in the different and superficially sleeker logics of
Western political and ideological systems, whose arrangements and
connections are generally supposed to be formalized, well defined,
and explicitly spelled out. In a Western world of passports, territorial sovereignty, and well-demarcated borders, what do we make of
borderlands that states tolerate precisely because their writ does not
entirely extend to such places—where lawlessness serves the mak-
ers of laws, and vice versa? How do we think about the existence of
frontier zones whose extreme violence periodically impinges on state
capitals and their elites but that are at the same time areas of wealth
creation, opportunity, and cultural innovation that those elites also
make use of?

In 2017, however, some of the conditions described in this book might seem uncomfortably familiar to Westerners, particularly when we shift the focus of our considerations a little. By the start of the twenty-first century, Western governments themselves had discovered the attractions of facilities that are situated in marginal places where the protections of national laws run only equivocally. The most famous of these Western legal borderlands is Guantanamo Bay, an American military base that through an accident of history is on Cuban soil and thus maintains an ambiguous status in terms of American law. Guantanamo's convenient legal status became famous as part of America's Global War on Terror: after the attacks of September 11, 2001, the use of Guantanamo as a detention facility was greatly expanded, as the United States and its allies gathered up suspected fighters and insurgents from across the globe. Crucially, the United States asserted sovereignty and legal jurisdiction over Guantanamo Bay, while at the same time claiming that elements of its judicial protections did not apply to those people being held there. Guantanamo has not been the only such detention facility operated by America in the twenty-first century; it merely constitutes the best-known location in a gray archipelago of prisons scattered across the world, under American control but somewhat beyond its laws, officially denied but traceable by the registration numbers of not-quite-anonymous passenger aircraft and documents released by leakers. Such activities are not limited to the United States: the United Kingdom, France, and Australia, at least, have benefitted from similar equivocal arrangements.

These Western examples may seem rather different from cases in the Lake Chad Basin, where precolonial states exerted control in their predation zones only during violent incursions. Modern nations and their leaders, not only Western ones but those in Africa and elsewhere, have far greater power available for the control of territory. They can decide where their writ will not run, or even—as America has done—expend vast amounts of money establishing complex, carefully calibrated jurisdictional systems within which some (but not all) national laws are not supposed to apply. And it is there that we see the parallels with modern circumstances in the Lake Chad Basin: states and their elites find advantage in the existence of accessible territories that are not entirely controlled, that are outside the full reach of the law or where law can be applied selectively. Western governments have learned the charms of a refusal to exert their jurisdictions. The very term "jurisdiction," after all, derives from the Latin *jus+ dictio*, law's speech and words, but what advantages may a state find when the law can sometimes be made to fall silent?

Comparing Guantanamo to the lands of Boko Haram may seem somewhat artificial, an academic point made about jurisdiction and the potential advantages of its absence. However, we can also see striking parallels between the human landscapes of the southern Lake Chad Basin and regions much closer to the experience of North American readers. The modern borderlands between Mexico and the United States provide us with a whole series of points of comparison with the Central African case. Those North American border regions are also frequently seen as "marginal" or "peripheral" in modern readings of cultural change (Adelman and Aron 1999; Frey 2003; Weaver 2001), even though they have been areas of cultural contact and combination for many centuries now. Archaeologists look at prehistoric sites like Casas Grandes/Paquimé in the northern Mexico state of Chihuahua as places of cultural encounter between Mesoamerican societies and communities in what is now the American Southwest, occupied and abandoned over about the same period as the DGB sites in the Mandara Mountains (Minnis and Whalen 2015). The borderlands continued as a zone of encounter and synthesis through the colonial period, as indigenous people and various European and Euroamerican populations struggled for control over different parts of the region and its resources.

The colonial history of the US-Mexico borderlands was marked by great vitality and by great violence, which included state expansionism that was in many ways comparable to those same processes during precolonial periods in the Lake Chad Basin—albeit with slave-raiding joined with the exploitation of silver mines for elite profit.[1] These borderlands were also arenas for new kinds of cultural identity formation, for example, among Comanche and other indigenous societies and with Tejano and other Hispanic American communities in the United States (Kavanagh 1996; Ramos 2009), and those identities remain important in reimagining regional histories today (Limón 1994; Marez 2001). That turbulent and vibrant history has continued through the twentieth and twenty-first centuries. It included substantial but fluctuating levels of immigration from Mexico into the

United States, as well as racist reactions from the American government, which periodically deported not merely illegal immigrants but also large numbers of legal immigrants and even Hispanic American citizens, particularly during the 1930s and 1950s.

More recently, the US-Mexico border has seen substantial industrial development in the *maquiladora* free-trade zones—and, of course, also the violence and lawlessness associated with cross-border movements, including the smuggling of drugs and the movement of undocumented migrants from Mexico into the United States and the smuggling of firearms from the United States into Mexico (Andreas 2001; Esparza and Weigend 2015; Gokee and de León 2014; Spener 2009). The institutional power exerted by the United States and the fact that the weapons are flowing southward across the border has meant that most of the overt, open violence associated with this illegal trade has been confined to Mexico, especially in the northern states of Sonora, Chihuahua, Coahuila, and Tamaulipas. I have a number of colleagues who continue to work in those Mexican states, and—as in the Lake Chad Basin during the period of banditry—it seems that the danger of violence exists in zones that are fairly well demarcated and well known; as long as it is possible to stay away from those areas, archaeologists can most often still do their work.

There appear to be significant relationships between Mexican governmental and other elites and the organizations responsible for the smuggling and violence, to the extent that in many areas of Mexico the administration and security services are severely compromised by association with drug cartels (Hernandez 2013). These relations between elites and illegal activity on the Mexican side of the border are covert and, it seems, even more dangerous to discuss openly than such relations in the Lake Chad Basin. On the American side of the border, positions are more overt: gun rights are so important ideologically that American politicians generally support the legal structures that allow weapons to be sold locally and then smuggled illegally into Mexico in large numbers. One of the major differences between the circumstances in the borderlands between the United States and Mexico on the one hand and the lands of Boko Haram on the other is that the New World conflict has been far deadlier. Between 120,000 and 130,000 people were murdered in drug-related violence (often with American small arms) between 2006 and 2014 in Mexico, perhaps eight times as many as in the Boko Haram insurgency, with more than twenty-five thousand others disappeared, while thousands of undocumented migrants have perished more or less unnoticed in the deserts of the American Southwest (Molloy 2013). The rates of killing have decreased somewhat since 2013, but sections of the borderlands remain dangerous places. Americans have more immediate connections to many of the themes of this book than they might at first realize.

There are relatively few ethnographies of the foot soldiers in this drug war along the Mexico-US border of the sort carried out in the Lake Chad Basin by Janet Roitman, Saïbou Issa, and Christian Seignobos; the focus of documentation in the Mexican example seems to be on cartel leaders. However, the research that has been done shows that similar calculations of poverty and hopelessness drive many of the activities of ordinary actors in the American borderlands. As in the Lake Chad Basin, the borderlands between Mexico and America are places of opportunity as well as violence (Muehlmann 2013), places where the poor, ruthless, and lucky may hope to become rich. Those foot soldiers also figure in cultural productions about the activities of drug traffickers, the *narcotraficantes*, particularly through a genre of songs called *narcocorridos* that chronicle their lives and histories. *Narcocorridos* have been the subject of a substantial amount of anthropological research (Edberg 2009), perhaps because it is less hazardous to interview musicians than the *narcotraficantes* who are the subjects of their songs. The recognition that comparable genres of popular music and oral history also memorialized the exploits of bandits in northern Cameroon during the colonial and independence periods first led me to think about other kinds of parallels between borderlands of the Lake Chad Basin and the US-Mexico borderlands (Issa 2001, 2009).

Jason de León, another archaeologist, examined the experience of undocumented migrants trying to cross into the United States in southern Arizona—the Tucson Sector of US Customs and Border Protection—through his work with the Undocumented Migration Project and in his masterful 2015 book *The Land of Open Graves*. In that book, de León shows that violence is not confined to the states of northern Mexico, and he demonstrates how US security forces make deliberate use of the border deserts to deter potential migrants and place border crossers in harm's way, with the result that thousands of desperate people have perished of dehydration and heatstroke after having crossed into the United States. The violence and suffering in *The Land of Open Graves* is graphic and disturbing, and de León's book has made me wonder whether I have over-intellectualized the real and horrific violence associated with Boko Haram, subsuming the tragedy into a historical model of cultural developments.

There is, however, an important difference involved in doing research in these two regions. De León's book about the American Southwest examines an area that Western readers may well assume is ruled by American bureaucratic logics of order, control, and concern for human welfare, and one of his aims is to make blatant the violence associated with border enforcement in that area. On the other hand, Western media tend to present conflict and life itself in the lands of Boko Haram (and in Africa more widely) as remote and Hobbesian, not governed by comprehensible cultural logics. The assumption of violence is inherent in Western views of the continent. I have avoided graphic descriptions of violence and tried to give a sense of the ways in which people in this region act according to comprehensible plans and goals—even if some of those plans appear to us to be misguided or reprehensible. The borders, though, and their dangers and opportunities form a common thread through de León's text and this one.

The future

I have no idea when I will return to the lands between the Mandara Mountains and Lake Chad that I have written about in this book. That is a strange feeling, since these are places that I first visited well over thirty years ago and have returned to many times in the years since then; they are a part of my own history. In 2014, my colleagues and I conducted fieldwork somewhat further to the south in Cameroon, and that research will continue in the near future. I hope that I will be able to carry out archaeological fieldwork around the Mandara Mountains as well, but who knows exactly when or under what circumstances that will happen? Of course, it's a big area that will get on perfectly well without my presence, and my disquiet matters not one whit when measured against the challenges that people who actually live there have to deal with these days. Telephone and the internet allow me to communicate with my friends there, and increasingly their children—some who were babies when I first visited—travel as well, going off to university and jobs in the cities. This is a very different sign of the global networks that encompass us all. One day, perhaps, some of them will come and visit me in North America.

In mid-2017, Boko Haram continues to control territory in and around the Mandara Mountains and along the shorelines of Lake Chad, and it still maintains a nebulous and ill-defined presence in communities across the region as a whole. The mountains and nearby plains on the Nigerian side of the border suffer from serious famine as a result of the violence and disruption of everyday life, while residents in neighboring areas in Cameroon and in Niger—themselves poor farmers—have displayed great generosity in assisting refugees. The world's attention has somewhat shifted to the challenges of integrating Boko Haram captives back into civil society if and when they are freed, particularly women and children and including the young women captured at Chibok. Reporters also note the terrible state of the IDP camps in northern Nigeria and ask if those will become a permanent part of the human landscape there.

What of Boko Haram itself? State governments in the region regularly predict the final defeat of the insurgency, but there is no real evidence that Boko Haram is finished yet. It may at some point in the future finally be eliminated, although this will probably be in part because regional elites have no use for the name anymore. Given recent history, it seems most likely to me that the Boko Haram insurgency will gradually fade into a condition of increased banditry, frontier lawlessness, and insurgency, as was the case in the region after the Chadian wars of the 1980s and early 1990s. At that time, men who had grown up "living by the gun" (Debos 2016) and who knew little of any other occupation were reluctant to give up the possibilities of wealth and power that armed action afforded for the lives of impoverished farmers or traders. Instead, they went into the bush that they were familiar with and continued their careers as rebels and *coupeurs de route*.

There is some evidence that the Boko Haram insurgents operating along the shores of Lake Chad are beginning to join forces with Chadian rebel groups that have used those environments as a refuge for decades. This implies the integration of some Boko Haram commanders and fighters into the networks of Chadian "politico-military entrepreneurs" and their factions described in chapter 5. This may well also extend that factionalism and the constant, low-level armed conflict associated with it to northern Cameroon and Nigeria, as has been the case in Darfur and the Central African Republic. That would be a somewhat ironic result, since the largest such faction—the Chadian military, commanded by the president, Idriss Déby—has gained a great deal of credibility in the West for its campaign against Boko Haram, and for its actions in Mali against Islamist insurgents there.

The *cascadeurs* and *coupeurs de route* that I have described in this book are mostly young men today, many really boys, with no future prospects, and the number of such young people is increasing all the time. The success of governments in providing support for such young people will probably go a long way to determining the degree to which these new cultural lessons are expressed violently. So far, this does not seem to be a major priority across the region: elites need desperate foot soldiers, after all, for all kinds of reasons. It is possible, in fact, that the dynamism and social possibilities described so well in Marielle Debos's *Living by the Gun in Chad*—what we might call the "Chadian model" of weaponized political life—will become increasingly attractive across the region, if "living by the gun" offers more opportunities to young men than the ossified social hierarchies characteristic of the region during colonial and postcolonial times.

That would virtually guarantee the continuation of armed violence over the longer term, and the continuing interpenetration of such violence and everyday political and social life. Such violence would depend to an even greater extent on frontier zones, as sanctuaries and rear areas for politico-military groups as well as spaces of wealth creation, as is the case for Chad's borders with Darfur and the Central African Republic today. The increasing involvement of outside powers—the United States, Israel, France, South Africa, and others— in conflicts in the Lake Chad Basin will probably contribute to that internationalization of regional conflicts. Today, the United States and France look to the Chadian military, with its kaleidoscopic relations with armed factions in the country, as a proxy force in wars against Islamic militants in different parts of West Africa. Men and boys "living by the gun," following faction leaders who are also army officers, have found themselves fighting not only in Nigeria and Cameroon but also in the deserts of northern Mali. It is very likely that this use of fighters from the area as Western proxies will continue, and some of the combatants may well be ex-insurgents of Boko Haram.

Future conflicts in the region will probably continue to be associated with religion as well; fighters may call themselves "Boko Haram" even if they are primarily acting as bandits or the clients of political faction leaders. This would be a significant change from the earlier periods of violence from the 1980s onward, which we might have called "secular" in nature. There seems to be less tolerance of religious difference in general throughout the southern Lake Chad Basin in recent decades, among both Muslims and Christians. Civil violence between Muslim "séléka" and Christian "anti-balaka" militias has torn the Central African Republic apart during the last five years, while Boko Haram's terrorism was extending through the lands south of Lake Chad.[2] If that sort of communal violence extended further in the region, where both Nigeria and Cameroon have Christian majorities in the south and Muslim majorities in the north, the consequences would be even more disastrous than the Boko Haram insurgency has been. At the same time, the ambiguities I have described in earlier chapters should make us suspicious of any easy dichotomies between religious worlds. We have seen, after all, Muslims killing each other over theological disputes, "pagan" amulets in Boko Haram camps, Christians converting to Islam and joining Boko Haram, Christians masquerading as Boko Haram while attacking other Christian congregations. Religion is as complex and as prone to reinterpretation in the Lake Chad Basin as anywhere else in the world.

We have also seen that one of the long-timescale processes operating in the Lake Chad Basin is globalization and its opposite, isolation, and that the degree of interconnection between the region and other parts of the world has varied on a timescale of centuries and millennia. In many ways, the present phase of globalization has its deepest roots in the late first millennium CE, and there seems to be no reason to think that it will not continue into the future. Globalization will continue to diffuse the effects of social and political conflicts in the Lake Chad Basin outward, via flows of migrants and refugees and culture. Young people will listen to songs in Kanuri and Hausa coming over the internet in neighborhoods across the world, in the United

States, in France, and in China, and their elders and neighbors will wonder what exactly those young people are listening to. They will become members of very different societies, and change those societies as they do so. Meanwhile, their compatriots at home in Nigeria, Cameroon, Chad, and Niger will imbibe global culture from all angles as well, just as their parents and grandparents watched *Baywatch* and Chinese martial arts movies and listened to Wahhabi sermons when I was working there—with all the disparate interpretations that one might expect from that process.

The lessons that they take away from such global contacts will be equally varied, refracted through the lenses of local understandings and local preoccupations. These changes will come at the expense of the more localized identities and practices that have very deep roots in the region's history. Powerful spirits of place like the Dala Nokwé rock that I described in chapter 5 will become less and less relevant to the people of Gréa as time goes on. In the same way, the growing power of global languages, states, and media are threatening the viability of smaller languages across the region, especially the very diverse Chadic languages in and around the Mandara Mountains. One of those languages, Zumaya, has gone extinct just during the thirty years I have worked in the region; others, like Baldamu and Hya, are critically endangered. I wonder whether and for how long Plata, the language of the community where I did my doctoral research, will continue to be seen as relevant by young people. Like beliefs in local spirits of places, these localized linguistic identities helped anchor communities in particular landscapes and ethnic milieus, which may be rendered less relevant as young people go out further into the world and as the world presses in more heavily on them.

Climate change will continue to play a role in the region's future, as it has in the past. It is impossible to predict exactly how climate change in the coming centuries, the shorter end of the timescales we have looked at in this book, will affect Lake Chad and the lands around it. In part, this is because less attention is paid to future climate change in sub-Saharan Africa than in many other parts of the world, and because the historical data vital to climate change models are rarer for that area. Global climate models are less precise on regional scales, and the models themselves thus sometimes disagree. It is almost certain that the region will become hotter than today, possibly by 1–3°C on average, while there is a great deal of disagreement between models for rainfall change.

The question is not so much averages in climate change but the greater frequencies of extreme events—droughts, floods, heat waves—and the capabilities of social and technological systems to cope with those extreme events. As we have seen particularly in chapters 2 and 3, people living in this region have proven themselves to be extraordinarily resilient and ingenious in coping with changing climates and environments in the past, although at some point such changes may overwhelm systems for coping. The Sahelian droughts of the 1970s and 1980s come to mind, with their great suffering and refugee flows. A future where such events become even more common would place great burdens on communities in the region, probably increasing the movements of refugees both within and beyond the African continent. Both African states and the international community will need to support those communities in coping with such changing environments.

Over longer timescales, the prediction of future trends and processes becomes more impressionistic and correspondingly less useful. I cannot predict how political processes or religious affiliations will change this region in the coming centuries, what the size of Lake Chad will be, or whether farming will continue in the Mandara Mountains. I have no idea what will come after Boko Haram. But there are some elements of this historical narrative that will certainly continue into the future, not particularly because they are unique to the Lake Chad Basin but simply because they are part of what humans do. Identities in the region will continue to be both persistent and dynamic: two hundred or three hundred years from now, there will still be Kanuri and Hausa people living in the lands south of Lake Chad—but they will live in other parts of the world as well, and their values and identities will be somewhat different from those of their predecessors who live today. Humans will continue to adopt new cultural identities and be transformed by them, while in turn transforming those preexisting identities in the process.

As long as states exist, their frontier zones will continue to be ambiguous spaces, places of opportunity and possibly danger, offering possibilities for changes in status and perhaps the reinvention or even redemption of individual or group identities.

People whose identities are associated with borderlands, who are too comfortable in such spaces, will continue to be viewed with unease and suspicion. Probably the most important element that we cannot predict is the continuing role of violence in the frontier zones that are now within the lands of Boko Haram. I hope for a future of peace and prosperity for this region and for its people, when they will be able to enrich themselves in security and plan for the future of their own children, but I am not sure when that will happen. The questions concerning proper relationships between citizens and the state and between the powerful and ordinary people that were raised in chapters 4 and 5 show no signs at all of being addressed in the region, now or in years to come. It seems likely that the *métier des armes*, the "ordinary job of weapons" —in all its legal and illegal, licit and illicit forms—will continue to be an important pathway toward status, wealth, and power in the Lake Chad Basin for the foreseeable future. There is that word, though, "foreseeable": none of us can foresee the future, and it may be that archaeologists in particular should not try to do so.

I would rather end this book on a positive note and emphasize that great resilience and resourcefulness that Lake Chad Basin populations have displayed throughout history. They have created vibrant and complex societies across the region, sometimes in the face of violence and dislocation, and that is as true in the early twenty-first century as it was in the past. The landscapes that people have fashioned there are some of the most beautiful and most interesting places I have ever seen in my life. I am proud to count some of the people I've met in Cameroon, Nigeria, and Chad as my friends. I hope to be able to travel back soon to the places that I have described in this book—no longer the lands of Boko Haram—in order to continue my research there, investigating the history and landscapes of this extraordinary part of the world.

LIST OF FIGURES

ACKNOWLEDGMENTS

This book is the product of more than three decades of research in the southern Lake Chad Basin. Over that time, I have been helped in my work in more ways that I can name, by more people than I can easily mention. Nicholas David began the Mandara Archaeological Project in 1984, and he introduced me to the region in the same year. His continuing engagement with Mandara communities is a wonderful example of good scholarly practice and humane commitment to the people with whom we live and who work beside us. Michel Kourdapaye Amba was my translator and friend throughout my PhD research; I know that he spent a fair amount of time explaining my faux pas to his neighbors and to people in the many communities we visited. What I remember best about that work was the unfailing welcome and kindness shown to me by people throughout the region, wherever we went.

Claire Bourges, Rébecca Janson, and Jean-Marie Datouang Djoussou each worked with me through multiple archaeological field seasons from 1992 onward, and that research would not have been possible without their efforts and expertise. I cannot individually thank the more than one hundred people, Cameroonians, Nigerians, Canadians, Americans, Poles, and Germans, who worked with us through those different field seasons in Cameroon and Nigeria, but their hard work, ingenuity, and good humor made that fieldwork successful. I would like to particularly acknowledge the insights of Christian Seignobos, Marielle Debos, Saïbou Issa, and Janet Roitman, without whom this work would have been much poorer.

I would like to thank Stefan Vranka of Oxford University Press for all of his work with me on the preparation of this book manuscript, as well as Nic David, Thomas Spear (University of Wisconsin–Madison), and an anonymous reviewer for their absolutely invaluable feedback and thoughtful comments at various stages during the process. This is a rather strange book—an examination of a modern terrorist organization that begins its coverage after the last Ice Age—and these readers' expertise has made it a much stronger work than it would otherwise have been. To my layperson reviewers, Mariana and Meredith, thank you so much as well: in this, as in everything, you have meant more than I can tell you.

This book is dedicated to the people who live in the lands of Boko Haram, and who continue to care for their families, help their neighbors, and welcome strangers as they always have. In a book about violence, we need to remember that the strength and goodwill of ordinary people stand as a potent counterweight to the violence that can too easily afflict society. I hope, above anything else, that life will be easier in the future for those people and their children.

NOTES

CHAPTER 1

1. See, for example, *Boko Haram: Islamism, Politics, Security, and the State in Nigeria*, edited by Marc-Antoine Pérouse de Montclos.
2. This religious fractiousness would also later contribute to the formation of splinter movements within Boko Haram, most importantly with the appearance in early 2012 of Ansaru (Jamāʿatu Anṣāril Muslimīna fī Bilādis Sūdān—"Movement for the protection of Muslims in black Africa"), led by Khalid al-Barnawi.
3. All French translations in the text are mine, unless noted otherwise.

CHAPTER 2

1. This insight led to a very famous French school of historical research, called the Annales school, that looks at history from precisely this multi-scalar perspective.
2. These include culturally driven changes, like the development of lactose tolerance among pastoral populations.

CHAPTER 4

1. There is limited evidence for people from the Lake Chad Basin being sold into the Atlantic slave trade; for example, a genetic marker that is quite distinctive in the Mandara Mountains was found in a single seventeenth-century burial in Saint Martin in the Caribbean (Schroeder et al. 2015). However, such cases seem to have been extremely rare.
2. We should remember that when researchers talk of "rulers" and "elites" in the Lake Chad Basin, they are in virtually all cases implicitly assuming such individuals to be males. This is in large part a function of the available data. There are very few mentions of female political roles in the written histories of the region, although semi-legendary female rulers are described in pre-Islamic Hausa and Wandala oral histories. However, one Islamic chronicler's contemporary account of the maneuverings of the *gumsu* (principal wife) of the "ruler of Margi" (Lange 1987), in support of her husband while he was being pursued by the ruler of Borno, certainly implies that elite women could play an important role in political relations in the area.

CHAPTER 5

1. We did make sure that we carried a significant amount of cash with us when going to work, since the bandits had circulated very public warnings to travelers that they needed to have ready money with them if they wanted to avoid injury. Fortunately, we never had occasion to test whether that theory worked.
2. "Dane guns" are any indigenously produced firearms made in West Africa, named for the long-barreled flintlock muskets introduced to the region by Danish traders in the eighteenth century. In the late twentieth and twenty-first centuries, they are

usually muzzle-loaders fired using percussion caps—although I was astonished to see recently made flintlocks in the area in the 1980s and gunflints for sale in markets.

3. As I noted in the introduction, by 2008 I had to institute a rule among the local people I had hired to excavate for me on the DGB sites, isolated up in the Mandara Mountains: they were not allowed to take telephone calls while working in the excavation units, or we would never get anything done.

CHAPTER 6

1. Weirdly enough, the Maggi bouillon cubes that the men were carrying were apparently forbidden by Mohammed Yusuf to Boko Haram members. This is supposed to have been because they were a well-known Western food, although it may also be associated with wider and long-standing suspicions of Maggi cubes and their ingredients in northern Nigeria (Renne 1996).

2. The last element of the trio of powerful technologies that I mentioned in the last chapter, cell phones, have proven themselves equally valuable to Boko Haram in planning and carrying out attacks, to the extent that security forces now regularly shut off cell phone service through the region, on both sides of the border.

3. Boko Haram is also apparently intervening in the important trade in dried fish from Lake Chad to surrounding regions, taking the side of Yedina fishermen against immigrant competitors.

4. There are, however, significant parallels between the history of Boko Haram and that of the Movement for the Emancipation of the Niger Delta (MEND), a non-Islamic group that has as its stated goal a shift in the use of the Niger Delta's oil wealth, toward the interests of the region's citizens. MEND is a similarly long-lasting, violent, and rather obscure movement, which seems to have important continuing connections to some Nigerian political groups and leading politicians. It specializes in attacks on foreign oil companies and the kidnapping of foreigners, while its leaders are said to periodically deploy their followers as foot soldiers in local political conflicts.

5. In northern Cameroon in 2014, a number of people also told me that they believed that elements in the Cameroonian government were tolerating the presence of Boko Haram camps on Cameroonian soil, in return for guarantees that the terrorist organization would not carry out large-scale attacks in that country. (If this was true, kidnapping of foreigners was presumably more acceptable. That is not at all far-fetched, given the history of kidnapping by bandits in the region during the previous two decades.) This claim was supported by their disbelief that Boko Haram could operate camps within populated areas, and especially in the relatively limited area demarcated by the towns of Kolofata, Koza, Ashigashiya, and Keroua, without being detected by security forces.

CHAPTER 7

1. The literature on these topics is vast, but see, for example, Brooks 2011; Mathers, Mitchem, and Haecker 2013; and Schlegel 1992.

2. Even that religious violence in the Central African Republic, however, seems to have at its heart the ambitions of political leaders and the control over resources like diamonds, which are now smuggled across the border into Cameroon and exported.

REFERENCES

Adeleye, R. A. 1971. *Power and Diplomacy in Northern Nigeria, 1804–1906: The Sokoto Caliphate and Its Enemies*. New York: Humanities Press.

Adelman, Jeremy, and Stephen Aron. 1999. "From Borderlands to Borders: Empires, Nation-States, and the Peoples In Between in North American History." *American Historical Review* 104 (3): 814–841.

Amnesty International. 2015. "Stars on Their Shoulders, Blood on Their Hands: War Crimes Committed by the Nigerian Military." Report, June 3. Available at https://www.amnesty.org/en/documents/afr44/1657/2015/en/.

Amnesty International. 2016. "Right Cause, Wrong Means: Human Rights Violated and Justice Denied in Cameroon's Fight against Boko Haram." Report, July 14. Available at https://www.amnesty.org/en/documents/afr17/4260/2016/en/.

Andreas, P. 2001. *Border Games: Policing the U.S.-Mexico Divide*. Cornell Studies in Political Economy. Ithaca, NY: Cornell University Press.

Argenti, Nicolas. 2008. *The Intestines of the State: Youth, Violence, and Belated Histories in the Cameroon Grassfields*. Chicago: University of Chicago Press.

Armitage, Simon J., Charlie S. Bristow, and Nick A. Drake. 2015. "West African Monsoon Dynamics Inferred from Abrupt Fluctuations of Lake Mega-Chad." *Proceedings of the National Academy of Sciences* 112 (28): 8543–8548.

Asad, Talal. 2007. *On Suicide Bombing*. New York: Columbia University Press.

Barkindo, Bawuro M. 1989. *The Sultanate of Mandara to 1902*. Stuttgart: Franz Steiner Verlag.

Barreteau, Daniel, and Michel Dieu. 2000. "Linguistique." In *Atlas de la Province Extrême-Nord, Cameroun*, edited by C. Seignobos and O. Iyebi-Mandjek, 64–70. Paris: Editions de l'IRD/MINREST.

Bauer, Wolfgang. 2017. *Stolen Girls: Survivors of Boko Haram Tell Their Story*. New York: New Press.

Beauvilain, Alain. 1989. *Nord-Cameroun: Crises et peuplement*. Paris: Alain Beauvilain.

Bolak Funteh, Mark. 2014. "Border Shutting and Shrivel of Human and Merchandise on the Nigeria-Cameroon Passage of Banki and Limani." In "Effets economiques et sociaux des attaques de Boko Haram dans l'extreme-nord du Cameroun," edited by Saïbou Issa. Special issue, *Kaliao: Revue pluridisciplinaire de l'École Normale Supérieure de Maroua*, November: 33–60.

Boulet, J., Alain Beauvilain, and P. Gubry. 1984. "Les groupes humains." In *Le Nord du Cameroun: Des hommes, une région*, edited by J. Boutrais, 103–157. Paris: Editions de l'ORSTOM.

Bourges, Claire. 1996. "Ceramic Ethnoarchaeology and Historical Process: The Case of Gréa, North Cameroun." MA Thesis, University of Calgary.

Boutrais, J., J. Boulet, A. Beauvilain, P. Gubry, D. Barreteau, M. Dieu, R. Breton, C. Seignobos, G. Pontie, Y. Marguerat, A. Hallaire, and H. Frechou. 1984. *Le nord du Cameroun: Des hommes, une région*. Paris: Editions de l'ORSTOM.

Breunig, Peter. 2014. *Nok: African Sculpture in Archaeological Context*. Frankfurt am Main: Africa Magna Verlag.

Breunig, Peter, Katharina Neumann, and Wim van Neer. 1996. "New Research on the Holocene Settlement and Environment of the Chad Basin of Nigeria." *African Archaeological Review* 13 (2): 111–143.

Brooks, J. F. 2011. *Captives and Cousins: Slavery, Kinship, and Community in the Southwest Borderlands*. Chapel Hill: University of North Carolina Press.

Brunk, Karsten, and Detlef Gronenborn. 2004. "Floods, Droughts, and Migrations: The Effects of Late Holocene Lake Level Fluctuations and Climate Fluctuations on the Settlement and Political History in the Chad Basin." In *Living with the Lake: Perspectives on History, Culture and Economy of Lake Chad*, edited by M. Krings and E. Platte, 101–132. Cologne: Rüdiger Köppe Verlag.

Campbell, John. 2013. *Nigeria: Dancing on the Brink*. Lanham, MD: Rowman and Littlefield.

Cohen, Ronald. 1991. "Paradise Regained: Myth and Reality in the Political Economy of the Early State." In *Early State Economics*, edited by H. Claessen and P. Van de Velde, 109–130. New Brunswick, NJ: Transaction.

Connah, Graham. 1981. *Three Thousand Years in Africa: Man and His Environment in the Lake Chad Region of Nigeria*. Cambridge: Cambridge University Press.

Cooper, Helen. 2016. "The Boy, the Ambassador and the Deadly Encounter on the Road." *New York Times*, December 17.

Damis, Fritz. 1929. *Auf dem Moraberge: Erinnerungen an die Kampfe der 3. Kompagnie der ehemaligen Kaiserlichen Schutztruppe fur Kamerun*. Berlin: Buchdruckerie B. Deuss.

Danjibo, Nathaniel Dominic. 2009. "Islamic Fundamentalism and Sectarian Violence: The "Maitatsine" and "Boko Haram" Crises in Northern Nigeria." *Peace and Conflict Studies Paper Series* 2:1–21.

David, Nicholas. 1996. "A New Political Form? The Classless Industrial Society of Sukur (Nigeria)." In *Aspects of African Archaeology: Proceedings of the Tenth Pan-African Congress*, edited by G. Pwiti and R. Soper, 593–600. Harare: University of Zimbabwe Press.

David, Nicholas. 1998. "The Ethnoarchaeology and Field Archaeology of Grinding at Sukur, Adamawa State, Nigeria." *African Archaeological Review* 15 (1): 13–63.

David, Nicholas. 2004. "Watch or Water Towers?" *Expedition* 46 (2): 30–35.

David, Nicholas. 2008. *Performance and Agency: The DGB Sites of Northern Cameroon*. Oxford: British Archaeological Reports.

David, Nicholas. 2012a. "A Close Reading of Hamman Yaji's Diary: Slave Raiding and Montagnard Responses in the Mountains around Madagali (Northeast Nigeria and Northern Cameroon)." Available online at http://www.sukur.info/Mont/HammanYaji%20PAPER.pdf.

David, Nicholas. 2012b. *Metals in Mandara Mountains' Society and Culture*. Trenton, NJ: Africa World.

David, Nicholas, and Judith Sterner. 2004. "Title Holders." In *Sukur: A Culture of the Mandara Mountains*. Available online at http://www.sukur.info/Soc/Titles.htm.

Debos, Marielle. 2011. "Living by the Gun in Chad: Armed Violence as a Practical Occupation." *Journal of Modern African Studies* 49 (3): 409–428.

Debos, Marielle. 2016. *Living by the Gun in Chad: Combatants, Impunity and State Formation*. Chicago: University of Chicago Press.

de León, Jason. 2015. *The Land of Open Graves: Living and Dying on the Migrant Trail.* Oakland: University of California Press.

deMenocal Peter B., and Jessica E. Tierney. 2012. "Green Sahara: African Humid Periods Paced by Earth's Orbital Changes." *Nature Education Knowledge* 3 (10): 12. Available online at http://www.nature.com/scitable/knowledge/library/green-sahara-african-humid-periods-paced-by-82884405.

Denham, Dixon, and Hugh Clapperton. 1826. *Narrative of Travels and Discoveries in Northern and Central Africa in the Years 1822, 1823, and 1824.* London: John Murray.

Djanabou, Bakary. 2014. "Insécurité transfrontalière, perturbation des échanges et léthargie des marchés." In "Effets economiques et sociaux des attaques de Boko Haram dans l'extreme-nord du Cameroun," edited by Saïbou Issa. Special issue, *Kaliao: Revue pluridisciplinaire de l'École Normale Supérieure de Maroua,* November: 61–80.

Drake, Nick, Roger M. Blench, Simon J. Armitage, Charlie S. Bristow, and Kevin H. White. 2011. "Ancient Watercourses and Biogeography of the Sahara Explain the Peopling of the Desert." *Proceedings of the National Academy of Sciences* 108 (2): 458–462.

Edberg, M. C. 2009. *El Narcotraficante: Narcocorridos and the Construction of a Cultural Persona on the U.S.-Mexico Border.* Austin: University of Texas Press.

Ehret, Christopher. 2006. "The Nilo-Saharan Background of Chadic." In *West African Linguistics: Studies in Honor of Russell G. Schuh,* edited by P. Newman and L. M. Hyman, 56–66. Columbus: Ohio University Press.

Ehret, Christopher. 2011. *History and the Testimony of Language.* The California World History Library. Berkeley: University of California Press.

Esparza, David Pérez, and Eugenio Weigend. 2015. "The Illegal Flow of Firearms from the United States into Mexico: A State-Level Trafficking Propensity Analysis." *Journal of Trafficking, Organized Crime and Security* 1 (2): 115–125.

Falchetta, Pierro. 2006. *Fra Mauro's World Map: With a Commentary and Translations of the Inscriptions, Terrarum Orbis TP 5.* Turnhout, Belgium: Brepols.

Ferme, Mariane, and Danny Hoffman. 2004. "Hunter Militias and the International Human Rights Discourse in Sierra Leone and Beyond." *Africa Today* 50 (4): 73–95.

Fonka Mutta, Beau-Bernard. 2015. "Boko Haram Targets Arabs in Reprisal for Chad Offensive." Reuters, May 12.

Forkl, Hermann. 1982. "Untersuchungen zur Geschichte des ostlichen Zentralsudan." Paper read at Sprache, Geschichte und Kultur in Afrika: Vortrage gehalten auf dem III. Afrikanistentag, 1983, Cologne.

Frey, R. Scott. 2003. "The Transfer of Core-Based Hazardous Production Processes to the Export Processing Zones of the Periphery: The Maquiladora Centers of Northern Mexico." *Journal of World-Systems Research* 9 (2): 317–354.

Ghienne, Jean-François, Mathieu Schuster, Armelle Bernard, Philippe Duringer, and Michel Brunet. 2002. "The Holocene Giant Lake Chad Revealed by Digital Elevation Models." *Quaternary International* 87:81–85.

Gokee, Cameron, and Jason de León. 2014. "Sites of Contention: Archaeological Classification and Political Discourse in the US-Mexico Borderlands." *Journal of Contemporary Archaeology* 1 (1): 133–163.

Gronenborn, Detlef. 1998. "Archaeological and Ethnohistorical Investigations along the Southern Fringes of Lake Chad, 1993–1996." *African Archaeological Review* 15 (4): 225–259.

Guyer, Jane, and Samuel Belinga. 1995. "Wealth in People as Wealth in Knowledge: Accumulation and Composition in Equatorial Africa." *Journal of African History* 36:91–120.

Hallaire, Antoinette. 1976. "Problemes de developpement au nord des Monts Mandara." *Cahiers ORSTOM, Serie Sci. Hum.* 13 (1): 3–22.

Harnischfeger, Johannes. 2008. *Democratization and Islamic Law: The Sharia Conflict in Nigeria.* Frankfurt am Main: Campus Verlag.

Harnischfeger, Johannes. 2014. "Boko Haram and Its Muslim critics: Observations from Yobe State." In *Boko Haram: Islamism, Politics, Security and the State in Nigeria,* edited by M.-A. Pérouse de Montclos, 33–62. Zaria, Nigeria: IFRA/Ahmadu Bello University.

Hernandez, Anabel. 2013. *Narcoland: The Mexican Drug Lords and Their Godfathers.* New York: Verso.

Hiribarren, Vincent. 2012. "From a Kingdom to a Nigerian State: The Territory and Boundaries of Borno (1810–2010)." PhD diss., University of Leeds.

Hiskett, M. 1973. *The Sword of Truth.* New York: Oxford University Press.

Hiskett, M. 1977. "The Nineteenth-Century Jihads in West Africa." In *The Cambridge History of Africa,* vol. 5, edited by J. Flint and R. Oliver, 125–169. Cambridge: Cambridge University Press

Holl, Augustin. 2001. *The Land of Houlouf: Genesis of a Chadic Polity, 1900 BC—AD 1800.* Memoirs of the Museum of Anthropology, University of Michigan 35. Ann Arbor: Museum of Anthropology, University of Michigan.

International Crisis Group. 2012. *Curbing Violence in Nigeria: The Jos crisis.* Brussels: International Crisis Group.

Issa, Saïbou. 2001. "*Sonngoobe*, bandits justiciers au Nord-Cameroun sous l'administration Francaise." *Ngaoundéré Anthropos* 6:153–173.

Issa, Saïbou. 2004. "La répression du grand banditisme au Cameroun: Entre pragmatisme et éthique." *Recherches Africaines: Annales de la Faculté des lettres, langues, arts et sciences humaines de Bamako* 3.

Issa, Saïbou. 2006. "La prise d'otages aux confins du Cameroun, de la Centrafrique et du Tchad: une nouvelle modalité du banditisme transfrontalier." *Polis/R.C.S.P./C.P.S.R.* 13 (1–2):119–146.

Issa, Saïbou. 2007. "Chad's Vicinity and Ethnic Warfare in the Logone and Shari Division (Far North Cameroon)." *Sociologus* 57 (1): 41–60.

Issa, Saïbou. 2009. "Banditisme et contestation de l'ordre allogène au Nord-Cameroun." *Afrique et histoire* 7:99–118.

Issa, Saïbou. 2010. *Les coupeurs de route: Histoire du banditisme rural et transfrontalier dans le bassin du lac Tchad.* Paris: Karthala.

Issa, Saïbou, ed. 2014. "Effets economiques et sociaux des attaques de Boko Haram dans l'Extreme-Nord du Cameroun." Special Issue, *Kaliao: Revue pluridisciplinaire de l'École Normale Supérieure de Maroua,* November.

Jones, Kimberley. 2001. "The Archaeology of Doulo, Cameroon." Master's thesis, University of Calgary.

Kavanagh, T. W. 1996. *The Comanches: A History, 1706–1875.* Studies in the Anthropology of North American Indians. Lincoln: University of Nebraska Press.

Kelley, Colin P., Shahrzad Mohtadi, Mark A. Cane, Richard Seager, and Yochanan Kushnir. 2015. "Climate Change in the Fertile Crescent and Implications of the Recent Syrian Drought." *Proceedings of the National Academy of Sciences* 112 (11): 3241–3246.

Kelly, Alice. 2013. "The Crumbling Fortress: Nature, Society and Security in Waza National Park, Northern Cameroon." PhD diss., University of California, Berkeley.

Kopytoff, Igor, ed. 1987. *The African Frontier: The Reproduction of Traditional African Societies.* Bloomington: Indiana University Press.

Lange, Dierk. 1977. *Le Diwan des sultans du (Kanem)-Bornu: Chronologie et histoire d'un royaume africain de la fin du 10e siècle jusqu'à 1808.* Stuttgart: Franz Steiner Verlag.

Lange, Dierk. 1987. *A Sudanic Chronicle: The Borno Expeditions of Idris Alauma, 1564– 1576.* Studien zur Kulturkunde 86. Weisbaden: Franz Steiner Verlag.

Lange, Dierk. 1988. "The Chad Region as a Crossroads." In *Africa from the Seventh to the Eleventh Century*, edited by M. el Fasi, 436–460. General History of Africa 3. London: Heinemann Educational Books.

Lange, Dierk. 1989. "Préliminaires pour une histoire des Sao." *Journal of African History* 30 (2): 189–210.

Lange, Dierk. 1993. "Ethnogenesis from within the Chadic State: Some Thoughts on the History of Kanem-Borno." *Paideuma* 39:261–277.

Langlois, Olivier. 1995. "Histoire du peuplement post-néolithique du Diamaré." Doctoral dissertation, Université de Paris I—Pantheon-Sorbonne.

Last, Murray. 1989. "The Sokoto Caliphate and Borno." In *Africa in the Nineteenth Century until the 1880s*, edited by J. F. A. Ajayi, 555–599. General History of Africa 6. London: Heinemann Educational Books.

Lebeuf, A. M. D., J.-P. Lebeuf, F. Treinen-Claustre, and J. Courtin. 1980. *Le gisement sao de Mdaga (Tchad): Fouilles 1960–1968.* Paris: Société d'ethnographie.

Lebeuf, Jean-Paul. 1962. *Archéologie tchadienne: les Sao du Cameroun et du Tchad.* Paris: Hermann.

Lebeuf, Jean-Paul. 1969. *Carte archéologique des abords du Lac Tchad (Cameroun, Nigeria, Tchad).* Paris: Editions du CNRS.

Légaré-Tremblay, Jean-Frédéric. 2016. "Les mutations d'une nébuleuse à la violence inouïe: Voués au djihad, les terroristes font de plus en plus dans le grand banditisme." *Le Devoir*, February 13.

Lembezat, Bertrand. 1949. *Administration des primitifs du Nord-Cameroun.* Centre des Hautes Etudes d'Administration Musulmane note no. 366.

Lembezat, Bertrand. 1950. *Kirdi—les populations païennes du Nord-Cameroun.* Yaoundé, Cameroon: IFAN.

Levtzion, Nehemiah, and J. H. Hopkins. 1981. *Corpus of Early Arabic Sources for West African History.* Cambridge: Cambridge University Press.

Limón, José Eduardo. 1994. *Dancing with the Devil: Society and Cultural Poetics in Mexican-American South Texas.* Madison: University of Wisconsin Press.

Lohr, Doris. 2003. "The Malgwa: A Historical Overview and Some Ethnographic Notes." *Borno Museum Society Newsletter* 56–57:23–43.

Loimeier, Roman. 2013. *Muslim Societies in Africa: A Historical Anthropology.* Bloomington: Indiana University Press.

Lovejoy, Paul E. 2012. *Transformations in Slavery: A History of Slavery in Africa.* Cambridge: Cambridge University Press.

Lovejoy, Paul E., and Jan S. Hogendorn. 1993. *Slow Death for Slavery: The Course of Abolition in Northern Nigeria, 1897–1936.* Cambridge: Cambridge University Press.

MacEachern, Scott. 1993a. "Archaeological Research in Northern Cameroon, 1992: The Projet Maya-Wandala." *Nyame Akuma* 39:7–13.

MacEachern, Scott. 1993b. "Selling the Iron for Their Shackles: Wandala-Montagnard Interactions in Northern Cameroon." *Journal of African History* 34 (2): 247–270.

MacEachern, Scott. 2000. "Genes, Tribes, and African History." *Current Anthropology* 41 (3): 357–384.

MacEachern, Scott. 2001a. "Setting the Boundaries: Linguistics, Ethnicity, Colonialism, and Archaeology South of Lake Chad." In *Archaeology, Language, and History: Essays on Culture and Ethnicity*, edited by J. Terrell, 79–101. Westport, CT: Bergin and Garvey.

MacEachern, Scott. 2001b. "State Formation and Enslavement in the Southern Lake Chad Basin." In *West Africa during the Atlantic Slave Trade: Archaeological Perspectives*, edited by C. DeCorse, 130–151. London: Leicester University Press.

MacEachern, Scott. 2011. "Enslavement and Everyday Life: Living with Slave Raiding in the Northern Mandara Mountains of Cameroon." In *Slavery in Africa: Archaeology and Memory*, edited by P. Lane and K. MacDonald, 109–124. Oxford: Oxford University Press.

MacEachern, Scott. 2012a. "The Prehistory and Early History of the Northern Mandara Mountains and Surrounding Plains." In *Metals in Mandara Mountains' Society and Culture*, edited by N. David, 29–67. Trenton, NJ: Africa World.

MacEachern, Scott. 2012b. "Wandala and the DGB Sites: Political Centralisation and Its Alternatives North of the Mandara Mountains, Cameroon." *Azania: Archaeological Research in Africa* 47 (2): 272–287.

MacEachern, Scott. 2015. "What Was the Wandala State, and Who Are the Wandala?" In *Ethnic Ambiguity and the African Past: Materiality, History, and the Shaping of Cultural Identities*, edited by F. Richard and K. MacDonald, 172–191. Walnut Creek, CA: Left Coast.

MacEachern, Scott, Claire Bourges, and Maureen Reeves. 2001. "Early Horse Remains from Northern Cameroon." *Antiquity* 75 (287): 62–67.

MacEachern, Scott, and Abubakar Garba. 1994. "Preliminary Results of Research by the Projet Maya-Wandala, Nigeria, 1993." *Nyame Akuma* 41:48–55.

Marez, Curtis. 2001. "Signifying Spain, Becoming Comanche, Making Mexicans: Indian Captivity and the History of Chicana/o Popular Performance." *American Quarterly* 53 (2): 267–306.

Marliac, Alain, Olivier Langlois, and Michèle Delneuf. 2000. "Archéologie de la région Mandara-Diamaré." In *Atlas de la Province Extrême-Nord, Cameroun*, edited by C. Seignobos and O. Iyebi-Mandjek, 71–76. Paris: Editions de l'IRD.

Matfess, Hilary. 2016. "The Wives of Boko Haram." *Foreign Affairs*, August 17.

Mathers, C., J. M. Mitchem, and C. M. Haecker. 2013. *Native and Spanish New Worlds: Sixteenth-Century Entradas in the American Southwest and Southeast*. Amerind Studies in Archaeology. Tucson: University of Arizona Press.

Minnis, Paul E., and Michael E. Whalen. 2015. *Ancient Paquimé and the Casas Grandes World*. Tucson: University of Arizona Press.

Mohamed, Kyari. 2010. *Borno in the Rabih Years, 1893–1901: The Rise and Crash of a Predatory State*. Cologne: Köppe.

Mohammadou, Eldridge. 1982. *Le royaume du Wandala ou Mandara au XIXe siecle*. Tokyo: Institute for the Study of Languages and Cultures of Asia and Africa.

Mohammed, Kyari. 2014. "The Message and Methods of Boko Haram." In *Boko Haram: Islamism, Politics, Security and the State in Nigeria*, edited by M.-A. Pérouse de Montclos. 9–32. Zaria, Nigeria: IFRA/Ahmadu Bello University.

Molloy, Molly. 2013. "The Mexican Undead: Toward a New History of the 'Drug War' Killing Fields." *Small Wars Journal*, August 21.

Morrissey, Stephen R. 1984. "Clients and Slaves in the Development of the Mandara Elite: Northern Cameroon in the Nineteenth Century" PhD diss., Boston University.

Muehlmann, S. 2013. *When I Wear My Alligator Boots: Narco-Culture in the U.S. Mexico Borderlands*. California Series in Public Anthropology. Berkeley: University of California Press.

Müller-Kosack, Gerhard. 2003. *The Way of the Beer: Ritual Re-enactment of History among the Mafa, Terrace Farmers of the Mandara Mountains (North Cameroon)*. London: Mandaras.

Müller-Kosack, Gerhard. 2008. "Concepts and Migrations." In *Performance and Agency: The DGB Sites of Northern Cameroon*, edited by N. David, 115–117. Oxford: British Archaeological Reports.

Müller-Kosack, Gerhard. 2010. "Contextualising the DGB Sites of Northern Cameroon." In *West African Archaeology: New Developments, New Perspectives*, edited by P. Allsworth-Jones, 127–138. Oxford: Archaeopress.

Newman, Paul. 2013. "The Etymology of Hausa 'Boko.'" Available at http://www.megatchad.net/publications/Newman-2013-Etymology-of-Hausa-boko.pdf.

Nigerian Army. 2016. "Troops Ambush Boko Haram Terrorists in Musafanari." Available at http://www.army.mil.ng/troops-ambush-boko-haram-terrorists-in-musafanari/.

Nossiter, Adam. 2015. "Abuses by Nigeria's Military Found to Be Rampant in War against Boko Haram." *New York Times*, June 4.

O'Brien, John D., Kathryn Lin, and Scott MacEachern. 2016. "Mixture Model of Pottery Decorations from Lake Chad Basin Archaeological Sites Reveals Ancient Segregation Patterns." *Proceedings of the Royal Society of London B: Biological Sciences* 283 (1827), DOI 10.1098/rspb.2015.2824.

Omonobi, Kingsley. 2014. "Boko Haram Sponsor: Ihejirika, El-Rufai Trade Accusations." *Vanguard*, August 29.

Patton, Adell. 1987. "An Islamic Frontier Polity: The Ningi Mountains of Northern Nigeria 1846–1902." In *The African Frontier: The Reproduction of Traditional African Societies*, edited by I. Kopytoff, 193–213. Bloomington: Indiana University Press.

Peccavi (pseud.). 2016. "Boko Haram's IED Campaign 2015." *Vox Peccavi* (blog), March 6. Available at https://peccaviconsulting.wordpress.com/2016/03/06/boko-harams-ied-campaign-2015/.

Pérouse de Montclos, Marc-Antoine. 2014. "Boko Haram and politics: from insurgency to terrorism." In *Boko Haram: Islamism, Politics, Security and the State in Nigeria*, edited by M.-A. Pérouse de Montclos, 135–166. Zaria, Nigeria: IFRA/Ahmadu Bello University.

Pieri, Zacharias P., and Jacob Zenn. 2016. "The Boko Haram Paradox: Ethnicity, Religion, and Historical Memory in Pursuit of a Caliphate." *African Security* 9 (1): 66–88.

Ramos, R. A. 2009. *Beyond the Alamo: Forging Mexican Ethnicity in San Antonio, 1821–1861*. Chapel Hill: University of North Carolina Press.

Reinert, M., and L. Garçon. 2014. "Boko Haram: A Chronology." In *Boko Haram: Islamism, Politics, Security and the State in Nigeria*, edited by M.-A. Pérouse de Montclos, 237–245. Zaria, Nigeria: IFRA/Ahmadu Bello University.

Renne, E. P. 2010. *The Politics of Polio in Northern Nigeria*. Bloomington: Indiana University Press.

Reyna, S. P. 1990. *Wars Without End: The Political Economy of a Precolonial African State*. Hanover, NH: University Press of New England.

Robinson, D. 2000. "Revolutions in the Western Sudan." In *The History of Islam in Africa*, edited by N. Levtzion and R. L. Pouwels, 131–152. Athens, OH: Ohio University Press.

Robinson, D. 2004. *Muslim Societies in African History*. Cambridge: Cambridge University Press.

Roelofs, Portia. 2014. "Framing and Blaming: Discourse Analysis of the Boko Haram Uprising, July 2009." In *Boko Haram: Islamism, Politics, Security and the State in Nigeria*, edited by M.-A. Pérouse de Montclos, 110–133. Zaria, Nigeria: IFRA/ Ahmadu Bello University.

Rohlfs, Gerhard. 1875. *Quer durch Afrika: Reise vom Mittelmeernach dem Tschad-See un zum Golf von Guinea*. Leipzig: F. A. Brockhaus.

Roitman, Janet. 2005. *Fiscal Disobedience: An Anthropology of Economic Regulation in Central Africa*. Princeton, NJ: Princeton University Press.

Roitman, Janet. 2006. "The Ethics of Illegality in the Chad Basin." In *Law and Disorder in the Postcolony*, edited by J. Comaroff and J. L. Comaroff, 247–272. Chicago: University of Chicago Press.

Rosen, Arlene. 1986. *Cities of Clay: The Geoarcheology of Tells*. Chicago: University of Chicago Press.

Salamone, Frank. 1985. "Colonialism and the Emergence of Fulani Identity." *Journal of Asian and African Studies* 20 (3–4): 193–202.

Sarkozy, Nicolas. Speech at Université Cheikh Anta Diop, Dakar, Senegal, July 26, 2007 2007. Available at http://www.lemonde.fr/afrique/article/2007/11/09/le-discours-de-dakar-de-nicolas-sarkozy_1774758_3212.html.

Schlegel, Alice. 1992. "African Political Models in the American Southwest: Hopi as an Internal Frontier Society." *American Anthropologist* 94: 376–397.

Schroeder, Hannes, María C. Ávila-Arcos, Anna-Sapfo Malaspinas, G. David Poznik, Marcela Sandoval-Velasco, Meredith L. Carpenter, José Víctor Moreno-Mayar, et al. 2015. "Genome-Wide Ancestry of 17th-Century Enslaved Africans from the Caribbean." *Proceedings of the National Academy of Sciences* 112 (12): 3669–3673.

Seignobos, Christian. 1982. *Nord Cameroun: montagnes et hautes terres*. Collections Architectures Traditionelles. Roquevaire, France: Éditions Parenthèses.

Seignobos, Christian. 1986. "Les Zumaya ou l'ethnie prohibée." Paper read at Relations Inter-Ethniques et Cultures Materielles dans le Bassin du Tchad, 1986, Paris.

Seignobos, Christian. 2011. "Le phénomène zargina dans le nord du Cameroun: Coupeurs de route et prises d'otages, la crise des sociétés pastorales mbororo." *Afrique Contemporaine* 2011/2013 (239): 35–59.

Seignobos, Christian. 2014. "Boko Haram: Innovations guerrières depuis les Monts Mandara; Cosaquerie motorisée et Islamisation forcée." *Afrique Contemporaine* 4/2014 (252): 149–169.

Seignobos, Christian. 2015. "Boko Haram et le Lac Tchad." *Afrique Contemporaine* 3/2015 (255): 93–120.

Seignobos, Christian. 2016. "Lac Tchad: Tout comprendre de la stratégie des terroristes de Boko Haram." *Le Monde*, April 29.

Sharpe, Barrie. 1986. "Ethnography and a Regional System: Mental Maps and the Myth of States and Tribes in North-Central Nigeria." *Critique of Anthropology* 6 (3): 33–65.

Sikes, Sylvia K. 1972. *Lake Chad*. London: Eyre Methuen.

Smith, Adam, and Nicholas David. 1995. "The Production of Space and the House of Xidi Sukur." *Current Anthropology* 36 (3): 441–471.

Smith, M. G. 1997. *Government in Kano, 1350–1950*. Boulder, CO: Westview.

Soares de Oliveira, Ricardo M. S. 2007. *Oil and Politics in the Gulf of Guinea*. New York: Columbia University Press.

Spener, D. 2009. *Clandestine Crossings: Migrants and Coyotes on the Texas-Mexico Border*. Ithaca, NY: Cornell University Press.

Sterner, Judith. 2008. "Representations: Indigenous Constructions of the Past." In *Performance and Agency: The DGB Sites of Northern Cameroon*, edited by N. David, 119–123. Oxford: Archaeopress.

Stewart, W. E. 1970. "Indirect Rule and the Political System in Northern Nigeria." *Genève-Afrique* 9 (2): 50–84.

Street-Perrott, F. Alayne, J. A. Holmes, M. P. Waller, M. J. Allen, N. G. H. Barber, P. A. Fothergill, D. D. Harkness, M. Ivanovich, D. Kroon, and R. A. Perrot. 2000. "Drought and Dust Deposition in the West African Sahel: A 5500-Year Record from Kajemarum Oasis, Northeastern Nigeria." *Holocene* 10 (3): 293–302.

Tijani, Abba Isa. 2010. *Tradition and Modernity: The Gamergu (Malgwa) of North-Eastern Nigeria*. London: Mandaras.

Tilouine, Joan. 2016a. "Cameroun: Comment les terroristes de Boko Haram se sont convertis à l'import-export." *Le Monde: Afrique*, August 3. Available at http://www.lemonde.fr/afrique/article/2016/07/11/cameroun-comment-les-terroristes-de-boko-haram-se-sont-convertis-a-l-import-export_4967769_3212.html.

Tilouine, Joan. 2016b. "Moi, Bouba Pété, contrebandier, mécène et notable du nord du Cameroun." *Le Monde: Afrique*, July 29. Available at http://www.lemonde.fr/afrique/article/2016/07/29/moi-bouba-pete-contrebandier-mecene-et-notable-du-nord-du-cameroun_4976358_3212.html.

Tishkoff, Sarah A., F. A. Reed, F. R. Friedlaender, C. Ehret, A. Ranciaro, A. Froment, J. B. Hirbo, A. A. Awomoyi, J. M. Bodo, and O. Doumbo. 2009. "The Genetic Structure and History of Africans and African Americans." *Science* 324:1035–1044.

Tomlinson, G. J. F. 1916. *Report on Dikoa District of the Northern Cameroons*. Colonial Office Report CO 879/118 (Correspondence Relating to the Territories of the Cameroons under British Administration and Their Boundaries), no. 14.

Umar, Haruna. 2016. "Villagers: Cameroon Troops Kill 40 in Pursuit of Boko Haram." Associated Press, January 26.

Umar, Muhammad. 2012. "The Popular Discourses of Salafi Radicalism and Salafi Counter-radicalism in Nigeria: A Case Study of Boko Haram." *Journal of Religion in Africa* 42:118–144.

United Nations High Commissioner for Refugees. 2016. "Minawao: Profile du Camp." United Nations High Commissioner for Refugees.

van Beek, Walter. 2012. *The Dancing Dead: Ritual and Religion among the Kapsiki/Higi of North Cameroon and Northeastern Nigeria*. Oxford: Oxford University Press.

Walker, Andrew. 2016. *"Eat the Heart of the Infidel": The Harrowing of Nigeria and the Rise of Boko Haram*. London: Hurst.

Weaver, Thomas. 2001. "Time, Space, and Articulation in the Economic Development of the US-Mexico Border Region from 1940 to 2000." *Human Organization* 60 (2): 105–120.

Wendt, Karl Peter. 1997. "Gajiganna-Stratigraphien und Keramik: Quantitative Analysen zu einem endsteinzeitlichen Keramikkomplex in Nordostnigeria." PhD diss., Johann-Wolfgang-Goethe Universität.

Yaji, Hamman. 1995. *The Diary of Hamman Yaji: Chronicle of a West African Muslim Ruler*. Translated by James Vaughan and Anthony Kirk-Green. Bloomington: Indiana University Press.

Zenn, Jacob. 2014. "Boko Haram and the Kidnapping of the Chibok Schoolgirls." *CTC Sentinel* 7 (5):1–8.

Zenn, Jacob. 2016. "Boko Haram: Two Years On Shekau and Buhari Still Face Pressure over the Chibok Schoolgirls." *Terrorism Monitor* 14 (10):8–11.

Zucker, Eve Monique. 2013. *Forest of Struggle: Moralities of Remembrance in Upland Cambodia*. Southeast Asia: Politics, Meaning, and Memory. Honolulu: University of Hawai'i Press.

INDEX